One Love

The Official Report of the 14th Meeting of the Anglican Consultative Council Jamaica 2009

Published by the Anglican Communion Office
St Andrew's House
16 Tavistock Crescent
London W11 1AP
England
Tel: +44 (0) 207 313 3900
Fax: +44 (0) 207 313 3999
Email: aco@aco.org
www.anglicancommunion.org

Printed in England
ISBN 978-0-9558261-8-4
Cover design by Tomoko Fujimura
Compiled by Yoshimi Gregory

Printed by Printondemand-worldwide
9 Culley Court, Bakewell Road, Orton, Southgate, Peterborough PE2 6XD

Contents

PART ONE   SERMONS & ADDRESSES

PART TWO   RESOLUTIONS

PART THREE   GENERAL BUSINESS

PART FOUR REPORTS

PART FIVE   APPENDICES

Preface by the Archbishop of Canterbury

I imagine that what a lot of people will remember about this year's ACC meeting in Jamaica is the Caribbean hospitality. On the first Sunday, virtually all the churches on the island were closed, and we joined with congregations from across the island in an enormous Eucharist in one of the national Sports Halls in Kingston. There were, I suppose, the best part of 8,000 people there altogether, and that was the beginning of the sense of being included in the life of the local church that was very distinctive and very positive. We were made to feel very much at home straight away, and on the second Sunday of the meeting, ACC members also got involved in local parishes located in different parts of the island. I had the great privilege of going to a village that had been more or less flattened by Hurricane Ivan in 2004. The original church had been destroyed and had since been rebuilt by the local people, and I was asked to go and rededicate the new church. The visit offered a little bit of a glimpse into the extraordinary resilience and strength of the local Church and people, and the way in which the Church in Jamaica is simply there for the people, in the middle of what can be very difficult circumstances.

The warmth and hospitality of the Church of Jamaica and the opportunity to be immersed in its life enabled, I think, ACC delegates to remain grounded and to see how the Anglican Communion carries on at a grass roots level. The agenda for ACC-14 had been shaped to make the best use of what had been learned from the Lambeth Conference, and some of the deep relationships that had been shaped last year have been worked on and developed through the meeting of the ACC. Although there continue to be tensions in the Communion, I believe that ACC-14 helped to build a framework of trust in which to discuss them. I would say that the interdependence of the Communion, our need of one another, both in theological reflection and in practical work, as in the healthcare network and the proposed Anglican Relief and Development Alliance, was reaffirmed very importantly and deeply. Work on the Anglican Communion Covenant was also affirmed and taken forward to the next stage, and the three-year project on 'The Bible in the Life of the Church' was endorsed, offering great potential for enlarging minds and hearts in its exploration of the ways in which the Bible is used in the Anglican Communion. And so I thank God for all we were given in two weeks of quite hard work, two weeks that were deeply, warmly encouraged and nourished by the hospitality of a wonderful local Church.

© Rowan Williams 2009

Foreword by the Secretary General

Posters at the airport welcomed ACC representatives from around the world to the Church of the Province of the West Indies, and specifically to the Diocese of Jamaica and the Cayman Islands. The warm welcome from our host church turned into closer friendships as the days unfolded.

ACC-14 was shaped around Mission - God's mission at work through the Provinces represented, through Anglican Communion Networks and Commissions, and through the local church. All were woven into a rich tapestry portraying the life of our churches around the globe. Who can forget the wonderful Opening Service in the Sports Arena, the presentation by the Networks at the Market Place, our daily worship and bible study, the engagement with parishes across the island, or the dignified Closing Service in the Cathedral in Spanish Town?

Worship shaped each day, when within a common structure, the prayer of several Provinces became the prayers of all; bible study drew us to the core of our faith; and music from the local church enabled our praise.

The Archbishop of Canterbury set a prayerful tone in his devotional morning before we began, and in his concluding address he set the business of ACC-14 in the context of wider life of the Communion.

The Networks of the Anglican Communion set the mood of the business session in the opening afternoon. Much is being achieved through their work on issues as diverse as Peace & Justice, Women, Family, Canon Law, and Health, and as we engaged with them, common threads emerged - a concern for the marginalised, justice, and ministry in situations of conflict and violence.

Work sessions came in various forms. Information plenaries introduced the text or texts under discussion, smaller discernment groups enabled each member to engage with the subject matter in some depth, which in turn informed the decision making plenaries where resolutions were considered and voted on.

The reports, resolutions and addresses in this book are offered to the Anglican Communion and the wider church as the fruits of ACC-14.

The Revd Canon Dr Kenneth Kearon
Secretary General of the Anglican Communion

Message from the Bishop of Jamaica
& The Cayman Islands

'The experience of a lifetime.' 'I never believed that I would live to meet, see, hear and inter-act with the Archbishop of Canterbury'; 'Words cannot express.' These are samples of the way in which many of the faithful in Jamaica have talked about the impact of ACC-14 held in Jamaica in May 2009.

I, personally, feel privileged and honoured to have been the Bishop at that particular time. The Diocese itself has been greatly encouraged and inspired by the fellowship we have enjoyed with our brothers and sisters from around the Globe. It is not automatic or easy for dioceses located in small and far flung islands to experience the vastness of this unique worldwide community of faith known as Anglicanism. Even in this global village of instant electronic communication, it is easy to become isolated, insular and introverted. We have to work intentionally to overcome this tendency. However, an opportunity to enjoy the fellowship and to see the cultural and even the spiritual diversity of our Church will contribute much to this process. We recognize that this tremendous diversity is a challenge that could lead to an intensification of divisions and alienation, but it could also lead to a wonderful mutual enrichment. Our own poet, Professor Mervyn Morris, in a hymn written specifically for the Opening Service, affirms the source of our diversity in God Himself. He wrote:

'Lord of our diversity
unite us all we pray;
welcome us to fellowship
in your inclusive way

Teach us that opinions which
at first may seem quite strange
may reflect the Glory of
your great creative range.'

We are grateful that the ACC generously made time for the local
Church. Firstly, to open up their Opening Service into a Provincial/Diocesan
Service and, secondly, by taking time out to visit as many as forty of our
Congregations. All of these visits were successful. Links and lasting
connections were made at grassroots level. Who would have believed that
the Archbishop of Wales, on his visit to St David's, Yallahs, would have
bonded with the people to the extent of co-signing their petition to the
Government asking for improvement to the roads leading to Llandewey.

Another highlight of these visits was the visit of Bishop Samson
Mwaluda of Kenya to St Paul's, Moore Town, our chief Maroon Church.
The Maroons are the original anti-slavery crusaders who refused to be
enslaved and retreated to the most inaccessible hills of the country where
they have maintained many features of their African heritage. The
Missionaries who founded St Paul's from as far back as 1804 discouraged
any manifestation of African culture. However, on May 10, 2009, when the
Maroons of Moore Town learnt that they were to be visited by a real African
Bishop, they were overjoyed. The Maroon Council, led by their Colonel, Mr.
Wallace Sterling, came with traditional dancers and drummers and, of course,
the Abeng. The Colonel led the team in a welcome dance, song and words
spoken in Kromanti, based on the Twi language of West Africa.

Stories like these abound. We ourselves did not realise how connected
we are with one another. Mention must be made of the impact of His Grace
The Archbishop of Canterbury for his accessibility, his gracious demeanour,
his wisdom and kindness. His great stature as a world leader was in no way
diminished by his willingness to share himself with the humble people of his
flock.

It is our prayer that ACC and, by extension, the Communion will have been as blessed as we have been by this coming together and that our present serious controversies may ultimately result in deeper understanding and wider fellowship.

Yours in Christ's love and service

The Rt Revd & Hon Alfred C Reid DD, OJ
Bishop of Jamaica & The Cayman Islands

Membership of ACC-14
& Ecumenical Participants

President
The Most Revd and Rt Hon Dr Rowan Williams

Chair
The Rt Revd John Paterson

Vice Chair
Professor George Koshy

Secretary General
The Revd Canon Dr Kenneth Kearon

Aotearoa, New Zealand and Polynesia
The Ven Turi Hollis ACC-14, 15, 16
Dr Anthony Fitchett ACC-14, 15

Australia
The Rt Revd Andrew Curnow ACC-14, 15
The Ven Dr Sarah Macneil ACC-14, 15, 16
Mr Robert Fordham ACC-14

Bangladesh
The Revd Sunil Mankhin ACC-14

Brazil
Professor Joanildo Burity ACC-14, 15, 16

Burundi
The Rt Revd Martin Nyaboho ACC-14

Canada
The Rt Revd Susan Moxley ACC-14, 15
The Revd Dr Stephen Andrews ACC-14
Ms Suzanne Lawson ACC-14, 15, 16

Central Africa
The Rt Revd Dr James Tengatenga ACC-14
Mr Daniel Taolo ACC-14

Central America
Miss Lisbeth Barahona ACC-14, 15, 16   *unable to attend*
Miss Maria Barahona Flores   *alternate Member for ACC-14*

Congo
The Rt Revd Kahwa Henri Isingoma ACC-14, 15
The Revd Joyce Tsongo ACC-14   *unable to attend*

England
The Rt Revd Michael Hill ACC-14, 15, 16
The Revd Rose Hudson-Wilkin ACC-14, 15, 16
Canon Elizabeth Paver ACC-14

Hong Kong
Mr Arthur Mo ACC-14, 15, 16   *unable to attend*
The Revd Peter Koon   *alternate Member for ACC-14*

Indian Ocean
The Revd Canon Razafindralambo Samitiana Jhonson ACC-14, 15, 16
Dr Michel Razafiarivony ACC-14, 15, 16

Ireland
The Revd Dr Maurice Elliott ACC-14, 15, 16
Miss Kate Turner ACC-14

Japan
The Rt Revd Laurence Minabe ACC-14, 15, 16

Jerusalem and the Middle East
The Rt Revd Azad Marshall ACC-14, 15, 16

Kenya
The Rt Revd Samson Mwaluda ACC-14, 15
Mr Amos Kiriro ACC-14

Korea
The Revd Abraham Kim ACC-14, 15

Melanesia
Ms Merilyn Tahi ACC-14, 15, 16   *unable to attend*

Mexico
Miss Sarai Osnaya-Jimenez ACC-14, 15, 16

Myanmar
Dr San Myat Shwe ACC-14, 15, 16

Nigeria
The Rt Revd Ikechi Nwachukwu Nwosu ACC-14, 15, 16
The Ven Dr Abraham Okorie ACC-14, 15, 16
Mr Abraham Yisa ACC-14, 15, 16

North India
The Revd Ashish Amos ACC-14, 15
Dr Vincent Kaushal ACC-14, 15, 16   *unable to attend*
Mr Kalyan Peterson   *alternate for ACC-14 and unable to attend*

Pakistan
The Revd Shahid Mehraj ACC-14, 15
Mr Humphrey Peters ACC-14, 15

Papua New Guinea
Member to be appointed ACC-14, 15, 16

Philippines
Mr Floyd Lalwet ACC-14, 15

Rwanda
The Rt Revd Josias Sendegeya ACC-14
Priest to be appointed ACC-14, 15, 16
Mrs Jane Mutoni ACC-14, 15

Scotland
Mr John Stuart ACC-14, 15

South East Asia
Dato' Stanley Isaacs ACC-14, 15

South India
The Most Revd John Gladstone ACC-14, 15
The Revd Moses Jayakumar ACC-14, 15
Mr J M Richard ACC-14, 15

Southern Africa
The Most Revd Thabo Makgoba ACC-14, 15, 16
Ms Nomfundo Walaza ACC-14, 15   *unable to attend*
The Revd Canon Janet Trisk ACC-14, 15, 16

Southern Cone
The Rt Revd Dr Bill Godfrey ACC-14, 15, 16

Sudan
The Rt Revd Ezekiel Kondo ACC-14, 15
The Revd Canon Enock Tombe ACC-14, 15

Tanzania
The Rt Revd Gerard Mpango ACC-14
The Revd Canon Dr R Mwita Akiri ACC-14, 15
Mrs Judith Ghemela ACC-14, 15, 16

The Episcopal Church
The Rt Revd Catherine Roskam ACC-14
The Revd Dr Ian Douglas ACC-14, 15, 16
Ms Josephine Hicks ACC-14, 15

Uganda
The Rt Revd Elia Luzinda Kizito ACC-14, 15   *unable to attend*
Priest to be appointed ACC-14, 15, 16
Mrs Jolly Babirukamu ACC-14

Wales
The Very Revd Christopher Potter ACC-14
Mrs Helen Biggin ACC-14, 15, 16

West Africa
Mrs Philippa Amable ACC-14, 15

West Indies
The Ven Cornell Moss ACC-14, 15, 16
Dr Barton Scotland ACC-14, 15

Co-opted members
The Revd Maria Christina Borges Alvarez ACC-14, 15
The Rt Revd Kumara Illangasinghe ACC-14, 15
The Rt Revd Carlos Lopez-Lozano ACC-14
Head Brother George Siosi ACC-14, 15
Mr Michael Tamihere ACC-14, 15
Ms Sarah Tomlinson ACC-14, 15, 16

Primates' Standing Committee Members

The Most Revd Dr Mouneer Anis	Jerusalem & Middle East
The Most Revd Dr Phillip Aspinall	Australia
The Most Revd Dr Katharine Jefferts Schori	The Episcopal Church
The Most Revd Dr Barry Morgan	Wales
The Most Revd Henry Orombi *unable to attend*	Uganda

Ecumenical Participants

The Roman Catholic Church
Monsignor Mark Langham, representing HE Cardinal Walter Kasper

The Orthodox Church
Metropolitan Nikitas, representing His All Holiness Ecumenical Patriarch Bartholomew

The Lutheran World Federation
Bishop Michael Pryse, representing the Revd Dr Ishmael Noko, Lutheran World Federation

The Old Catholic Church
Professor Dr Harald Rein, representing the Most Revd Dr Joris Vercammen Archbishop of Utrecht

The Moravian Church
The Revd Paul Gardner, Moravian Church in Jamaica

The World Council of Churches
The Revd Dr John Gibaut, Director of Faith and Order

ACC–14 Group Photo

ACC-14 Opening Service at the National Arena

Bishops gather around the Eucharistic Table at the Opening Service

Congregation at the Opening Service

ACC-14 Provincial
Banners

Drummers at the
Opening Service

Members of
Congregation at the
Opening Service

The Rt Revd
Robert Thompson
Bishop of Kingston

Ecumenical Participants with the Archbishop of Canterbury

Diocesan staff and ACC-14 volunteers with the Archbishop of
Canterbury

Network representatives with the Archbishop of Canterbury

ACC members in a Discernment Group

Part One
Sermons and Addresses

The Archbishop of Canterbury's Opening Address at the Welcome Plenary

Friends,

Welcome to this session of the Anglican Consultative Council. I am very delighted that we are able to meet here in Jamaica and not only to meet but to share something of the life of the local church. In our small group this afternoon a number of people raised the question of what the ACC has to do with local churches around the world. How do you actually explain to people in the parishes of the communion why we're here, what we're doing and why we matter. The answer to that is quite a long one. But part of it surely, is that when we do meet we attempt to listen to the immediate reality of a local church, and I know that we are going to be very deeply enriched by our experience of the church in this Island.

And I would very much like to repeat Bishop John's warm thanks to our hosts here to those represented on the platform who have made us already in the last few days so very, very welcome. Those of us who have been here meeting as the Finance committee and Joint Standing Committee have already experienced something of the warmth of Jamaican hospitality and we are very delighted that as I've said we should not only be treated to parties and the delights of Jamaican social life, but also able to see something of other aspects of the Kingdom of God at work on this Island. Given that I hope you believe in the good Gospel sense, parties and social life have something to do with the Kingdom of God.

However, we're not here simply for parties and social life as a Consultative Council. This is quite a full agenda as you heard but we have attempted so to scale it and scope it, that it won't feel we hope and trust too packed and too pressurised.

We have in this attempted to learn some lessons from the experience of last year's Lambeth Conference. And among those lessons one of the most important I think, was this; in large groups people will for the most part only speak if they can trust those around them to hear and they'll only trust those people around them to hear what they are saying if they've had some experience at depth, talking, praying and relating together. During the course of the Lambeth Conference many very precious relationships were created in that way, sustained and deepened, and we hope that the structure of this Council meeting will repeat something of what was possible at Lambeth last year. That's to say we hope that the experience of smaller groups, bible studies, discussion and discernment in smaller groups will enrich and focus our plenary discussions.

However, unlike the Lambeth Conference we do have a constitution and that constitution requires us to make certain decisions with clarity. And so you'll see in the construction of our programme a fairly clear distinction between different kinds or levels of meeting. Those of you who have the programme may like to look again at the final page - page 12 of that programme and I'll just very briefly run over the rationale of what is said there.

Those notes on the programme begin appropriately by speaking of worship and bible studies. And one of the aspects of the hospitality offered to us here is of course the chaplaincy provided for our meeting by the local church, especially through the ministry of Canon Collin Reid. Our Bible studies will take us through St Mark's Gospel, the beginning of the Gospel of Jesus Christ the Son of God. And as in other meetings of the Communion it must be our hope and prayer that that framing of our business in worship and bible study will permeate everything that we do. So that in all things God maybe glorified, in all things we may be seeking daily and hourly to open ourselves to Gods word, that in all things our work maybe in occasion for thanksgiving and growth in the holy spirit.

But in terms of the way we do our business you'll see a distinction drawn there between information plenaries, discernment groups, decision making plenaries, in the first instance. Information plenaries are exactly what they say they are, there are occasions for all of us to be updated on where some of the business of the communion is and I'll say a word later on about particular significant subjects involved there.

These plenaries are intended to clarify what is before us to give people opportunity to ask the questions they need to ask so that our discussion and decision maybe honest and clear headed. But just as important in that process will be the discernment groups, groups of 20 or so members meeting at different points in the programme so that they may discuss in smaller units the business that will be before the council as a whole. And those groups rather like the Indaba groups at Lambeth will be animated and steered by people trained in facilitating a discussion where everybody maybe heard.

And those two together information plenaries and discernment groups make up the back drop to the decision making plenaries where the business is finally dealt with. You will note the two other categories there the network groups and the ecumenical streams.

Networks of the Communion report to the Consultative Council and the network groups are simply an attempt to find the best and most creative way of engaging members of the council and this work. Similarly with the ecumenical streams, where once again we expect reports to this council and we're trying to find ways of making it possible for as many people as managed to interact directly to those responsible for the networks, matters of concern and the ecumenical agenda.

If you look at the subjects touched on in the programme you'll see that apart from the ecumenical streams which are a huge importance of course, there is a strong predominance of the early part of the meeting to a large scale of business to the communion, in particular the proposal to an Anglican Covenant, a final draft to which is now before you and some of the recommendations which have emerged from the Windsor Continuation group. The group which I charged some 18 months ago, with commenting on and steering the whole implementation of the Windsor Report and its business.

We hope that out of this council will come some clear direction about the future of the Covenant and also some clear direction about what the instruments of communion might be doing to respond to the challenges of the Windsor Report and move forward in new and perhaps more responsive, flexible and user friendly ways to the crises which the communion continues to face.

In all, I simply ask for your prayers and the prayers of the local church that our discernment maybe faithful, careful and clear. But as the agenda moves on you will notice in the last few days there are some new and I hope challenging elements introduced. A week today we should be hearing about the project for the Bible in the Life of the Church, part of our attempt as a communion to penetrate more deeply into the mysteries of Gods word and

4

find out what has been said in the church today in response to Gods self communication and how we share ways of interpreting across the communion. See that there's also opportunity also for reflection of what we have seen of the mission of the local church.

You'll note that on Monday the 11th there will be opportunity to hear about the Evangelism and Church growth initiative. So my own hope for this session of the council is that we should be moving through some of the difficult business of the communion structures, towards a proper focus on theology and on mission. A proper focus on theology as creative and converting engagement with Gods revelation; a proper focus on mission as one of the elements that most securely and profoundly binds us together as a communion not just as an assembly of local enterprises.

To strengthen the life of the Communion is not an end in itself. We are not meeting here to design more and better committees. To strengthen the life of the Communion is surely only important if it strengthens the mission of the Communion. That is why the agenda moves in that direction, why I hope that by the time we have got to the end of this taxing - I hope properly challenging agenda, we should be moving away from here, renewed in a sense of the mission that does bind us together and what that makes possible for us and those with whom we choose to share the good news with together.

So to conclude once again you are very welcome here to this meeting. I look forward personally very much to sharing with you in the days to come, hearing of your experiences, your wisdom, your challenges. I look forward to our engagement with the local church. I look forward to what ACC14 is going to contribute to the life and health, the faithfulness and vigour of our Communion together under God.

Thank you very much.

© Rowan Williams 2009

The Archbishop of Canterbury's Sermon at the Opening Eucharist at the National Arena

The Lord is Risen, Alleluia!
He is risen indeed, Alleluia!

Dear brothers and sisters, I greet you in the name of the risen Jesus and I pray that my words and the thoughts of all our hearts will be acceptable in the sight of our God and Father. Amen.

First of all, let me say on behalf of the Anglican Consultative Council, your guests in these days, how profoundly grateful we all are, not only for the welcome you have given us, but for the opportunity we have to share this morning with you in the worship of Almighty God at his table. Thank you for showing yourselves, brothers and sisters, to us in this way. We give thanks to God for your witness, we give thanks to God for the largeness of your heart, and we rejoice to be with you on this occasion.

In this morning's reading from the Acts of the Apostles, we heard a story that was very like the story of Pentecost. The Apostles are gathered together and suddenly the place where they are is shaken by the coming of the Holy Spirit. The Spirit renews in them their vision and their courage – they speak the word of God with boldness. This story reminds us that when the Holy Spirit comes, the Holy Spirit gives us the power to speak in a way that changes the world we live in; to speak with such boldness that lives are changed.

And as the story continues, we hear what the effect is of the coming of the Holy Spirit and the speaking of the word. And the effect of this great earth shattering gift of the Spirit of the word, the effect of this is that a new kind of community is born. Immediately we have heard about the coming of the Spirit, we are told something about how the Christian community lived together. And we are told that among the believers in Jerusalem there was not one needy person. Now that immediately tells us something about what is at the heart of our life as a Christian community. When the Spirit comes, when the word is spoken, the human family comes into being where there are no needy persons; the Church is a community where there are no persons in need. And because the Church is a kind of hint, a foretaste of God's purpose for all human beings, we can conclude from that that the world God wishes us to see is a world in which there is no one in need.

We as a Church have to be the kind of community which shows what God's promise is for the whole of humanity, and we shall do that by asking ourselves day by day and year by year: 'Is ours a community in which there are still people in need?'. Well, the answer sadly is 'yes', isn't it? In the Church and in the world there is need wherever we look. We are still on the way to becoming the Church that God wants us to be, and so we are still on the way to expressing the fullness of the gift of the Spirit, and the fullness of speaking the word in boldness.

And the first challenge which this reading from the Acts of the Apostles puts before us, is are we as a Christian community here in this island, across the world, are we prepared for working to be a community where there is no needy person? Are we prepared to be a community where we are so attentive, so careful to notice the needs of others that our instinct is always to go out to them, to ask what their hunger is and to meet it? And in this way, and in this way alone, the Church will be able to challenge the whole world and say, 'God's purpose for the world is a human family where there is no one in need'.

God knows that in this island you have felt the effects of international debt and the way in which the economy of our world seems to turn its back on those in need. God knows that in many different societies represented here in our Anglican Communion that experience is the same, as if the world has turned its back on need. And so for us, as a Christian family worldwide, this must be at the heart of our witness and our message. Are we prepared so to be shaken by the Holy Spirit, so to hear the word of God that we become a community where the need of all is seen and understood, and felt and met?

So brothers and sisters, I ask your prayers for the meeting of our Anglican Consultative Council this week, that in all we do we may assist our Anglican family to become more deeply a community shaken by the Holy Spirit, speaking the Word of God with boldness – a community where the needs of the poorest are always before our eyes, where we seek to create a community in which there is no needy person.

But as soon as we have said that, we may very well remember some other words of Scripture. It is not by bread alone that human beings live. The needs that are around in the Church, the needs that are around us in the world are not only the need for material wealth, the need for food or healthcare. Our needs go deeper. We need forgiveness, we need reconciliation, we need justice; as Jesus himself says, 'Those who are hungry and thirsty for justice are blessed'. And that is a reminder of how deep that need is. We need to hear from one another words of hope.

And once again this is a challenge to us as a Christian family and a challenge to us as a human family. Are we in our own context meeting one another's need to hear words of hope, meeting one another's need for a word of reconciliation?

In the Church we must constantly be asking: 'Whose forgiveness do I need? Who needs my forgiveness? Who is it who is hungry for a word of hope from me? Who is it that I am hungry to hear a word of hope from?' When we look at the deep conflicts of our world, at the terrible tragedies that divide so many countries – the anguish of Palestine and Israel, of Sudan, of Sri Lanka – those are not situations where all that is needed is bread or healthcare. There is, as the prophet says, a hunger for the word of the Lord, there is a hunger for the word of hope and of forgiveness. And so we, as Christians, must begin by asking ourselves within our own community, 'Who needs from me that word of hope? From whom do I seek forgiveness?'

And once again, I ask your prayers, dear friends, for our meeting in these days, that in our Anglican Communion too we shall find the words and the prayers that will unleash, unseal the power that comes seeking and offering forgiveness. That we may ask ourselves as an Anglican family how we speak of hope to one another, how we meet that need, the word of transforming mercy. Because at the heart of it all lies our need for the overwhelming reality of love, which is God revealed in Jesus Christ our Saviour. We cannot speak about that need for God unless we also make it real in our lives in terms of the need for solidarity, the need for compassion, the need for forgiveness and for words of hope. God is there to meet that deepest need. God speaks the greatest and the fullest word of hope and reconciliation that we could imagine. In the Cross and the Resurrection of our Saviour, God offers himself as food for our hunger, the hunger of Spirit and body alike. God does not simply meet our needs by sending manna from heaven as he once did for the Israelites. God meets our material needs now by touching the hearts of his people so that they are moved to give and to serve. This morning as we gather to be fed at this the Lord's Table we must let ourselves be fed by a power that drives us to feed others, to see their material need and to see their spiritual hunger.

And we must go from here committed yet again, renewed in the vision yet again that God's purpose is a world where needs are met, where the poverty and wretchedness of people is met by love and generosity of neighbours, where the despair and the violence of people is met by the transfiguring word of hope and reconciliation. By God's grace and goodness we have so many stories in our Christian family that we can share, of that powerful word spoken across the gap of hunger and fear and despair. May those stories become our stories too. Because finally the key to all this is given to us in the words of today's Gospel: God has met our need by putting himself completely at our service. God's own life in Jesus Christ is laid down so that we may live. God holds nothing back in pouring himself out into the need of his creation. And God has swept us into his action and his life so that our own love, weak and frail as it is, is carried forward by the great action of his love into the service of the world's need; into the act of mercy and the word of promise.

The Holy Spirit comes upon us as a Church so that our actions, our loves, our hopes, our feelings, are caught up into the action of God in Jesus Christ; so that our weak power is overwhelmed in the power of God to give and to serve. And we, caught up in that self-giving love of God in Jesus Christ, we begin to understand that the hunger and the need of this world is met not simply by policies, not by words, not by documents, but by the gift of ourselves in prayer and in love. And to give ourselves means a great risk – letting go of what makes us feel safe. Sometimes, as we all know, it makes us feel safe to ignore the needs of others. 'They are needy, but I am safe.' Sometimes, sadly, in conflict with others, I can say, 'I am right and that makes me feel safe, so I have no need of reconciliation.' God help us when we deny our needs like that, because it is that refusal of God's act of transfiguring love that holds us back from giving ourselves in and through the love of God into the life of God's world. There is no needy person in the company of Jesus' friends in Jerusalem.

There it is – a huge challenge for us as a Church, and a challenge that we as a Church give to all our neighbours. A challenge to imagine a world where poverty is not ignored and the needy are not forgotten. But a challenge also to imagine a world in which we truly understand how deep in human beings is the hunger, the passionate devouring hunger to hear words of hope; to hear the possibility of reconciliation. We have come here to be fed. To be shaken by the Holy Spirit and fed by the Word of God. To share in the Holy Sacrament of Christ's Body and Blood. And as we go from this place, we go committed to feed others with that life we have received. We go in the commitment to a world where there are no people dying forgotten because of their hunger for food, and dying forgotten because of their hunger for reconciliation. As we put out our hands to be fed by Jesus Christ, so we take into our hearts the life and the promise that is in him, our Good Shepherd, feeding and nourishing the life of the whole world to which we are sent.

And now to Christ, our Good Shepherd, to his Father, and his transfiguring Holy Spirit, in praise and thanksgiving, Glory and Majesty forever. Amen.

© Rowan Williams 2009

The Archbishop of Canterbury's Presidential Address

What have we achieved? What are the challenges we've discovered? What are the lessons we've learned?

There's no absolute measure for achievement. In critical times quite small things may be quite large achievements. And so, if we reflect on what we've done in the last ten days, then it may be that even some apparently very routine things are real achievements. We've got up every morning; and we've prayed every morning; we've read scripture together; we've affirmed our will to stay in relation; and we've done some planning. We have sent forward work on the aid and development alliance, on theological education, on evangelism and church growth, on the Bible in the Church. We've agreed on the follow-up to the work of the Windsor Continuation Group. We've even agreed on the substance of the Covenant, including, and we should remember this, the timescale for that work.

Now, if someone diagnosed as terminally ill had prayed and planned, and given evidence of new energy, and rising from their bed to make and begin new things, we might just possibly question a diagnosis of terminal outlook. There's been very little hint in the last ten days that, for example, unless Section 4 of the Covenant were delivered now in exactly the form proposed, none of the rest would matter; that work together on development or theological understanding or on the Bible in the Church depended on getting all the rest sorted at this moment, and I'll say a bit more about that later. But it remains true, I believe, that our willingness in certain areas to act as one and to discover more deeply how we pray as one, is, by God's Grace and Gift, and for no other reason I'm sure, an achievement. Small things, but life-giving things. And the Bible has a great deal to say about the day of small things and the work of God in small things and apparently routine things. So I do want to begin this evening's reflection in gratitude: that we have been given the grace, the charity, and the liberty to plan together and pray together. To put it in a slightly different way, we have not in this meeting given evidence of any belief that we have no future together.

The question is of course what that future will look like, and needless to say, that is where we pass on to the challenges. Because there's no point in being too sanguine. Nobody's moved very much in the last ten days. Our problems are not guaranteed a solution through what we have done, and while we thank God with all our hearts for what has been given to us, by God in our prayer, through our fellowship with each other, there remains in a good few areas an intensely felt stand-off between groups in our Communion. The other day we were giving quite intense attention to the situation in the Holy Land, and at moments in that discussion I thought there are echoes of language we hear nearer home; echoes of perceptions around. Emergencies means all the rules and standards are suspended. We can't discuss while there are tanks on the lawn. We can't discuss when there are facts on the ground. We've conceded something and you haven't moved. If you were where we are, you'd see the absolute moral imperative of acting as we've done. Well, thank God our divisions and our fears are not as deep and as poisonous as those between communities in the Holy Land. But I think you may see why some of the language occasionally awakes echoes, and I don't even begin to speculate on who might like to identify themselves with which party in this debate, except to say that on the whole we identify with the victims who are their victims.

But looking at the Holy Land may also give us one or two clues about how life continues to be at work. What is it in that tragic and terrible situation in the Holy Land that gets underneath that rhetoric of rival victim sufferings, rival resentments? Many of you will have quite direct experience of some of what does get under that in the Holy Land. I've spoken in other contexts about the extraordinary work of the Families Forum in the Holy Land – the way in which people who have suffered traumatic loss in the conflict in the Holy Land have been able to meet one another on the basis of that very loss; have been able to find one another in the very depth of the suffering that they've endured. Something begins to shift when people who bear the heaviest cost on both sides of the conflict are somehow able to recognise one another. A couple of years ago in my study at Lambeth I listened to two people sitting on the sofa in the study – one an Israeli mother whose son had been killed by a Palestinian sniper, the other a young Palestinian man whose brother had been killed by an Israeli soldier. They were travelling in Britain together to speak about the absolute imperative necessity of being with one another.

Now, who are the people who bear the deepest costs in our conflicts in the Anglican Communion? It's a question to which there is actually no short answer, but I simply put it before you for some reflection. But there are some who would say that in this conflict the credibility of Christianity itself is at stake. There are some who bear the cost in this way: they will say that Christian credibility is shattered by the sense of rejection and scapegoating which they experience, and that includes a great many of our gay and lesbian brothers and sisters in the Body of Christ. The cost they feel is often they cannot commend the Christianity that they long to believe in because they feel that they are bound up in a system and a community where scapegoating and rejection are very deeply engrained. And then there are those for whom the credibility of Christianity is at stake in another way, those for whom the cost is felt like this: that the decisions that others have made in other parts of the world have put them in a position where they cannot commend the Christianity they long to share with their neighbours with any ease or confidence because they feel that fellow Christians have somehow undermined their witness. Deep cost – different costs – but here is the first big challenge. How can those who share that sense of cost and that sense of profound anxiety about how to make the Gospel credible – how are they to come together at least for some recognition and respect to emerge? How are they to come together so that they can recognise the cost that the other bears,

12

and also recognise the deep seriousness about Jesus and his Gospel that they share? As with so many observations of this sort, I have to add immediately I know that won't solve the problem. All I know is that it's part of the imperative of dealing with this in a Christian way, not just in terms of managing something or glossing over something.

And really it's in that context that some of our earlier remarks might make sense. If we talk about moratoria or, God help us, ceasefires, or whatever. If we talk about all the immensely complicated and tangled web of stuff that we're dealing with around the Windsor Continuation Group and the Covenant. If we want to talk about that at all, it is only useful and serious if it is part of the background for that exercise of recognition: the recognition of the reality of the cost, the recognition of the reality of a passion about Jesus. And as we go back to our Provinces thinking about the work we've done, and thinking about the quagmires of detail and procedure that we waded through last Friday, the only thing we can say, I suspect, in defence of all that is something like this: we did it because we hoped that through all these procedures, Christian people would be able to recognise each other a bit more fully, a bit more generously, and a bit more hopefully. So as we try and bracket, just for a moment, the idea that we're bound to be betraying something central by even trying to find where these encounters can happen, if we bracket that for a bit, that challenge remains. The Listening Process, yes, but of course good listening is a listening that really allows the other person to speak. It hardly needs saying, but I say it all the same. Archbishops are employed to tell you what you know already really.

But then what about a second challenge, because I think that is coming up over the horizon as we speak about all this, and it is even in some ways more uncomfortable. We've talked about the Covenant, and we have sanctioned a measure of delay about some of its details, though as I said earlier, we have affirmed our commitment to the basic timetable. And in connection with that I would want to say with great emphasis, don't please put off discussion of the Covenant simply because of that detail we are finalising. The texts are out there. Please pray them through and talk them through, starting now. The official processes will no doubt take longer and be more complex. We are trying – and the Secretary General and I have already discussed a timetable for this in some detail – we are trying to make sure that any delay is as brief as possible. But meanwhile the texts are on the table.

Talk about them. Begin the discernment. Begin that intelligent engagement with those texts as soon as you can.

But of course, one reason why I suspect we are just a bit reluctant, some of us, many of us, to start engagement with the detail is that of course much of what we've been thinking about the Covenant does underline for us that the possibility of division is there. The possibility at least of certain kinds of division. Some people speak of the future of the Communion as a federation – a much more dispersed association than it now is. An association within which some groups are more strongly bound to one another and some groups less strongly bound. I suspect that may very well be if not all Provinces do sign up to the Covenant, and I hasten to add that's not what I hope. It is what I think we have to reflect on as a real possibility. But if that is a possibility – that the Communion shifts towards an agglomeration of more strongly bonded and less strongly bonded Provinces or constituent parts – if that is where we are heading – the second challenge is how do we preserve the structures that will allow us to do what we still want to do together? Because I said at the beginning, it is quite clear that there is an awful lot that we do want to do together, and I believe very strongly that even if we are facing a more diverse or divided future, we shall still want to do those things. I really don't believe that if not every Province signs up to the Covenant in the years ahead, that means that the development or the educational work we do together instantly disappears; that we shall no longer want to do that with each other.

So what are the structures, the protocols that will allow those relations to continue? How do the Instruments of Communion – this body, the Primates' Meeting, the Lambeth Conference – how do they continue as organs of life-giving exchange, even if other coalitions and other alliances emerge? Because, believe me, we are going to need organs of life-giving exchange whatever happens. So my plea is, don't write off those Instruments of Communion whatever may happen in the years ahead. In your Provinces and in your relations with one another and your conversations with each other, keep thinking about how the most life-giving kinds of exchange are made possible. Oh, and think also about what makes life-giving exchange impossible, because what makes it impossible is a ceaseless rhetoric of fear and competition directed backwards and forwards in our fellowship. And that is fatal to life-giving exchange if all we have to speak of is fear or competition, rivalry and resentment, there will not be the flow of life and so we will not be able to do together the things we shall still, believe me, want to do together. So we behave with each other as hopefully and respectfully as we can, and dare I say it, we ought to behave together as Anglicans as hopefully and respectfully as if we were dealing with other kinds of Christians, because we are nine times out of ten a great deal more polite about other Christians than we are about each other in the Communion these days!

But that takes us into the final area – what have we learned? And I don't simply mean what have we learned in terms of process, though it does seem to me that we've learned yet again that one of the things we're not terribly good at is resolution passing. I'd suggest, purely practically that for the next ACC we might very well have a little briefing in advance about procedures, and perhaps some time right at the beginning of the meeting – it's a highly practical suggestion and very modest – right at the beginning of the meeting to explain a bit about how resolution procedures work. But that's a smallish thing. I think that we have learned, as many of us learned at the Lambeth Conference, to recognise that relations need to be deep enough, worked at enough, to survive possible shifts in structure and alignment. We've learned something of our value to one another, not only in terms of cooperation on the kind of practical projects I've suggested, but simply in terms of learning about God from one another. In case we've forgotten, it's worth reminding ourselves that the Bible seems fairly clear that we are given to one another as believers so that we may know and experience more of God than we would on our own. Basic New Testament theology, I believe. And so we've learned, unsurprisingly that we need to work on those relations if we are to be able to receive what God wants to give us.

But I think we've also learned a good deal from the degree to which we've found ourselves rooted for this time in the life of our host Church. It's not only the particular things we've learned from engaging with our brothers and sisters here in Jamaica, it's also that we've been I think quite simply conscious that here is a local Church and local Churches matter. Indeed, they are what matters in many, many ways. We've simply been privileged to see what an ordinary local Church does, and I'm sure that our hosts won't mind if I say that the Church in this island and this Province is in most respects neither greatly better nor greatly worse than local Churches in many other parts of the world. You are, happily, Christians like us – that is, intermittently holy and intermittently a mess. And God be thanked for that. We've been reminded of what the real Church looks like, and saving your presence, the real Church doesn't always look like the ACC at work, any more than it looks like the Archbishop of Canterbury I hasten to add. The real Church happens here on the ground. And the experience of this real, local Church offers us at least one very striking and very potent metaphor for what we're all about. This is a part of the world where natural devastation makes structures very vulnerable. Structures – physical structures – come and go. Earthquakes and hurricanes deal with them repeatedly, and yet the Church continues, and renews its pledge of divine faithfulness to the place where it is set. Now that's something that I certainly want to take away and pray and think about a great deal. And it's a reminder that Anglicanism does indeed have a deep investment in the particularities of places and cultures, not in an exclusive, fearful way, but simply in a recognition that the Gospel truly is a word that can be translated into any language. And perhaps in recent years, for understandable reasons, we've become so preoccupied with talking about the autonomy of Provinces in a defensive way that we've lost sight of the positive side of that, which is the particularity of Provinces. Talk about autonomy and you are already, so to speak, defending against incursion. Talk about particularity and you're talking about the gift you have to share. And somehow we have to balance that out a bit again, I believe.

But that learning which we've been going through in our happy and fruitful relationship with our host Church here, that learning has been underpinned by what I hope and trust is the deeper learning that has come through our engagement with the Gospel of St Mark in these days. And the last thing I want to say is really based on Mark. The other day in one of the Bible Studies, we were reminded of those marginal characters in Mark's Gospel who see the point when the disciples don't. Mark's Gospel has been called many things – it's been called a Passion story with an extended preface, and it's been called a celebration of the stupidity of the twelve. The people who see the point – the Syrophoenician woman, blind Bartimaeus, and of course the centurion of the cross, whose words we heard earlier this evening – the people who see the point are the people the disciples do not expect to see the point. Their obsessiveness about getting their questions answered and their future sorted out and their status assured, their obsessiveness is challenged again and again by the clear simplicity of those who simply see in Jesus where there is bread to be had for nourishment. The Gospel of Mark is bad news for Christian elites, all of whom need to grow by being humbled: Archbishops, ACC members, experts of whatever kind, even commentators on the Anglican Communion. This is a learning that is focused on success and failure – how to understand them and how to misunderstand them. An English Roman Catholic nun, Maria Boulding, wrote memorably a few years ago that the alternatives for Christians were not success or failure, but glorious failure and miserable failure. Glorious failure is the recognition that we fall again and again and have a Lord and Saviour whose promise is so inexhaustible that we can pick ourselves up and begin the world all over again, newly created. Miserable failure takes many forms, including the form of telling ourselves that we haven't really failed at all. The Apostles of Mark are greatly at risk of being miserable failures, but presumably Mark's Gospel is written because the Apostles finally decided they were going to be glorious failures. That is, they finally decided that the story they were going to tell was of how they had misunderstood and abandoned and betrayed their Lord who had still loved them and returned to them. That is what I call being a glorious failure – that's the story if you believe the ancient tradition that St Peter handed on to Mark the Evangelist. The story of a glorious failure.

So if as we look back on these ten days we ask ourselves has this been a failure or a success, maybe we should step back and think a few Mark-shaped thoughts. And maybe if we ask is the Anglican Communion at the moment a failure or a success, we should ask the same thing. Because the Gospel seems to be saying to us: first face your failure; your failure, not your neighbour's; your failure, your turning away; not theirs, not his, not hers; then ask how can it be made glorious? And maybe that's another thing to take back to our Provinces. They're going to love you for this, if you go back to your Province and say, 'What we really need to be talking about is our failures in this Province'. You will be so popular – they'll never send you to a meeting again! But perhaps, just perhaps, thinking about those potentially glorious failures, opens us out onto the prayer that turns us back to Christ-like self-giving that lets the glory through. That's what we hope for in our fellowship, our very fragile, very flawed, very precarious Anglican fellowship. We hope for the failure that lets the glory through, because we face it, we name it, we open ourselves to God and say, 'Do with us what you will so that your name may be glorified and your kingdom advanced'.

Let us bless the Lord.

© Rowan Williams 2009

17

The Chairman's Report

Part A The Joint Standing Committee of Primates and ACC

1.   Membership

The membership of the Standing Committee of the ACC has remained constant since ACC-13 met in Nottingham June 2005.

Chair	The Rt Rev John Paterson	Aotearoa, NewZealand & Polynesia
Vice Chair	Professor George Koshy	South India
Members	Mrs Philippa Amable	West Africa
	Mrs Jolly Babirukamu	Uganda
	Mr Robert Fordham	Australia
	The Rt Rev Kumara Illangasinghe	Ceylon
	Canon Elizabeth Paver	England
	The Rt Rev Dr James Tengatenga	Central Africa
	Ms NomfundoWalaza	Southern Africa

There have been some changes in the membership of the Primates Standing Committee, and the following Primates have served:

President & Chair The Most Revd & Rt Hon Dr Rowan Williams
England

Members
2003 ~	The Most Revd Dr Barry Morgan	Wales
2006 ~	The Most Revd Orlando Santos de Oliveira	Brazil
2006/7	The Most Revd Bernard Malango	Central Africa
2007 ~	The Most Revd Dr Mouneer Anis	Jerusalem & the Middle East
2007 ~	The Most Revd Dr Phillip Aspinall	Australia
2007 ~	The Most Revd Dr Katharine Jefferts Schori	The Episcopal Church
2007 ~	The Most Revd Henry Orombi	Uganda

2.   Meetings

The Joint Standing Committee has met six times since ACC-13. Three of those meetings (March 2006, March 2008 and November 2008) were held at St Andrew's House in London. In February 2007 the meeting was held in Dar-es-Salaam, Tanzania, prior to a meeting of the Primates, and in response to a resolution of ACC-13 (Resolution 4b), and in September 2007 the meeting was held as guests of The Episcopal Church in the Diocese of Louisiana, City of New Orleans, USA in association with a meeting of the House of Bishops of The Episcopal Church. The Joint Standing Committee has also met here in Kingston, Jamaica immediately prior to the meeting of ACC-14.

3.   Staff

The Secretary General, the Revd Canon Kenneth Kearon has attended all meetings and seen to the preparation of the Agenda and the necessary follow-up to decisions made by the Joint Standing Committee. The Deputy Secretary General, The Revd Canon Gregory Cameron has also attended each meeting, but this will be his last meeting of the ACC as a staff member, as he has recently been consecrated to be the Bishop of St Asaph in the Church in Wales. Gregory has carried a great deal of responsibility since his appointment in 2005 both in the ecumenical portfolio and in a number of added tasks as the Secretary of a number of Commissions which have been created for specialist consideration of issues in the Anglican Communion, notably the Lambeth Commission which produced *The Windsor Report,* the Windsor Continuation Group, and the Covenant Design Group. Canon Cameron has served the Anglican Communion with great distinction in these various roles, and the ACC will have an opportunity to thank him and wish him well in his new appointment.

Mr Andrew Franklin, the ACC Director of Finance has attended each meeting, as did Mrs Deirdre Martin until her retirement as a member of staff in December 2008. Deirdre's long service was recognised by the Joint Standing Committee at a Dinner Function marking St Andrew's Day 2008. We bade farewell to another long serving staff member in December 2008, when The Revd Canon James Rosenthal, formerly Director of

Communications for the Anglican Communion, resigned. Archdeacon Taimalelagi Fagamalama Tuatagaloa Leota attended a number of meetings in her capacity as the Anglican Observer at the United Nations until her term of office concluded at the end of 2006. Archdeacon Tai has since been ordained as a deacon in the Diocese of Polynesia, and I will be assisting at her ordination to the priesthood in July of this year. Another long-serving staff member to retire during this period was Miss Marjorie Murphy, who held responsibility as the Director of Mission and Evangelism for nine years, and retired in June 2006.

The Revd Canon Andrew Norman attended each meeting in his capacity as the Archbishop of Canterbury's Anglican Communion Staff Officer. Canon Norman was appointed to head Ridley Hall, Cambridge at the end of 2008, and Mr Chris Smith, Chief of Staff at Lambeth Palace has attended in his place. Ms Sue Parks, the Manager of the Lambeth Conference attended a number of meetings in that capacity.

4.   Joint Standing Committee Business

The Minutes of each meeting of the Joint Standing Committee are sent to ACC members and to the Provincial Office of each Province and Member Church of the Communion. In that sense the decisions of the Committee are in the public domain, and need not be rehearsed in great detail in this Report. Major items that have been considered are as follows:

4.1 Evaluation of ACC-13

It was clear from the Evaluation Forms at Nottingham that there was some dissatisfaction at what had taken place, and that consideration should be given to the design of such meetings for the future. A special meeting of the Joint Standing Committee in November 2008 worked on this matter and Mr Stephen Lyon, who had been instrumental in the shaping of the 2008 Lambeth Conference, was present to help in the design of ACC-14.

4.2 Staffing Portfolios

A considerable amount of time at each ordinary meeting of the Joint Standing Committee is given to the written Reports of the Directors of each of the 'desks' in the Anglican Communion Office.

- We have thus considered many detailed reports on ecumenical affairs presented by Canon Cameron and the meetings of the Inter-Anglican Standing Commission on Ecumenical Affairs (IASCER).
- We have given careful attention to Mission and Evangelism and Marjorie Murphy's reports and the material from IASCOME - the Inter-Anglican Standing Commission on Mission and Evangelism. Subsequently The Revd John Kafwanka was appointed to the desk and has been surveying these matters and has reported accordingly in the lead up to the Lambeth Conference.
- We have looked in detail at the matter of Communications, its high I mportance in the life of the Communion, and the rapid changes in technology which require new and specialised knowledge in relation to the best and most effective ways of telling our stories to one another and to those who do not belong.
- Mrs Clare Amos has reported in detail on her work in relation to Theological Education in the Communion, and gratitude was expressed to Trinity Church, Wall Street, New York, for a grant which enabled this work to be carried out.
- Mrs Amos has also had responsibility for the work of NIFCON, the Network for Inter Faith Concerns, and has brought these matters also to the attention of the Joint Standing Committee.
- The Anglican Observer at the United Nations has reported in detail on her work. Dr Hellen Grace Akwii Wangusa from Uganda was appointed to this post and was duly installed in January 2007.
- Canon Phil Groves was appointed in 2006 to take responsibility as Facilitator for *The Listening Process*. He has reported faithfully and well on his work.
- Andrew Franklin as Director of Finance and Administration has worked with the Inter-Anglican Finance and Administration Committee and has reported in detail on our financial matters, and these will be the subject of a separate Report to the ACC.

- The Revd Terrie Robinson has recently been appointed as Co-ordinator of the Anglican Communion Networks, the ACC Women's Desk Officer and ACO Translation Coordinator.

4.3 Matters considered

- The Province of Hong Kong was thanked for its wonderful gift of funds to enable the completion of the costs of renovation for St Andrew's House.
- Canon John Rees has attended meetings in his capacity as Legal Advisor to the ACC, and in particular has continued to guide our consideration of constitutional matters.
- The Joint Standing Committee has also received reports regularly from a number of the Anglican Communion Networks, and has tried to ensure that each Network has a liaison person who is a member of the Joint Standing Committee.
- The Compass Rose Society has continued to work with the Secretary General, and provides a great deal of financial assistance and encouragement for the work of the Communion.
- Consideration has continued to be given to the matter of the possible formation of new Provinces, and particularly in relation to Central Africa and West Africa.
- The Windsor Report has been the subject of much discussion, and the Joint Standing Committee established a small group to report on the response of the General Convention of The Episcopal Church to that Report. The Panel of Reference has also given rise to extra work for the Secretariat and the Deputy Secretary General in particular. The subject of Cross-Boundary Interventions as a very real threat to communion also received consideration, and Primates were encouraged to resist requests for such interventions.
- Much attention has been given over the period covered by this Report to the proposals for an Anglican Covenant. ACC-14 is to be asked to consider this matter as an important item on its Agenda.
- The Place and Role of Women in the Structures of the Anglican Communion is an ongoing exploration arising in particular from Resolution 33 of ACC-13. We have considered matters arising from the Inter Anglican Women's Network, and greeted the appointment of the Revd Terrie Robinson as Women's Desk Officer in the ACO.

- Discussions have continued with those involved in the International Anglican Liturgical Consultation.
- A study of hermeneutics and the place of the Bible in the Church has been encouraged and will form an item for discussion at ACC-14.
- The Windsor Continuation Group posed some specific questions for the Joint Standing Committee to help in the work of that Group.
- The Joint Standing Committee looked at some specific matters from the 2008 Lambeth Conference, and in particular the proposal for a Pastoral Forum and Pastoral Visitors which had come from the Windsor Continuation Group.
- A proposal for the formation of an Anglican Healthcare Network was considered and further information was requested.
- A proposal to form an Anglican Relief and Development Agency was considered, and suggestions made as to ways to co-ordinate such matters in the Communion.
- The Joint Standing Committee approved the mandate for an Inter-Anglican Standing Commission on Unity, Faith and Order (IASCUFO). The formation of the Commission is proceeding and the appointment of a Director is a matter of some urgency. Much of the work of this Commission will include Ecumenical Relations, the work of the former Theological and Doctrinal Commission, and the various bodies associated with the Windsor process.

Part B

Responsibilities of the Chair

In addition to the tasks associated with the chairing of meetings of the Joint Standing Committee, which at times have been shared with Professor George Koshy as Vice-Chair, the Chair of the ACC has also served as Chair of the Inter Anglican Finance and Administration Committee, but this is not an ex officio appointment. In that capacity I have been a Trustee of the Archbishop of Canterbury's Anglican Communion Fund, and also a Trustee of the Anglican Investment Agency. It has been useful for the Chair to have been associated with those two bodies, given that an overview of the Anglican Communion from the viewpoint of the ACC has been a worthwhile perspective to offer.

23

I have also represented the Anglican Communion perspective as a member of the Canterbury Cathedral Council, largely because of that Cathedral's unique position in the Anglican Communion.

I have been a member of the Advisory Council for the Anglican Observer at the United Nations since its inception, both to represent the ACC and also because two of the Observers have come from the Anglican Church in Aotearoa, New Zealand and Polynesia.

Following ACC-13 I resolved to meet with the Primate / Presiding Bishop and the Executive Councils of both the Anglican Church in Canada and The Episcopal Church, to explain the actions and decisions of ACC-13, and those visits were met with sincere appreciation.

Within a year of the appointment of Canon Kenneth Kearon as Secretary General, I conducted an initial review of his appointment, as a result of which the appointment was confirmed. In very recent times at the request of the Joint Standing Committee I have conducted a four year review of that appointment, including a focus on the relationship with Lambeth Palace.

In the course of my frequent trips to London I have greatly appreciated the convenience and the hospitality offered by St Andrew's House, and I have tried to maintain a pastoral ministry with all the staff there, many of whom work extremely hard to further the very varied work of the Anglican Communion office.

It has been a privilege to serve the Anglican Communion in this role. I first was elected as a member of the ACC in 1988, so this meeting brings to an end my involvement lasting twenty-one years.

+ John Paterson
Chair
April 2009

The Chairman's Closing Sermon

Mark 16: 1-8

This morning the Bible Study for the ACC looked in detail at the Gospel reading for this service, and the much-debated question of the abrupt ending to St Mark's Gospel. Did Mark really finish in mid-sentence, or, as the old Sunday School joke would have Eve saying to Adam in the Garden of Eden is there a leaf missing?

Despite Janet's carefully crafted Bible Study this morning, I take the view that the last piece of Mark's manuscript has gone missing, and that he did not intend to leave the women trembling in fear and silence. Mark makes the point that these same women witness the death and burial of Jesus. These were strong, courageous, loving women who went to the tomb at first light without their men, intending to see to the necessary preparation of Jesus' body, expecting to have trouble with the massive stone, but hoping no doubt that someone stronger would be around to help. You see, they were not going there in order to witness Jesus' resurrection from death. They had no idea that any such thing was even thinkable. They were going to complete the primary burial tasks, the anointing of his body as their one last act of service to him, sad but necessary, leading to eventual permanent entombment.

And they got the shock of their lives. The stone was already rolled away. 'The stone was rolled back' – an example perhaps of Mark's use of the passive voice to avoid speaking directly of God. We are to understand that the entire event is God's doing.

I like to ponder about that stone. Mark makes the point that it was extremely large, yet when the women arrived, they found that it had been rolled away. Are there any large stones in our lives? 'Who will roll the stone away?' the women asked. Who can roll the stone away from the death, from the negativity that so easily causes us to stumble and even to stop? Who will roll the stone away from those places where death and decay have us locked in, have us trapped? Are we looking for the experience of triumph or hoping for the experience of presence? Does the empty tomb represent the assurance that God is present in our times of limits and losses? Have we manufactured any large stones and are now unable of our own strength to roll them away?

Have we manufactured a large stone called 'An Anglican Covenant' that will seal off creative, faithful life in the Communion? I trust not. Perhaps there are other large stones with different labels that we might wish God to roll away – stones that might be labeled 'conservative', 'liberal', 'orthodox', 'Windsor', 'Gafcon' – are a few possibilities. Will God roll those stones away in order to let new life, new light, new hope emerge.

The women enter the tomb and find a young man whose message is perhaps the central message of Mark's entire Gospel – 'he has risen, he is not here'. The message brings dramatic reversal to a tragic narrative, which had seemed to end in the abandonment and death of the Son of God. The tragedy though is turned upside down. Looking among the dead for the one crucified, the women are assured that they are looking in the wrong place. 'The place where they laid him' Mark says is empty. In this emptiness is expressed the futility of every effort to capture, to contain, to possess the Nazarene, the frustration of every quest of the historical Jesus. To see Jesus, the women and the disciples must look ahead, as the second part of the message makes clear. He would see them again in Galilee, and they are to go and inform the disciples and Peter – the man who had missed Good Friday. Even after those catastrophic denials, Peter was not to be regarded as being beyond redemption.

The falling away of the disciples and the denials of Peter are not the end of God's plans for them. In this command to the women lies the promise of forgiveness and restitution, a renewed call and a fresh start for disciples chastened by failure but empowered by the resurrection.

One of the things that some of us have noticed about Mark's Gospel is that people are often told to remain silent. Particularly people whom Jesus has healed are charged with maintaining silence. But they seldom take heed. For Mark the revelation of Jesus of Nazareth is not complete until the resurrection has occurred – only then is the command issued, and it is by the youth in the tomb – 'go and tell'. And the supreme irony of the ending of Mark's Gospel is that they do just the opposite. 'They said nothing to anyone'.

Overcome by ecstasy, fear and trembling, the women flee from the tomb. Emotionally, they are overwhelmed with joy, but physically they are shaking with the enormity of what they have learned. 'And they said nothing to anyone, for they were afraid'. The revelation for Mark has been completed, and at last the command can be given – 'Go and tell'. The silence of the women, in Mark's abrupt ending, then for me is inexplicable. Some scholars inform us that the real ending of this Gospel is for the reader to write.

'But go and tell his disciples and Peter, that he is going ahead of you to Galilee. You will see him there, just as he told you.' At one level, the mention of Galilee functions in both a literal and a geographical sense. Other evangelists understood it in those terms, and Mark Chapter 13 presupposes that some such meeting must have occurred. A reflection perhaps of a life setting in which restored disciples are engaged in mission to all nations in the face of severe opposition and persecution.

As we celebrate the ending of this fourteenth meeting of the Anglican Consultative Council, pack our bags to begin the journey home, perhaps we could also reflect on a different reading, on a different understanding of the significance of Galilee. Janet made this explicit this morning. At the level of discourse between the text and the reader could we not also understand Galilee as the Galilee of the Gentiles, the locus of mission to the nations? For Galilee is the place from which the disciples and the women came – Galilee is their home turf, the place of their daily life, their daily routine. So the place where we as readers of Mark's Gospel must write the fuller ending, is precisely there also – at home, at our place of mission and ministry, and not simply here in this historic Cathedral in Kingston, Jamaica.

There is much for us to process as we return home, much that we have both contributed and learned in these eleven days together. For some of us it is also the last occasion that we will be together in an ACC gathering as members. Those whose ACC journey began in Hong Kong with ACC-12, and continued through ACC-13 in Nottingham, have finished their usual term of membership here in Kingston. In my case a journey from ACC-8 in Cardiff through twenty years until Kingston Jamaica and ACC-14.

I have sat alongside three Archbishops of Canterbury in that time, and three Secretaries General, during seven full meetings of the ACC. It was one of those Archbishops, Robert Runcie, who spoke of the 'bonds of affection' which used to hold the Anglican Communion together, and that certainly was my experience of these gatherings, certainly up until our meeting four years ago in Nottingham, when our holding together was severely challenged. But thanks to our wonderful hosts here in Jamaica, thanks to the magnificent way in which you have made us feel good to be here, thanks to the outstanding manner in which you have made us feel proud once again to be Anglican in your midst, in your worship, in your hospitality, in the broad smile of a Caribbean welcome, those bonds of affection are back in place. Thank you, Diocese of Jamaica and the Cayman Islands, thank you Church of the Province of the West Indies. That in itself is a gift of great value, perhaps another aspect of that pearl of great price with which Archbishop Rowan began his time with us ten days ago.

When the members of ACC-10 arrived in Panama in 1996 and checked into the Hotel that was to be our home for the next two weeks, we were confronted by a large sign which said 'On checking in to this Hotel, guests are required to leave their guns and weapons at the door'. Our Jamaican hosts have helped us to do just that once again. Our meeting has been characterized by some rigorous debates, but with respect and even affection across the floor of the house. As your outgoing Chair, I have been deeply grateful for that. And that surely is one of the many gifts that we can return home with, knowing that the ACC has met well, and the renewed confidence we can have in the strength and the life of the Anglican Communion. In my own case, ACC experiences over 21 years have provided me with wonderful friendships in many parts of the Anglican world, and those will always be treasured.

As well as being part of the ACC for so long, I have also had experience of two of the other 'Instruments of Communion'. Only the Archbishop of Canterbury can have experience of all four Instruments, but some of us are able to claim experience of three of those four bodies. I served a six-year term as Primate, and attended a Primates' Meeting in each of those six years. I have had the privilege and the pain of attending two Lambeth Conferences. The fact that the ACC is the only truly representative gathering under a Constitution agreed to by all the Member Churches, the only one of those four instruments where laity and clergy other than bishops can have a voice and a vote, is of lasting significance.

28

Anglican polity has always held that it is bishops in synod, or bishops in council, that are able to make decisions that guide the life of the church locally. For the Communion, the Primates' Meetings cannot do that, although we should be able to look to our Primates for wise guidance and theological insights, but in my view that is quite different from making binding decisions from which the rest of the Church is excluded.

We have now moved to seeing what we have known as the Joint Standing Committee of the Primates and the ACC become more simply the Standing Committee of the Anglican Communion, possibly meeting more than once a year, with the right balance of Primates, clergy and laity represented. That is a significant advance in the tightening of our structures, a significant advance in helping the four 'Instruments of Communion' work more cohesively together, without taking anything away from any of those Instruments.

So I wish Bishop James Tengatenga and Elizabeth Paver well as they take up their new responsibilities as Chair and Vice Chair respectively. I have occupied both of those positions, and so I know something of what you will experience. When I was the Vice Chair I held Bishop Simon Chiwanga of Tanzania in very high regard as the Chair of the ACC, but I privately would address him as 'the Artful Dodger' because of the way he very skillfully would get me to do most of the donkey work. So, Elizabeth, be careful!

I look forward to helping to organise the hosting of ACC-15 in three years time in the context of the Anglican Communion's best-kept secret – i.e. the Anglican Church in Aotearoa, New Zealand and Polynesia. I will not have to concern myself with the deliberations, the by-laws, the Constitution, the Budget, nor the politics that have sometimes been all too present in these meetings. But the major challenge, which will face us as hosts, is to try and maintain the extremely high standards of welcome and hospitality, which have been set here in Jamaica, and were most certainly also set seven years ago in Hong Kong. Our hosts will know that I mean the Black Caps batsmen face the challenge of the West Indies fast bowlers. I know Anglicans in Aotearoa, New Zealand and Polynesia, will gladly face the challenge of hosting the ACC but, perhaps a barrel or three of Bishop Reid's rum punch would help, and I need to talk to the Bishop about that.

The abrupt ending to Mark's Gospel invites readers to write their own. Well - here is one such attempt: 'The disciples - the members of the ACC went out and flew home from Jamaica. Trembling and panic had not seized them, other than going through Customs and Immigration. They told everyone they met that Christ is alive and living in Jamaica, and they fully expected him to accompany them on their journey, and to meet him when they arrived home. And what is more, they said, the Anglican Communion is alive and well, and functioning faithfully and effectively in places right around God's world, in places of fear and strife, in places of poverty, places of wealth, places of natural disaster. Anglicans everywhere are following our Lord's beckoning to meet him there in Galilee, in the places where they live and work, in the midst of God's creation, which so badly needs our care. Alleluia, Christ is risen! He is raised indeed! Alleluia let us keep the Feast. Amen.

+ John Paterson
Spanish Town, Jamaica
May 2009

The Secretary General's Report
The Revd Canon Dr Kenneth Kearon

Those of you who were at the last ACC Meeting, ACC-13 in Nottingham, England, may well feel like myself that that event lies in the far distant past. At that time, the Windsor Report had just been published and the Episcopal Church and the Anglican Church of Canada had agreed to the request of the Primates' Meeting to voluntarily withdraw their members from that meeting of the ACC. At that time it felt that that crisis within the Communion was permeating each part of our ACC meeting. In the past four years since then much has happened to strengthen our common life within the Anglican Communion. There has been a very successful Lambeth Conference and an enormous amount of work has been done on the Covenant at which we will be looking at during this meeting.

WINDSOR PROCESS

Its possible to divide up the Windsor Report recommendations into two. First of all, there were proposals aimed to address the immediate tensions and issues facing our Communion at that time. There was the request for three moratoria: the first on the election and consent to any candidate to the episcopate living in a same-gender union; second, the request for a moratorium on the authorisation of public rites of blessings of same-sex unions; and thirdly, a request for a moratorium on interventions into other provinces. There was also a request that the listening process, first requested at the Lambeth Conference 1978, listening to the experience of gay and lesbian people within the Church, should begin without delay.

The second part of the Windsor Report recommendations concern our common life together as a communion and the nature of that communion. You will remember that that report addressed the concepts of autonomy and communion and explored what it meant to be a communion, given the diversity of experience within our common life.

With respect to the immediate issues, (i) a request to initiate a listening process in the Communion came before the meeting of the ACC in 2005 and following that meeting and the mandate that was received there a facilitator for the listening process was appointed to monitor and share resources on listening throughout the provinces of the Communion. (ii) The Windsor Continuation Group report, which was received by the Archbishop of Canterbury earlier this year, reflected on where the Communion was with the three moratoria.

It said:

It was the judgement of the Joint Standing Committee of the Anglican Consultative Council and the Primates and Moderators of the Anglican Communion (JSC)[9] that the first moratorium (On the Consecration of Bishops) is effectively in place in the communion. Although there continues to be some debate whether the wording of the resolution B033 of the 75th General Convention and its subsequent interpretation by the TEC House of Bishops at New Orleans in 2007 exactly meets the wording of the recommendation in the Windsor Report, such a moratorium does, in fact, exist; an interpretation agreed by both the strongest supporters and opponents of B033.

It is the judgement of WCG (Windsor Continuation Group) that the same is significantly, but not universally, true of the second moratorium on the authorisation of public Rites of Blessing of same sex unions. In The Episcopal Church up to a dozen dioceses out of the 110 dioceses of the Church are actively pursuing the exploration of such Rites within the life of the Church (10%). They do this with only the passive consent of General Convention[10], which has until now refused to take positive steps towards the recognition of such Rites. The remainder of the dioceses of TEC either explicitly or implicitly are living by the Windsor recommendation. While this situation cannot be characterised as a wholehearted embrace of the Windsor recommendation by TEC, neither should it be characterised as a determined movement by the whole Church to carry forward the agenda to see such Rites firmly established in the life of the Church. It remains a pattern of isolated instances.

It is in respect to the third moratorium (on interventions) that there has been the least discernable response. As noted in the JSC Report of October 2007, there has apparently been an increase in interventions since the adoption of the Windsor/Dromantine recommendations by the unanimous voice of the Primates. The adoption of dioceses into the Province of the Southern Cone, inconsistent with the Constitutions both of TEC and the Southern Cone; the consecration of bishops for ministry in various forms by different Provinces and the vocal support of such initiatives by the Primates associated with the Gafcon have all taken place, apparently in contradiction of the 2005 Dromantine Statement, although in each case, the primates involved would cite a conviction that their actions were provisional, born of necessity, and reactive rather than taking the initiative. From their perspective, some of the intervening Primates have indicated that they will hand back those within their care as soon as the underlying causes have been resolved (WCG Report paras 29, 30 & 33).

To those immediate responses by the Windsor Report should be added to the requests by the Primates' Meeting 2005 for the setting up of a Panel of Reference 'for parishes which find it impossible in all conscience to accept the direct ministry of their own diocesan bishop or for dioceses in dispute with their provincial authorities'. The task was a difficult one, but progress was made, and the Panel completed its work some time ago.

The work of the Listening Process has been very worthwhile with virtually every province in the Communion engaged in a way appropriate to its situation and culture to which it finds itself, engaged in some form of listening both to the experience of gay and lesbian people within the Church and also to those who have sincere and deeply held opinions or difficulties with their recognition. A sub-project of that process called 'Don't Throw Stones' was also established to enable more theological conversations and resources to be developed. A book was published in time for the Lambeth Conference outlining resources for listening, and giving theological biblical resources for such listening and conversation. Later on during this meeting you will hear a report the listening process, and the next phase which it is hoped will begin very shortly.

With respect to the longer term, the Windsor Report recommended that a text for the Anglican Covenant be developed within the Communion and much work has been done on this, so much so that draft texts have been considered by both the Lambeth Conference and the Primates' Meeting, and now come to this meeting of the ACC for your consideration.

ECUMENICAL WORK

One of the major areas of work of this office has always been our ecumenical dialogues with our partners churches. The Lambeth Conference often provides a watershed for such ecumenical conversations and the Conference of 2008 was no different. Before that Conference a final text was agreed by the Anglican-Roman Catholic Commission on Unity and Mission (IARCCUM) entitled 'Growing Together in Unity and Mission', and also the long running Anglican-Orthodox Dialogues produced a report entitled 'The Church of the Triune God'. In parallel with these dialogues, relationships among our churches have grown and deepened extensively. In particular, we should mention relations with the Lutheran World Federation, the Methodist Church worldwide, the Roman Catholic Church and the Orthodox Churches.

MISSION DESK

Mission has always been a priority for the Anglican Communion and over the last few years following the retirement of Marjorie Murphy as Director of Mission and Evangelism a review of this whole area of our work was instigated. It was decided to appoint a Project Officer, the Revd John Kafwanka from Zambia to work to resource bishops in terms of mission at the Lambeth Conference and also to explore what the future shape of a mission desk at the Anglican Communion Office might look like. The Desk at the Anglican Communion Office has been renamed the 'Mission Desk' and two working groups dealing with two very different aspects of mission have been set up. One is entitled 'Evangelism and Church Growth Initiative' and we will hear more about this during the Council meeting, and the other one, particularly picking up a proposal from the Lambeth Conference aims to develop a strategy for Anglican Relief and Development worldwide. This aspect of work is being jointly supported by the Mission Desk and Lambeth Palace International Development Office. Another dimension of the work of mission in the Anglican Communion is the work of the official Anglican Communion Networks of which we have already heard a lot during this Conference. A Co-ordinator for our Networks has been appointed within the Anglican Communion Office to strengthen and raise the profile of our Networks and to ensure coordination of their activities.

COMMUNICATIONS

A major review of our Communications strategy will begin shortly at the Anglican Communion Office. In part this was triggered by the fact that we had to cease publication of Anglican Episcopal World a couple of years ago for financial reasons but also to acknowledge the increasing use of the web, and the extent to which people now use web-based resources in terms of communications. The fruits of that review will be seen shortly.

UNITED NATIONS OBSERVER

We have always been an outward looking Communion and one of the ways in which we look outward is through our engagement with work of the United Nations. Since 1990, the Anglican Communion has had an Observer at the United Nations based in New York. 2006 saw the retirement of Archdeacon Tai and after an extensive recruitment process Dr Hellen Wangusa from Uganda was appointed to this position. The role of the UN Observer is becoming increasingly important in our globalised world to enable Anglican voices, opinions and perspectives to be raised in the corridors of the United Nations and also to communicate to the Anglican Communion the relevant work within the United Nations.

THEOLOGICAL EDUCATION

At the last meeting ACC meeting in 2005 you received a report on theological education. You may be aware that this is one of the priorities for Archbishop Rowan's ministry as Archbishop of Canterbury and there was a strong sense that this area needed to be better resourced and strengthened in our common life. Since then additional resources have been found and the work of theological education has increased apace from the Anglican Communion Office. A Director of Theological Issues has been appointed; textbooks on Anglicanism have been identified and disseminated; a textbook suitable for use in parishes and seminaries has been identified and translated into several languages. What are called the 'grids', common standards of education attainment in the area of theological education have been worked on and commended to the Communion and a working definition of what the Anglican Way means today in our common life has been drawn up. We are at the end of the first phase of our work on Theological Education and about to begin a second new strategic phase, where the emphasis will be resourcing and support for theological educators. Again, you will hear about the work of theological education during this meeting.

INTER FAITH ISSUES

It won't surprise you when I say that inter faith issues have become a very significant part of our life in the Communion and while you will hear proposals later on you will hear much about inter faith work in the Communion. It is clear to me that this is an area in need of substantial resources into the future. Up to now this has been delivered through the work of a Network for Inter Faith Concerns (NIFCON). The title is important, as that Network looks to the whole range of our experience of inter faith engagements, from dialogue to the support of Christians living in situations where inter faith issues are difficult and sometimes engender violence. We are grateful for what have been done already but we do recognise that much more needs to be done in this area.

Theological reflection in this area led to the publication of '*Generous Love:* the truth of the Gospel and the call to dialogue', an important statement of an Anglican theology of inter faith relations, and how and why we engage with people of other faiths. A study guide is now being prepared. In all of this our staff work closely with Lambeth Palace staff, especially in support of the Archbishop in his engagement in dialogue.

SUPPORT FOR WOMEN

An important resolution at ACC-13 concerned the role and place of women in the structures of the Anglican Communion of the Standing Committee. Appointments to most of the structures of the Communion are not made by the ACC itself, except in one area – the appointment of its own Standing Committee, and there women are well represented.

However the Standing Committee also recognised that behind this resolution is the more serious issue of how we as a Communion support women especially in areas of marginalisation, violence and economic disadvantage. These are crucial issues and have been named and identified in the work of our Observer at the United Nations and by several of our Networks – especially the Anglican Women's Network and the Family Network.

STANDING COMMISSIONS

In the past, two commissions have addressed important issues for our common life in the Communion and in our relationships with other churches. One is the Inter-Anglican Standing Commission on Ecumenical Relations (IASCER), which oversaw ecumenical dialogues and the way in which we related to our partner Christian Churches throughout the world. The other was the Inter-Anglican Theological and Doctrinal Commission (IATDC), which addressed basic questions of in our Anglican teaching and identity. It has been decided to gather the issues addressed by both these bodies, together with the many issues arising from the Windsor Process and make them the responsibility of one much bigger Standing Commission. Last November the Joint Standing Committee authorised the Archbishop of Canterbury and the Secretary General to begin the process of appointing an Inter-Anglican Standing Commission on Unity Faith and Order (IASCUFO). This body, I am sure, will make an important and significant contribution to our own self understanding as Anglicans within a global communion and to a theological and doctrinal understanding of ourselves as Anglicans in our relationships with other Christian churches.

An important proposal will come before this meeting – that we set up a study process – 'the Bible in the Life of the Church'. Scripture is at the heart of all that we are, and all we do as churches. How does the Bible shape our lives as individuals and as church committee? How do Anglicans engage Scripture with our everyday lives? You will hear more about this important project later.

LAMBETH CONFERENCE

Numerically the biggest of the Instruments of Communion is the Lambeth Conference, occurring every 10 years, most recently in 2008. Planning for that Conference was the responsibility of a Lambeth Design group – a group of bishops, clergy and lay people from around the Communion. The Secretary General is the Secretary of the Conference, so the organisational responsibility lies with the Anglican Communion Office. A Lambeth Conference Manager, Sue Parks, was recruited in late 2004, soon to be joined by 3 assistant managers – David Craig, Anna Potts and Emily Horrocks. A Lambeth Conference Company was formed as a vehicle for financial, legal and administrative aspects of the Conference.

The format of the Conference was new and proved engaging for the bishops there, and almost all judged the Conference to be an important unifying event in the life of our Communion. Costs of the Lambeth Conference exceeded £5million, and at one stage there was the possibility of a funding shortfall of up to £1million. Happily this turned out not to be the case, and the current shortfall is just under £200,000.

ANGLICAN COMMUNION OFFICE

All of this activity is resourced by a comparatively small staff at the Anglican Communion Office in London. As Secretary General, I would like to pay tribute to each and every one of those staff. The years bring changes and we have seen over the while the retirement of Marjorie Murphy, Director of Mission and Evangelism for quite a number of years, and we thank her for work and we are grateful that she has maintained her links and contacts with the office. For almost 20 years Canon Jim Rosenthal has been Director of Communications and after the Lambeth Conference he too has ceased to work at the Anglican Communion Office. He will in the minds of many always be associated with 'Anglican Episcopal World', and for his work with this publication and all other aspects of communications we are immensely grateful. For very, very many years, 32 years in fact, the voice and face of the Anglican Communion has been Deirdre Martin, Executive Assistant to the Secretary General. She has served the Anglican Communion through four Lambeth Conferences, four Archbishops of Canterbury and four Secretaries General. After the last Lambeth Conference she decided to retire at the end of 2008. It is important that we pay tribute to her, to Marjorie and to Jim for all they have done for the Communion over those years.

This meeting marks the end of Gregory Cameron's ministry as Deputy Secretary General and Director of Ecumenical Affairs, as he is now Bishop of St Asaph in the Church in Wales. He came to the Anglican Communion Office just before the appointment of the Lambeth Commission which led to the Windsor Report, and readily took on that work in addition to Ecumenical Affairs. Since then the Windsor Process has piled on more and more commissions, panels and working groups on to him. Without doubt he has made quite remarkable contribution to shaping the Anglican Communion in the troubled times, and to steadying our common life. His skill, good humour and resolute impartiality has infused all his work. We at the Anglican Communion Office miss him already, and I am losing a wonderful colleague and friend. St Asaph's has truly chosen wisely!

Part Two
Resolutions

The Resolutions of ACC-14

ACO PROGRAMMES

Resolution 14.01: Ecumenical Affairs (Ecumenical)
Resolved, 09.05.09, 11.05.09(clause b)

The Anglican Consultative Council:
(a) thanks the members and staff of the Inter-Anglican Standing Commission for Ecumenical Affairs (IASCER) for their fruitful labours over the last ten years, and commend the Report *'The Vision Before Us'*, compiled on behalf of the Commission by the Revd Sarah Rowland Jones, for study as a benchmark ecumenical volume in the Provinces of the Anglican Communion;
(b) endorses the 'Four Principles of Anglican Engagement in Ecumenism' set out in that Report as a key description of the Anglican approach towards ecumenical activity and goals, adopts the following shorthand to describe them, and commends them to the Churches of the Communion;
1. The Goal: the full organic unity of the Church
2. The Task: recognising and receiving the Church in one another
3. The Process: unity by stages
4. The Content: common faith, sacraments and ministry
(c) welcomes the Resolutions of IASCER set out in the Report, endorses those relating to the administration of the *'the two sacraments ordained by Christ himself – Baptism and the Supper of the Lord'(Lambeth Quadrilateral)* and urges their adoption throughout the Anglican Communion in the light of the importance of convergence on the administration of these sacraments in ecumenical relations;
(d) reaffirms the *'Guidelines on Ecumenical Participation in Ordinations'* set out in the report of IASCER as describing the best practice for Anglicans in this area;
(e) requests the Standing Committee to commission a review of the processes for the reception of ecumenical texts, as recommended in the Resolution 02.08 of IASCER;
(f) welcomes the continuing work of the various dialogue commissions of the Anglican Communion at present operating, namely the

Anglican Old Catholic International Co-ordinating Council, the Anglican Lutheran International Commission and the Anglican Methodist International Commission for Unity in Mission;

(g) looks forward to the Report of the ARCIC Preparatory Commission, and the commissioning of a third phase of the Anglican Roman Catholic International Commission, and the resumption of the work of the International Anglican Roman Catholic Commission for Unity and Mission and the International Commission for Anglican Orthodox Theological Dialogue;

(h) urges the resumption of the work of the Anglican Oriental Orthodox International Commission along the lines set in IASCER Resolution 04.04 point 4;

(i) noting the favourable response recorded in the Lambeth Indaba Reflections to the reports '*The Church of the Triune God*' of the International Commission for Anglican - Orthodox Theological Dialogue and '*Growing Together in Unity and Mission*' of the International Anglican Roman Catholic Commission for Unity and Mission, commends them to the Provinces of the Communion for study and response as detailed in IASCER Resolutions 07.08 and 08.08, and requests that Provincial responses be submitted to the Anglican Communion Office by the end of June 2011 for consideration by the subsequent meeting of the Inter-Anglican Standing Commission for Unity, Faith and Order;

(j) welcomes the IASCER Report with respect to the World Council of Churches and urges the Churches of the Anglican Consultative Council to continue their support of, and their participation in, the life of the WCC;

(k) urges Anglican Christians around the world to gather informally with other Christians around God's Word, in prayer and in service.

Resolution 14.02: Evangelism and Church Growth Initiative (Mission)
Resolved 09.05.09

The Anglican Consultative Council:
(a) notes the aspirations and desire of the Bishops at the 2008 Lambeth Conference 'to develop a worldwide vision and strategy of church planting, growth and mission' (Lambeth Indaba P.13),

(b) welcomes the renaming of the department from Mission and Evangelism to Mission Department,

(c) endorses Resolution 2 of the Joint Standing Committee of the Anglican Consultative Council and the Primates of the Anglican Communion of November 2008 and the work already undertaken to set up an Evangelism and Church Growth Initiative.

Resources
Resolution 2: Mission Desk at the Anglican Communion Office

THAT the Joint Standing Committee of the Primates of the Anglican Communion and the Anglican Consultative Council receive the report on the future of the Mission Desk at the Anglican Communion Office, agree to its renaming and encourage the Secretary General to proceed with the setting up of and Evangelism and Church Growth Network.

Resolution 14.03: Anglican Relief and Development Alliance (Mission)
Resolved, 11.05.09

The Anglican Consultative Council:
(a) acknowledges the request from the Bishops at the 2008 Lambeth Conference to enhance a more collaborative approach to existing relief, development and advocacy activities in the Anglican Communion, and the support for this initiative from the Primates' meeting in Alexandria in February 2009,

(b) welcomes and receives the report from the Anglican Relief and Development Consultation in January 2009;

(c) affirms the recommendation to form an alliance of Anglican relief and development agencies to improve co-ordination in development, relief and advocacy work across the Communion, and to share experiences of best practice;

(d) encourages the steering group, established after the January 2009 Consultation, with the Anglican Communion Office and Lambeth Palace, to advance this recommendation, seeking the widest Communion participation.

Resolution 14.04: Local efforts in Relief and Development (Mission)
Resolved, 12.05.09

The Anglican Consultative Council asks the Anglican Communion Office to investigate means by which relief and development initiatives at local level, in congregations, dioceses, provinces and other groups across the Communion might be encouraged and strengthened.

Resolution 14.05: Sixth Mark of Mission (Mission)
Resolved 11.05.09

The Anglican Consultative Council
  (a) endorses the request from the Anglican Church of Canada and the 2009 Mutual Responsibility and Mission Consultation in Costa Rica to add a sixth 'Mark of Mission' that relates to peace, conflict transformation and reconciliation to the current list of five,
  (b) requests the Mission Department of the Anglican Communion Office to take this process forward and report to ACC-15.

Resolution 14.06: 'The Bible in the Life of the Church'
(Theological Studies)
Resolved, 09.05.09

The Anglican Consultative Council:
  (a) welcomes the presentation by Archbishop Phillip Aspinall and the Director of Theological Studies on the proposed project 'The Bible in the Life of the Church';
  (b) asks the Archbishop of Canterbury and the Secretary-General to appoint a Steering Group to direct the project until ACC-15;
  (c) encourages the development of the project along the lines presented, asking that the Steering Group take account of the work of, and work collaboratively with, the Listening Process and the Inter-Anglican Standing Commission on Unity, Faith and Order;
  (d) asks Provinces to contribute to the ongoing costs of the Project over the next three years;
  (e) asks that a report on the project be presented to ACC-15.

Resolution 14.07: Network on Inter Faith Concerns (Theological Studies)
Resolved, 09.05.09
The Anglican Consultative Council:
(a) welcomes the varied work done by NIFCON in the field of inter faith concerns;
(b) commends the report *Generous Love: the truth of the Gospel and the Call to Dialogue* for study in the Anglican Communion
(c) endorses NIFCON's priorities for the next phase as set out in their Report, in particular its desire to offer training resources in the field of engagement with other faiths, and to assist the Anglican Communion in responding more effectively to the situation of Christian minorities living in difficult contexts.
(d) welcomes the appointment of the Most Revd Mouneer H Anis and the Rt Revd Tim Stevens as Presidents of NIFCON.

Resolution 14.08: Theological Education in the Anglican Communion (Theological Studies)
Resolved, 11.05.09

The Anglican Consultative Council:
(a) thanks the current members of TEAC for their work and contribution to the development of theological education in the Anglican Communion;
(b) welcomes the new phase of the Working Party;
(c) endorses the proposed structure and tasks as set out in the submission received;
(d) welcomes the establishment of the informal network 'Connecting Anglican Women in Theological Education' and asks those responsible for the work of TEAC to support and encourage its further development;

WINDSOR PROCESS RESOLUTIONS

Resolution 14.09: The Windsor Continuation Group
Resolved, 08.05.09

The Anglican Consultative Council:
  (a) thanks the Archbishop of Canterbury for his report on the work and recommendations of the Windsor Continuation Group,
  (b) affirms the recommendations of the Windsor Continuation Group,
  (c) affirms the request of the Windsor Report (2004), adopted at the Primates' Meetings (2005, 2007 and 2009), and supported at the Lambeth Conference (2008) for the implementation of the agreed moratoria on the Consecration of Bishops living in a same gender union, authorisation of public Rites of Blessing for Same Sex unions and continued interventions in other Provinces;
  (d) acknowledges the efforts that have been made to hold to the moratoria, gives thanks for the gracious restraint that has been observed in these areas and recognises the deep cost of such restraint;
  (e) asks that urgent conversations are facilitated with those Provinces where the application of the moratoria gives rise for concern;
  (f) encourages the Archbishop of Canterbury to work with the Standing Committee and the Secretary General to carry forward the implementation of the Windsor Continuation Group Report recommendations as appropriate,
  (g) asks the Inter-Anglican Standing Commission on Unity, Faith and Order to undertake a study of the role and responsibilities in the Communion of the Archbishop of Canterbury, the Lambeth Conference, the Anglican Consultative Council and the Primates' Meeting; the ecclesiological rationale of each, and the relationships between them, in line with the Windsor Continuation Group Report, and to report back to ACC-15;
  (h) calls the Communion to pray for repentance, conversion and renewal; leading to deeper communion.

Resolution 14.10: IASCUFO Study
Resolved, 11.05.09

The Anglican Consultative Council, in the light of the Resolution 14.09 of ACC-14 on the WCG Report, asks that the report of the study undertaken by IASCUFO includes a study of the existing papers developed within our Communion and of current best practices in governance for multi-layered complex organizations, and makes recommendations to ACC-15 on ways in which the effectiveness of the Instruments of Communion may be enhanced.

Resolution 14.11: The Anglican Communion Covenant
Resolved, 08.05.09
The Anglican Consultative Council:
  (a) thanks the Covenant Design Group for their faithfulness and responsiveness in producing the drafts for an Anglican Communion Covenant and, in particular, for the Ridley Cambridge Draft submitted to this meeting;
  (b) recognises that an Anglican Communion Covenant may provide an effective means to strengthen and promote our common life as a Communion;
  (c) asks the Archbishop of Canterbury, in consultation with the Secretary General, to appoint a small working group to consider and consult with the Provinces on Section 4 and its possible revision, and to report to the next meeting of the Standing Committee;
  (d) asks the Standing Committee, at that meeting, to approve a final form of Section 4;
  (e) asks the Secretary General to send the revised Ridley Cambridge Text, at that time, only to the member Churches of the Anglican Consultative Council for consideration and decision on acceptance or adoption by them as The Anglican Communion Covenant;
  (f) asks those member Churches to report to ACC-15 on the progress made in the processes of response to, and acceptance or adoption of, the Covenant.

Resolution 14.12: The Listening Process
Resolved, 06.05.09

The Anglican Consultative Council
(a) thanks Canon Philip Groves for his facilitation of the Listening Process since 2005 and for his report to Anglican Consultative Council;
(b) recognises that listening is a long term process and is linked to the 'gracious restraint' asked for in the Windsor Continuation Group Report;
(c) notes that the report requested that the Instruments of Communion to commit themselves to a renewal of the Listening Process, and a real seeking of a common mind upon the issues which threaten to divide us (paragraph 25);
(d) welcomes the proposal for a Continuing Indaba Project and urges its implementation as soon as possible;
(e) expresses its profound thanks to Dr David Satcher, Director of the Satcher Health Leadership Institute at the Morehouse School of Medicine, for his generous financial support for this project.

NETWORK RESOLUTIONS

Resolution 14.13: Colleges and Universities of the Anglican Communion (CUAC)
Resolved, 06.05.09

The Anglican Consultative Council
(a) gratefully acknowledges the work of the CUAC (the Colleges and Universities of the Anglican Communion) network in supporting and enlarging educational ministry throughout the Communion
(b) asks that Provinces
i.   identify and support Anglican-related institutions of higher learning in their region
ii. urge such institutions to participate in the CUAC network in order to effect mutually useful student and faculty study experiences and exchanges

iii. give attention to the training and experience of future leaders and scholars for Anglican institutions of higher education in their regions;
(c) asks the network to encourage and advise on the establishment of new institutions of higher education in Provinces where no such institutions exist.

Resolution 14.14: Theological Institutions (from CUAC)
Resolved, 06.05.09

The Anglican Consultative Council notes that there is an evolving field of knowledge in contemporary Anglican Studies, and that both current and future leaders of the Communion would benefit from learning about Anglicanism in more than one context. It therefore encourages

- schools of theology, seminaries and programmes of ministry to develop inter-Anglican courses which involve the study and research of the variety of Anglican contexts, and specifically to include inter-Anglican study projects with students of at least one other very different Province
- the ACO Department of Theological Studies, to co-operate with CUAC in the development of such programmes
- theological colleges, seminaries and programmes of study to explore the possibility of using these relationships to develop a permanent inter-Anglican network of institutions of theological studies.

Resolution 14.15: Anglican Communion Environmental Network
Resolved, 11.05.09

The Anglican Consultative Council supports the Archbishop of Canterbury in his thoughtful reflection and witness in the areas of the environment, the global economy and our support of vulnerable people and communities, and encourages Provinces:
(a) to weigh the environmental as well as the financial costs of all church activities;
(b) to assist transition to a carbon-neutral world by accepting, year on year, a five percent reduction in the carbon footprint of the Churches;
(c) to celebrate a liturgical 'Season of Creation' as an integral part of the church's yearly pattern of worship and teaching;
(d) to advocate access to drinkable water as an inviolable human right;

(e) to encourage faith communities to understand that energy is part of God's provision, and that renewable energy should become the standard and fossil fuels be used only when renewable energy is temporarily unavailable;

(f) to provide means for Anglicans to develop competencies in environmental stewardship and theological reflection on the sustainability of creation and the appropriate use of science and technology;

(g) to advocate sustainable restorative economies with national governments, the United Nations through the Anglican Observers Office, and local constituencies.

Resolution 14.16: International Anglican Family Network
Resolved, 05.05.09

The Anglican Consultative Council affirms the value of International Anglican Family Network's work to the Communion, particularly the publication of their newsletters, welcomes the network's proposal to hold a third regional consultation on family issues in Oceania in 2010 and urges Provinces to support this proposal in every way they can.

Réseau /Resolution 14.17:
Le Réseau francophone de la Communion anglicane/
Resolution of the Francophone Network of the Anglican Communion

Résolu/resolved, 05.05.09

(en français)

Le Conseil Consultatif Anglican demande au Comité Ad Hoc d'explorer les moyens d'encourager la traduction de travaux théologiques anglicans fondamentaux dans des langues autres que l'anglais ainsi que leur dissémination, de même que de soutenir la formation de professeurs pour les collèges théologiques de ces provinces et diocèses dont la langue nationale est autre que l'anglais.

(in English)
> The Anglican Consultative Council requests the Standing Committee to explore ways of encouraging the translation of basic Anglican theological works into languages other than English, and their dissemination, as well as supporting the formation of teachers for the theological colleges of those provinces and dioceses whose national language is other than English.

Resolution 14.18: Anglican Health Network
Resolved, 05.05.09

The Anglican Consultative Council
  (a) welcomes the establishment of the Anglican Health Network as an official Network of the Anglican Communion
  (b) commends the objectives of the Network to the Provinces.

Resolution 14.19: Anglican Indigenous Network
Resolved. 05.05.09
The Anglican Consultative Council:
  (a) asks those member Churches whose governments have not yet signed the United Nations Declaration on the Rights of Indigenous Peoples to encourage their governments to become signatories;
  (b) asks that, where there exist indigenous people who are minorities, member churches cooperate with indigenous Anglican leaders to ensure the provision of theological education and ministry training at all levels that takes account of indigenous cultural contexts and traditions;
  (c) calls upon member Churches to value, honour and incorporate the wisdom of the elders of indigenous peoples in their midst in efforts to address global climate change and the sustainability of creation;
  (d) recognizes the on-going disastrous effects that colonialism has had on indigenous peoples and their families and calls on member Churches, where there exists indigenous people who are minorities, to take appropriate and necessary steps to assist the healing of indigenous families, including the protection of women and children from violence and human trafficking.

References

United Nations Declaration on the Rights of Indigenous Peoples: (http://www.un.org/esa/socdev/unpfii/en/drip.html)

Resolution 14.20: Anglican Communion Legal Advisers' Network (ACLAN)
Resolved, 05.05.09

The Anglican Consultative Council
  (a) thanks the Anglican Communion Legal Advisers' Network for the work undertaken so far;
  (b) commends the *Principles of Canon Law Common to the Churches of the Anglican Communion* for study in every Province;
  (c) invites Provinces and others to submit comments on the *Principles of Canon Law Common to the Churches of the Anglican Communion* to the Convenor by 30 June 2010;
  (d) requests the Editorial Committee of the network to submit a report on the responses received to the following meeting of the Standing Committee; and
  (e) encourages the Provinces to use the network as a resource in dealing with legal issues in their Provinces.

Resolution 14.21: International Anglican Liturgical Consultations
Resolved, 11.05.09

The Anglican Consultative Council receives with thanks the Report of the International Anglican Liturgical Consultations.

Resolution 14.22: The Anglican Episcopal Church of Brazil

(from the Anglican Peace and Justice Network [APJN])
Resolved, 08.05.09

The Anglican Consultative Council expresses solidarity with the Anglican Episcopal Church of Brazil (Igreja Episcopal Anglicana do Brasil) in its prophetic stand on behalf of rural black and *quilombo* communities who 'are experiencing a delicate and tense moment due to imminent judgment of ADI No. 3239 by the Brazilian Federal Supreme Court.'

Resources: letter from the Primate of Brazil - to be added

Resolution 14.23: Community Rebuilding *(from APJN)*
Resolved, 11.05.09

The Anglican Consultative Council:
a. acknowledges with admiration and gratitude the vital work of local churches in rebuilding communities that have been devastated by violence and conflict;
b. urges Anglican and Episcopal development and aid agencies and other Church and secular NGOs, where appropriate, to increase their support through local churches, in order to hasten the implementation of social development programmes that address food security, education, sustainable livelihoods, health care, women's development and internally displaced persons.

Resolution 14.24: Conflict (from APJN)
Resolved, 12.05.09

The Anglican Consultative Council:
(a) remembers people in places of conflict and injustice everywhere, especially in
- Pakistan, where blasphemy laws allow persecution under law of Christians, and encourage religious extremism
- Philippines, where killings and disappearances of church workers and others working in civil society have occurred
- Sri Lanka, where a humanitarian crisis threatens hundreds of thousands of innocent civilians on the north eastern coastal belt of Sri Lanka
- Sudan, where its peoples desperately seek an end to conflict, suffering and death
- Zimbabwe, where previous government policies have created intolerable conditions that have destroyed the infrastructure of the country
- Other places, including Democratic Republic of Congo, India, Madagascar, Nepal, and Nigeria
(b) commends the efforts and witness of the Churches in all these areas

(c) encourages the Provinces of the Anglican Communion to support prayerfully and practically fellow Christians and all who live in situations of conflict, hostility and injustice

(d) calls upon the Provinces of the Anglican Communion to pursue, with their governments and all other parties, the end of these and all other conflicts and injustices.

Resolution 14.25: Korea *(from APJN)*
Resolved, 12.05.09

The Anglican Consultative Council:

(a) notes the suffering arising from the continued division of Korea,

(b) offers its prayers and support for the continuing efforts of the Anglican Church of Korea for reunification;

(c) commends the humanitarian efforts of the Anglican Church of Korea for the relief of the starving population in North Korea and expresses its gratitude for the international co-operation demonstrated in this project;

(d) laments that the political situation in the Korean peninsula and the surrounding nations has worsened in recent months;

(e) considers that re-engagement in dialogue and collaboration is the best forward to achieve reunification and calls on all countries involved to desist from confrontation and to re-open conversations and collaboration;

(f) supports the recommendations of the worldwide Anglican Peace Conference entitled 'Towards Peace in Korea' (TOPIK) in 2007, organised in response to resolution ACC13.49, and asks the Standing Committee to consider the ways in which these recommendations may be carried forward;

(g) urges the continuation of TOPIK initiatives until a permanent peace is reached on the Korean peninsula.

Resources:
for the TOPIK report:
http://www.anglicancommunion.org/acns/news.cfm?mode=entry&entry=
5DD5CD02-96C6-814E-5BBA61139628A8F9

The recommendations are set out there as follows:

To Member Churches of the Anglican Communion
- Utilize existing Anglican resources, particularly the Anglican Peace and Justice Network, for learning about and sharing information on peacemaking.
- Create a task force, authorized by the Archbishop of Canterbury and working with the Anglican Peace and Justice Network, to initiate future programs, including a similarly-designed peace conference in another part of the world such as the Middle East.
- Authorize that task force to create peace-focused educational and liturgical materials for churches throughout the Communion.
- Build on the work of the World Council of Churches' 'Decade to Overcome Violence.'
- Provide programs in conflict resolution for those in theological and ministry formation, specifically creating an Institute for Peace-Training within the Anglican Communion.
- Encourage the development of grassroots, parish-based peace training programs.

To The Anglican Church of Korea
- Organize a further peace conference which would include a wider range of participation, particularly from North Koreans, young people, women, those of other faiths and those from regions under-represented at this conference.
- Sponsor the translation and publishing of the stories of Koreans' experiences into at least English and Japanese.

To The Anglican Consultative Conference and Lambeth Conference
- Initiate a specifically Anglican follow-up to the WCC Decade to Overcome Violence.
- Provide time in the agenda for Lambeth 2008 for discussion of the issues raised by this conference.

Resolution 14.26: Middle East *(from APJN)*
Resolved, 09.05.09

The Anglican Consultative Council meeting in Kingston, Jamaica between May 2-12, 2009, in response to the challenge in a sermon on May 3, 2009, of the Archbishop of Canterbury to be a people of hope to those in need of justice, forgiveness and reconciliation,

a. deplores violence wherever it is used in conflict in the land of Israel/Palestine and affirms its desire that a robust peace process in the Palestinian/Israeli conflict leading to a two state solution should be pursued by all parties without delay

b. expresses its deep concern about recent and continuing events in Gaza, and supports and draws attention to the 'Statement on the situation in Gaza' issued by the February 2009 Primates meeting.

c. laments the fact that current Israeli policies in relation to the West Bank, in contravention of UN Security Council resolutions, have created severe hardship for many Palestinians and have been experienced as a physical form of apartheid.

d. noting that a just peace must guarantee the security and territorial integrity of both Israel and the future state of Palestine so that all the people of the area can live in peace and prosperity, applauds President Barack Obama for his commitment to work for a just peace for both Palestinians and Israelis, and calls on him and all governments of the Middle East to work in co-operation with the United Nations for the creation of a Palestinian state alongside the State of Israel as defined by UN Security Council Resolutions,

e. welcomes the Arab League statements which indicate a readiness to make peace with the state of Israel, the resolution of the Arab-Israeli conflict, and the normalization of relations, and calls on the Israeli government to respond favourably to the Arab proposal in an effort to end all forms of belligerence on the basis of international law.

f. calls on Israel to
   (i) end its occupation of the West Bank and the Gaza Strip
   (ii) freeze immediately all settlement building with the intention to abandon its settlement policy in preparation for a Palestinian state
   (iii) remove the separation barrier (wall) where it violates Palestinian land beyond the Green Line

(iv) end home demolitions, and

(v) close checkpoints in the Palestinian territories

g. recognising that the city of Jerusalem is holy to Christianity, Islam and Judaism and is not therefore the monopoly of any one religion, upholds the view that members of all three faith groups should have free access to their holy sites.

h. calls on all people of faith and good will to pray and work for peace so that justice and reconciliation may be achieved for all the people of Palestine and Israel.

Resolution 14.27: Peace-making Dialogues *(from APJN)*
Resolved, 05.05.09

The Anglican Consultative Council:

a. urges Anglicans everywhere to be bold in preaching reconciliation and facilitating peace-making dialogues in every situation of war and conflict;

b. supports the concept of healing through the processes of truth-telling, repentance, and restorative justice;

c. urges all in provincial leadership positions, especially those in theological education, to implement programmes of conflict-resolution skills training as a contribution to developing effective and bold prophetic voices for God's justice in all societies;

d. commends to the Provinces of the Anglican Communion the educational resources on conflict transformation and reconciliation identified and promoted by the Anglican Peace and Justice Network on the ACO website.

Resolution 14.28: Post-Conflict Resolution *(from APJN)*
Resolved, 05.05.09

The Anglican Consultative Council:

a. welcomes with appreciation the report of the Anglican Peace and Justice Network entitled *'Community Transformation: Violence and the Church's Response,'* and thanks the provinces of Rwanda and Burundi for hosting the APJN in September and October 2007

b. celebrates the leadership exercised by the Provinces of Burundi and Rwanda, as well as Congo, Sudan, and Melanesia, in establishing post-conflict programs of reconciliation and healing, as highlighted in the report

c. calls for increased solidarity from member Churches of the Anglican Communion with the Provinces in the Great Lakes Region, and recommends the establishment of partner relationships, where common witness and support may help in the prevention or resolution of conflicts in the region and communities may be more immediately rebuilt.

Resolution 14.29: Sudan *(from APJN)*
Resolved, 05.05.09

The Anglican Consultative Council:
a. draws the attention of member Churches to the Statement on Sudan issued by the Primates at their meeting in Alexandria in February 2009;
b. asks its member Churches to urge the African Union, the United Nations, and their own governments to be more assertive in seeking a commitment from the Government of Sudan to implement the Comprehensive Peace Agreement without further delay;
c. urges its members to offer continued prayers and advocacy for a cessation of violence in Darfur, for resumption of peace talks with the Lord's Resistance Army and the disarming of other marauding groups, for safe passage for aid organizations, and for the protection of civilian populations throughout the country;
d. appeals to those Anglican leaders who are in dialogue with Muslim leaders around the world to share from their experience, insights and wisdom on how best the interreligious dimensions of the conflict in Sudan can be reduced.

Resolution 14.30: Towards Effective Anglican Mission *(from APJN)*
Resolved, 11.05.09

The Anglican Consultative Council expresses appreciation for the Towards Effective Anglican Mission (TEAM) Gathering in Boksburg, South Africa in March 2007 and commends the TEAM report to the Provinces as a resource in addressing the Millennium Development Goals and the alleviation of poverty in its many forms.

Resolution 14.31: Anglican Refugee and Migrant Network
Resolved, 05.05.09

The Anglican Consultative Council
(a) welcomes the re-establishment of the Anglican Refugees and Migrant Network as an official Network of the Anglican Communion,
(b) thanks the Province of Hong Kong for hosting the Network, and
(c) commends the objectives of the Network to the Provinces.

Resolution 14.32: Anglican Urban Network
Resolved, 12.05.09

The Anglican Consultative Council affirms the work of the Anglican Urban Network.

Resolution 14.33: The International Anglican Women's Network (IAWN)
Resolved: 05.05.09

The Anglican Consultative Council:
(a) receives the report from International Anglican Womens Network, commends the network for its work and commitment, and encourages it to continue to raise and promote women's concerns in church and society;
(b) urges full implementation of ACC Resolution 13.31 (b.ii) across the Communion and encourages Provinces, through the IAWN Provincial links, to report on further progress made to ACC-15;
(c) requests that appointments to all Inter-Anglican Standing Commissions, and all other inter-Anglican Committees, design groups, or appointed bodies follow resolution ACC 13.31 (b.i) to provide equal representation of women on each body;
(d) unequivocally supports the elimination of all forms of violence against women and girls, including trafficking, and encourages all Provinces to participate in programmes and events that promote the rights and welfare of women, particularly as expressed in the Beijing Platform for Action and the United Nations Millennium Development Goals;

(e) recognising the importance of appropriate allocation of financial resources, recommends implementation of the principles of gender budgeting throughout the Communion, and requests Provinces to report on progress made to Anglican Consultative Council-15.

References

(ACC Resolution 13.31.b) Anglican Consultative Council acknowledges the MDG goal for equal representation of women in decision making at all levels, and so requests:

i.　　　the Standing Committee to identify ways in which this goal may appropriately be adapted for incorporation into the structures of the Instruments of Unity, and other bodies to which the Anglican Consultative Council nominates or appoints

ii.　　　all member churches to work towards the realisation of this goal in their own structures of governance, and in other bodies to which they nominate or appoint and to report on progress to ACC-14

For the Beijing Platform: www.un.org/womenwatch/daw/Beijing/platform
For the MDGs: www.un.org/millenniumgoals

Resolution 14.34: International Anglican Youth Network
Resolved, 05.05.09

The Anglican Consultative Council:
(a) urges every Province to ensure that at least one person, actively involved in youth ministry in their Province, participate in the International Anglican Youth Network;
(b) encourages every Province to dedicate one Sunday each year as 'Ministries with Young People Sunday';
(c) requests each Province to take up a special offering annually to support ministries with young people, of which a part would be for the work of the International Anglican Youth Network;
(d) requests each Province to contribute financially to the work of the International Anglican Youth Network.

OTHER RESOLUTIONS

Resolution 14.35: The Compass Rose Society (CRS)
Resolved, 11.05.09

The Anglican Consultative Council:
(a) thanks Bishop Philip Poole, President of the Compass Rose Society, for his presentation on behalf of the Society;
(b) thanks the Society for its generous financial support for the work of this Council and for mission in the Anglican Communion;
(c) asks the Provinces to consider how they might support the work of the Compass Rose Society, including recruiting new members
(d) asks the Standing Committee to consider and implement steps to strengthen the relationship between the Compass Rose Society and the Anglican Consultative Council, including:
  i.   identifying areas of Anglican Consultative Council work that may be supported by CRS;
  ii.   appointing a liaison person from Anglican Consultative Council to the Board of CRS
  iii. working with the Secretary General to plan strategic visits to further mission in the Anglican Communion and the mission of the CRS, and
  iv.   inviting regular reports from the CRS to the Standing Committee.

Resolution 14.36: Finance
Resolved, 11.05.09

The Anglican Consultative Council:
(a) adopts and approves the Statement of Accounts for the years ending 31 December 2006-2008;
(b) approves the budget presented to the meeting for 2009 and the projections for the years 2010 and 2011;
(c) asks each Province to meet its requested budget contribution, which includes a projected increase of 3% each year.

Resolution 14.37:
The Iberian Churches and the Extra-Provincial Jurisdictions
Resolved, 12.05.09

The Anglican Consultative Council:
(a) noting the long history of communion of the Spanish Reformed
Episcopal Church and the Lusitanian Church with the Churches of
the Anglican Communion, requests the Standing Committee to
consider their admission to full membership of the Anglican
Consultative Council;
(b) asks the Standing Committee to set up a review of the relationship of
all the extra-provincial jurisdictions with the Anglican Consultative
Council.

Resolution 14.38:
Anglican Consultative Council and the Primates' Meeting
Resolved, 12.05.09
The Anglican Consultative Council:
(a)   welcomes the presence of the primatial members of the Standing
Committee as full members of the Anglican Consultative Council,
and
(b)   asks the Primates to include an equal number of non-primatial
members of the Standing Committee as non voting participants in
the Primates' Meeting.

Resolution 14.39: Terminology (Standing Committee)
Resolved, 12.05.09

The Anglican Consultative Council
(a) notes that the former 'Joint Standing Committee' is named as the
'Standing Committee' under the new constitution;
(b) amends the resolutions of this Anglican Consultative Council
meeting so that the title 'Joint Standing Committee' is replaced with
the title 'Standing Committee' wherever appropriate.

Resolution 14.40: Resolution of Thanks
Resolved, 12.05.09

The Anglican Consultative Council expresses its profound thanks for the hard work and leadership of those who take leave from us especially
o   The Rt Reverend John Paterson for his gentle and steady hand as Chair, Vice-Chair and member of the Anglican Consultative Council since 1990
o   Professor George Koshy as Vice-Chair and member of Anglican Consultative Council since 1990
o   The Rt Reverend Gregory K Cameron as Director of Ecumenical Affairs since 2003 and Deputy Secretary General since 2004.

Resolution 14.41: Resolution of Thanks
Resolved, 12.05.09

The Anglican Consultative Council adopts the following letter, greetings, and expression of thanks.

TO THE ANGLICANS OF JAMAICA

This Anglican Consultative Council meeting in Kingston Jamaica gives thanks to the people of the Diocese of Jamaica and the Cayman Islands for their exceptionally warm welcome and generous hospitality.   Led by the Bishop of Jamaica, the Rt Revd Alfred Reid, together with the suffragan bishops of Jamaica, the Rt Revd Harold Daniel, Bishop of Mandeville; the Rt Revd Howard Gregory, Bishop of Montego Bay, the Rt Revd Robert Thompson, Bishop of Kingston, those belonging to the diocese have gone out of their way to welcome the participants in this meeting of the Anglican Consultative Council and have been exceedingly generous with their time and resources. The service of welcome in the Sports Arena on Sunday 3 May, and the visits to some 32 parishes of the diocese over the weekend of 9-10 May were highlights for many and will long stay in the memory of those who participated. Such events as ACC-14 take a huge amount of planning and we are hugely indebted to the work of the Local Arrangements Committee led by Bishop Robert Thompson and all those others who worked alongside him in these services, and in all the other arrangements so necessary to the smooth running of the meeting.

Daily worship and prayer frame the life of Anglican Consultative Council meetings. Canon Collin Reid headed the Chaplaincy Team which ably led our morning and evening worship, and were available daily as chaplains to the meeting. Our thanks go to those who led the music: we all go home with new songs in our hearts to share with our congregations on our return home.

Volunteers, led by the Revd Michael Elliott, from local churches have hugely assisted the smooth running of the meeting. We are indebted to them for their assistance in so many ways and for being available at all times to do what was needed in the office, and as ushers, information givers, providing transport - the list is endless. Thank you.

While members of ACC-14 were engaged in the business of the Council, those accompanying them enjoyed the programme of visits and excursions arranged for them by the local hosts. All those involved in this programme greatly enjoyed and valued the opportunities to see something of Jamaican life and culture. We recognise the huge amount of work involved in making the arrangements and would like to extend our thanks.

We are extremely grateful for all that you have given us. We wish to assure the people of Jamaica that we will continue to hold them and the work and witness of the Anglican Church of Jamaica in our hearts and prayers.

PRAYERS AND GREETINGS

The members of the Anglican Consultative Council received with appreciation greetings from the President of the Pontifical Council for Promoting Christian Unity, Cardinal Walter Kasper, on behalf of His Holiness Pope Benedict XVI; from the Ecumenical Patriarch, His All Holiness Bartholomew, Archbishop of Constantinople New Rome; from the President of the International Old Catholic Bishops' Conference of the Union of Utrecht, Archbishop Joris Vercammen, Archbishop of Utrecht, and from the Obispo Maximo of the Iglesia Filipina Independiente, the Most Revd Godfredo J David.

The Council was pleased to welcome as ecumenical participants: Canon John Gibaut and the Revd Paul Gardner [from the World Council of Churches]; Monsignor Mark Langham [the PCPCU]; Metropolitan Nikitas [The Ecumenical Patriarchate] and Bishop Michael Pryse [Lutheran World Federation]. We extend our thanks to our ecumenical participants for their willingness to stand alongside us and to offer prayer, greetings and participation as their gift to us. We assure them of our continued prayer commitment to them as fellow sisters and brothers in the body of Christ.

The Anglican Consultative Council sends greetings to our ecumenical dialogue partners, to His Holiness Pope Benedict XVI, to His All Holiness Bartholomew, Ecumenical Patriarch, to Archbishop Joris Vercammen, to Ishmael Noko, General Secretary of the Lutheran World Federation, and to George Freeman, General Secretary of the Methodist World Council, and to all faithful Christians and we wish to assure them of our prayers for their work and witness and for the unity of the Church.

EXPRESSION OF THANKS

This meeting gives thanks for the work of all those whose God-given gifts have contributed to this meeting and whose dedication and service have enabled the Council to do its work, at this meeting and in the period since ACC-13 on behalf of the Anglican Communion.

Our thanks go to:
The President, the Most Revd and Rt Hon. Dr Rowan Williams,
The Chair, the Rt Revd John Paterson,
The Vice Chair, Professor George Koshy,
The Secretary General of the Anglican Communion, Canon Kenneth Kearon,
the members of the Joint Standing Committee 2005 -2009, and
the members of Inter-Anglican Finance and Administration Committee 2005 – 2009

Additionally, in the conduct of this meeting, our thanks go to: those who led the bible studies (Clare Amos, Kumara Illangasinghe and Janet Trisk) those who led the discernment groups (Mwita Akiri, Josephine Hicks, Rose Hudson-Wilkin, Ezekiel Kondo, Humphrey Peters) and the ecumenical streams (John Gladstone, Sue Moxley, Elizabeth Paver, James Tengatenga), and the members of the Resolutions Committee (Tony Fitchett *Chair*, Philippa Amable, Ian Douglas, John Gladstone, John Stuart and Gregory Cameron, *Secretary*)

We offer particular thanks for the innovative design of the Anglican Consultative Council meeting, and for those responsible in developing and sustaining this, to the Secretary General and to Stephen Lyon and Sue Parks.

Our thanks go to the members of the Anglican Communion Networks who gave freely of their time to resource and inspire this meeting by sharing the work of the Networks. Their presence greatly enhanced and informed our deliberations. Additionally, this Council notes that a great deal of the work and witness of the Anglican Communion is undertaken through the Networks of the Anglican Communion. We thank them for their faithfulness and commitment to God's mission.

THE CONFERENCE STAFF

This meeting of the Anglican Consultative Council expresses its profound thanks to those who have staffed this Conference, and through their work – before, during and after the meeting – have enabled the smooth running of ACC-14:

Kenneth Kearon (*Secretary General*), Gregory K Cameron (*Deputy Secretary General*), Michael Ade, Clare Amos, Stuart Buchanan, Lynne Butt, Rachel Carnegie, Christine Codner, David Craig, Suminder Duggal, Paul Feheley, Andrew Franklin, Yoshimi Gregory, Phil Groves, Gill Harris-Hogarth, Ian Harvey, John Kafwanka, Stephen Lyon, Fiona Millican, Sue Parks, Dorothy Penniecooke, Terrie Robinson, Joanna Udal, Neil Vigers, Hellen Wangusa. *Interpreters:* Paul Cho, Dominique Macneill, Eddie Marques-Picon

We also thank the staff and management of the Jamaica Pegasus Hotel who provided a comfortable home in which to do our work.

Part Three
General Business

Election of Officers

The following elections were made by the Council:

Chair

The Rt Revd Dr James Tengatenga   Central Africa

Vice-Chair

Canon Elizabeth Paver   England

ACC Members of the Standing Committee

The Revd Dr Ian Douglas	The Episcopal Church
Dr Tony Fitchett	Aotearoa, New Zealand & Polynesia
Dato' Stanley Isaacs	South East Asia
The Rt Revd Azad Marshall	Jerusalem & the Middle East

Inter-Anglican Finance and Administration Committee Report

General Fund Reserves have increased from £44,010 at the end of 2004 to £104,216 at the end of 2008

It was not possible for ACC to make any contributions to the Lambeth Conference during this period. The Lambeth Conference company was formed in January 2007 and from then on was accounted for separate from ACC.

The funding of the alterations to our headquarters building St Andrew's House are now completed. A big debt of gratitude is due to the Province of Hong Kong who had loaned £500,000 to enable the work to be finished and who turned this into a grant in March 2006.

Following a resolution of ACC-13, additional funds from General Fund had to be found to finance the continuing Windsor Process including the cost of appointing the Facilitator of the Listening Process and the setting up of a Panel of Reference.

An increase in 10% in the Inter-Anglican Budget Contributions was called for at ACC-13. Few provinces met this ask and as a result ACC struggled to balance its General Fund core budget in 2006 and 2007, not helped by the continuing strength of the sterling pound against the US dollar.

Due to the prevailing financial circumstances and the low circulation, the Anglican and Episcopal World magazine ceased publication at the end of 2007.

The Windsor Process continued in 2007 with the appointing of a Covenant Design Group and a Windsor Continuation Group.

The Primates' Meeting has been meeting every two years while the provision in the ACC budget is really only sufficient for meetings to be held every three years.

The Department of Theological Studies was established in 2006 with Clare Amos appointed as Director. Financial support was provided not by the core budget by a grant from Trinity Church, Wall Street.

Hellen Wangusa was appointed as UN Observer in January 2007 and the costs of that ministry cannot be funded from the core budget either.

Notes to be read in conjunction with Inter-Anglican budget 2009

Incoming Resources

- **Inter-Anglican Budget Contributions £1,282,900**

This the main source of income to fund the Council's work and is paid by the member provinces. Ideally all the work of the Council should be funded by this method.

- **Compass Rose Donations £180,000**

The Compass Rose Society are faithful supporters of the Anglican Communion and meet annually usually in London before going on a Mission visit.

- **Grants and Other Donations £292,400**

This figure is made up as follows:

£79,000 of grants to pay for the Theological Issues ministry.
£155,000 of grants and donations to pay for the budgeted cost of the UN Observer Office of £200,000 with the balance being provided by from the ACC Core budget of £25,000 and a drawdown of £20,000 from Endowment Funds.

£50,000 of donations to the Personal Emergencies Fund to cover the budgeted cost of claims.

£84,00 shown in General Fund column is a rebate from our US travel agent.

- **Miscellaneous Income £54,000**

This is largely income from guests staying at St Andrew's House and when the house is used for meetings. We encourage all friends of the Anglican Communion to stay at St Andrew's House when they have cause to visit London

- **Endowment Drawdown £20,000**

Part of the cost of the UN Observer Office ministry is funded by an endowment.
Initially the endowment raised in excess of US $ 1 million.

Resources Expended

Secretary General Office £258,882 is the cost of staffing the office with the Secretary General supported by two executive officers (but see also Secretariat Services).
Also included here are the direct attributable expenses e.g. travelling and accommodation.

ACC is the cost of ACC14 meeting in Jamaica including the Finance and Joint Standing Committees that precede it. The cost of the meeting is budgeted at **£380,000** and has been affected by the fall in the value of sterling. As meetings of ACC normally take place every three years funds are set aside (designated) from the General Fund annually to spread the cost.

We intend to contribute **£5,000** to the **Anglican Centre in Rome.**

The Joint Standing Committee wish to resume making contributions to future **Lambeth Conferences** from their budget. The 2009 contribution may have to be applied towards the deficit of the 2008 conference. Budgeted **£30,000**.

Windsor Process £58,146 is the staff and direct overhead costs of the Listening Process and meeting expenses of Covenant Design and Windsor Continuation Groups.

Ecumenical Affairs £101,641 is the staff and direct overhead costs of the Ecumenical Affairs plus in the designated column **£90,000** for the meeting costs of the conversations that are expected to happen in 2009.

Mission & Evangelism £54,300 is the staff and direct overheads costs of the department.

Personal Emergencies Funds £50,000 is the cost of approved medical emergency claims. This is funded by outside donations given specifically for this purpose and is not a claim on the core budget.

Theological Issues £89,000 is the cost of the Theological Studies department. This ministry cannot be funded from the core budget and we are grateful for grants, notably from Trinity Church Wall Street, New York, which enable this ministry to happen.

UN Observer Office £200,000 shown in the restricted column is the cost of this ministry based in New York in the offices of TEC. Only £25,000 of this cost is currently met by a transfer from the ACC core budget and the remainder is funded by grants and donations. and shown in the Restricted Column.

Finance and Administration £292,214 The salaries of four people including the IT Manager working in the section, all the office expenses e.g. telephone, equipment rental and maintenance, audit and professional fees and depreciation are included here.

Secretariat Services £211,962 Included here are the salaries of the Travel Manager, Meetings Manager, Guest House Manager plus domestic staff and St Andrew's House expenses including utilities and insurance, building repairs and maintenance.

Depreciation of Refurbishments £106,917 The cost of the alterations to St Andrew's House are being depreciated over the remaining term of the lease which ends on 30 June 2022.

Transfers to Designated Funds are annual designations from General Funds for ACC £194,000, Primates £25,000, Ecumenical £83,000.

Transfer to Restricted Funds covers transfer to UN Observer from core budget £25,000 and £30,000 to cover cost of transfer of funds to Lambeth Conference.

Andrew Franklin
Director of Finance & Administration

ACC-14
Notes to the Financial Statements For the Year Ended 31st December 2008

Since the Accounts were closed off Inter-Anglican Budget Contributions for 2008
have been received from Brazil, Bangladesh, and North India

Inter-Anglican Budget Contributions		Received 2008		Received
	Request	Re Prior Years	Re 2008	2007
Aotearoa New Zealand & Polynesia	38,700		38,700	37,200
Australia	153,100		100,836	92,885
Brazil	4,300	61	-	2,300
Burundi	400		409	700
Canada	104,200		69,056	60,280
Central Africa	10,400		-	3,500
Central America	2,200		-	2,992
Ceylon	2,000		500	1,250
Congo	900		-	-
England	481,000		405,000	393,000
Hong Kong	30,100		30,100	28,900
Indian Ocean	4,300		-	635
Ireland	38,800		43,364	37,300
Japan	21,400		21,966	17,848
Jerusalem & the Middle East	6,000	11,400	6,000	-
Kenya	13,100		-	-
Korea	5,800	5,600	5,800	-
Melanesia	2,100		2,100	3,900
Mexico	2,200		2,288	2,480
Myanmar	2,100		-	1,900
Nigeria	24,900		-	-
Papua New Guinea	2,000		1,238	1,238
Philippines	2,700		2,467	2,596
Rwanda	2,000		-	1,900
Scotland	26,100		23,940	23,240
South East Asia	6,100		6,100	7,950
Southern Cone	4,200		-	4,000
Southern Africa	20,300		12,500	12,948
Sudan	4,200		-	-
Tanzania	8,600		1,000	1,000
Uganda	8,600		-	495
TEC	464,400		363,903	331,552
Wales	38,800		36,600	35,400
West Africa	3,300		-	-
West Indies	17,000		17,000	16,388
Bangladesh	900		-	2,272
North India	2,000		-	-
Pakistan	2,000		-	-
South India	2,700		-	2,600
Bermuda	2,600		2,600	2,500
The Lusitanian Church	900		982	796
The Spanish Ref'md Episc Church	900		-	800
	1,568,300	17,061	1,194,449	1,134,745

73

Anglican Consultative Council Financial Summary 2006/2008

	2006 General £	2006 Designated £	2006 Restricted £	2007 General £	2007 Designated £	2007 Restricted £	2008 General £	2008 Designated £	2008 Restricted £	Total 2008 £
INCOME										
Inter Anglican Budget Contributions	1,129,496			1,134,745			1,211,510			1,211,510
Compass Rose Donations	134,232		25,554	176,622		23,809	162,525		1,515	164,040
Grants and Other Donations	2,488	61,694	410,514	267	15,766	392,921	1,473	451	369,335	371,259
Gift from Hong Kong			500,000							-
Magazine	30,364			11,285						
Investment Income	10,228	28,293		8,156		7,589	9,553		8,507	18,060
Miscellaneous Income	39,320	2,552	8,817	64,341	2,968	1,221	57,044	3,478	2,342	62,864
Endowment Drawdown						36,000			8,640	8,640
Exchange /Investment Gains		14,848	100,003			4,468	28,027		5,832	33,859
Total	**1,346,128**	**107,387**	**1,044,888**	**1,395,416**	**18,734**	**466,008**	**1,470,132**	**3,929**	**396,171**	**1,870,232**
EXPENDITURE										
Secretary General Office	301,122		8,510	322,183		23,940	344,485	-	1,104	345,589
ACC		40,004			42,971			40,459	-	40,459
Primates		4,003			59,127			5,505		5,505
Anglican Centre in Rome		-		3,000			5,000		-	5,000
Lambeth Conference		159,621								-
Windsor Process	34,270	35,282	3,577	38,079	20,793	14,531	41,784	47,561	16,434	105,779
Ecumenical	120,909	86,149		118,207	85,562		122,696	55,379	-	178,075
Mission and Evangelism	39,359	9,992	28,944	31,743		57,158	54,478		36,470	90,948
Personal Emergencies Fund			28,337			47,938			75,166	75,166
Communications	155,521		61,173	148,987		26,110	189,005		9,469	198,474
Magazine	83,134			60,785			2,356			2,356
Theological Issues			76,279			108,333			93,363	93,363
UN Observer's Office			168,902			156,948			192,529	192,529
Finance and Administration	264,629		-	262,249			272,446			272,446
St Andrews House Expenses	109,165		10,158	119,550			127,847			127,847
Depreciation of Refurbishments			106,917			106,917			106,917	106,917
Exchange /Investment Losses	9,242			466					48,112	48,112
Total Resources Expended	**1,117,351**	**335,051**	**492,797**	**1,105,249**	**208,453**	**541,875**	**1,160,097**	**148,904**	**579,564**	**1,888,565**
Net Incoming /(Outgoing) pre transfers	**228,777**	**(227,664)**	**552,091**	**290,167**	**(189,719)**	**(75,867)**	**310,035**	**(144,975)**	**(183,393)**	**(18,333)**
Transfer to Lambeth Conference Co	(215,000)	215,000			(595,709)	(800,772)				
Transfer Designated Funds				(240,793)	240,793		(249,000)	249,000		-
Transfer Restricted Funds	(30,500)		30,500	(30,424)		30,424	(70,210)		70,210	-
Net Movement in Funds	**(16,723)**	**(12,664)**	**582,591**	**18,950**	**(544,635)**	**(846,215)**	**(9,175)**	**104,025**	**(113,183)**	**(18,333)**
Opening Balance	111,164	736,741	2,199,233	94,441	724,077	2,781,824	113,391	179,442	1,935,609	2,228,442
Closing Balance	**94,441**	**724,077**	**2,781,824**	**113,391**	**179,442**	**1,935,609**	**104,216**	**283,467**	**1,822,426**	**2,210,109**

74

Anglican Consultative Council - Budget Summary 2009

	General £	Designated £	Restricted £	Budget Total 2009	Actual 2008
INCOME					
Inter Anglican Budget Contributions	1,282,900			1,282,900	1,211,510
Compass Rose Donations	180,000			180,000	164,040
Grants and Other Donations	8,400		284,000	292,400	371,259
Investment Income	10,000			10,000	18,060
Miscellaneous Income	54,000			54,000	62,864
Endowment Drawdown			20,000	20,000	8,640
Exchange Gains					33,859
Total	1,535,300	-	304,000	1,839,300	1,870,232
EXPENDITURE					
Secretary General Office	258,882			258,882	269,589
ACC / Joint Standing Committee		380,000		380,000	40,459
Primates		70,000		70,000	5,505
Anglican Centre in Rome	5,000			5,000	5,000
Lambeth Conference			30,000	30,000	
Windsor Process	40,146	18,000		58,146	105,779
Ecumenical Affairs	101,641	90,000		191,641	178,075
Mission and Evangelism	54,300			54,300	90,948
Personal Emergencies Fund			50,000	50,000	75,166
Communications	151,655			151,655	198,474
Magazine	10,000			10,000	2,356
Theological Issues			89,000	89,000	93,363
UN Observer's Office			200,000	200,000	192,529
Finance and Administration	292,214			292,214	272,446
Secretariat Services	211,962			211,962	203,847
Depreciation of Refurbishments			106,917	106,917	106,917
Investment Losses					48,112
Total Resources Expended	1,125,800	558,000	475,917	2,159,717	1,888,565
Net Incoming /(Outgoing) pre transfers	**409,500**	**(558,000)**	**(171,917)**	**(320,417)**	**(18,333)**
Transfer Designated Funds ACC	(194,000)	194,000		-	
Primates	(25,000)	25,000		-	
Ecumenical	(83,000)	83,000		-	
Transfer Restricted Funds UN Observer	(25,000)		25,000	-	
Transfer Lambeth Conference	(30,000)		30,000	-	
Net Movement in Funds	**52,500**	**(256,000)**	**(146,917)**	**(320,417)**	**(18,333)**
Opening Balance	104,216	283,467	1,822,426	2,210,109	
Closing Balance	156,716	27,467	1,675,509	1,889,692	(18,333)

Anglican Consultative Council - Projections 2010/2011

Projections 2010/2011	2009 Budget	2010 General £	2010 Designated £	2010 Restricted £	Total 2010	2011 General £	2011 Designated £	2011 Restricted £	Total 2011
INCOME									
Inter Anglican Budget Contributions	1,282,900	1,282,900			1,282,900	1,321,400			1,321,400
Compass Rose Donations	180,000	180,000			180,000	180,000			180,000
Grants and Other Donations	292,400	8,400		285,000	293,400	8,400		295,000	303,400
Investment Income	10,000	10,000			10,000	10,000			10,000
Miscellaneous Income	54,000	54,000			54,000	54,000			54,000
Endowment Drawdown	20,000			20,000	20,000			20,000	20,000
Total	1,839,300	1,535,300	-	305,000	1,840,300	1,573,800	-	315,000	1,888,800
EXPENDITURE									
Secretary General Office	258,882	269,580			269,580	273,950			273,950
ACC	380,000		40,000		40,000		40,000		40,000
Primates	70,000				-				-
Anglican Centre in Rome	5,000	5,000			5,000	5,000			5,000
Lambeth Conference	30,000			50,000	50,000			50,000	50,000
Windsor Process	58,146	41,350			41,350	42,600			42,600
Ecumenical	191,641	103,670	110,000		213,670	107,450	110,000		217,450
Mission and Evangelism	54,300	56,200			56,200	58,500			58,500
Personal Emergencies Fund	50,000			50,000	50,000			50,000	50,000
Communications	151,655	151,000			151,000	155,500			155,500
Magazine	10,000	10,000			10,000	10,000			10,000
Theological Issues	89,000			100,000	100,000			100,000	100,000
UN Observer's Office	200,000			200,000	200,000			210,000	210,000
Finance and Administration	292,214	301,000			301,000	310,000			310,000
Secretariat Services	211,962	218,000			218,000	224,000			224,000
Depreciation of Refurbishments	106,917			106,917	106,917			106,917	106,917
Total Resources Expended	2,159,717	1,155,800	150,000	506,917	1,812,717	1,187,000	150,000	516,917	1,853,917
Net Incoming /(Outgoing) pre transfe	(320,417)	379,500	(150,000)	(201,917)	27,583	386,800	(150,000)	(201,917)	34,883
Transfer Designated Funds	-	(275,000)	275,000			(275,000)	275,000		
Transfer Restricted Funds	-	(85,000)		85,000		(85,000)		85,000	
Net Movement in Funds	(320,417)	19,500	125,000	(116,917)	27,583	26,800	125,000	(116,917)	34,883
Opening Balance	1,822,426	156,716	27,467	1,705,509	1,502,009	176,216	152,467	1,588,592	1,917,275
Closing Balance	1,502,009	176,216	152,467	1,588,592	1,529,592	203,016	277,467	1,471,675	1,952,158

The Secretary General in
the Plenary Session

ACC members at
Plenary Sessions

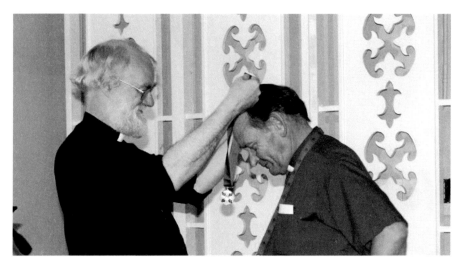

The Rt Revd John Paterson, Chair of ACC, receiving the
Cross of St Augustine from the Archbishop of Canterbury

Professor George Koshy, Vice Chair of ACC, at the Farewell Reception

Parish Visits

St Michael's Church

St Jude's, Stony Hill

St Andrew's Parish
Church

St Andrew's Parish
Church

Parish Visits

The Archbishop of Canterbury
with the Bishop of Jamaica &
The Cayman Islands

St John's Portland Cottage

Cultural Evening in Jamaica

Choir at the Closing
Service

80

The Closing Service

Part Four
Reports

Mission and Evangelism

Evangelism and Church Growth Initiative

(St Andrew's House, 9 - 11 February 2009)

Introduction

Right from the first ACC-1 meeting in Kenya, Mission and Evangelism has been an important strand of the work of the Anglican Communion Office. Evangelism was particularly emphasised during the Decade of Evangelism and through the Commissions. In preparing for the 2008 Lambeth Conference, the Office of Mission and Evangelism at the Anglican Communion carried out a survey on mission and evangelism issues around the Communion and produced a booklet, Holistic Mission. Out of this report many Self Select Sessions were prepared for the bishops and the spouses at the Lambeth Conference.

The Anglican understanding of mission is holistic as affirmed within the Five Marks of Mission.[1] As evangelism is an integral part of mission, and not separate from it, it was agreed by the recent Joint Standing Committee meeting (November 2008) that in future the office should be known as the 'Mission Office' and not the 'Mission and Evangelism Office'. To make sure that the emphasis upon evangelism was not lost, the Joint Standing Committee requested the Secretary General of the Anglican Communion to establish a 'network' of evangelism and church growth.[2] This resolution by the Joint Standing Committee followed the aspirations and desire of the Bishops at the 2008 Lambeth Conference 'to develop a worldwide vision and Strategy of church planting, growth and mission'.[3]

---

[1] The **Five Marks of Mission** are: To proclaim the Good News of the Kingdom; To teach, baptise and nurture new believers; To respond to human need by loving service; To seek to transform unjust structures of society; To strive to safeguard the integrity of creation and sustain and renew the life of the earth.

[2] **RESOLUTION 2: MISSION DESK AT THE ANGLICAN COMMUNION OFFICE THAT** the Joint Standing Committee of the Primates of the Anglican Communion and the Anglican consultative Council......encourage the Secretary General to proceed with the setting up of an Evangelism and Church Growth Network.

[3] "We acknowledge the growth of the Church in areas of the southern hemisphere and the many fresh expressions of church in the whole Communion. At the same time we are called as a Communion to develop a worldwide vision and strategy of church planting, growth, and mission. While we encourage these strategies we must be conscious of those diocese and provinces which are yet to achieve self-sufficiency and respond in appropriate ways to address the areas of need." P.13 and paragraph 42 (**Programmatic concerns**) of 'Lambeth Indaba'.

The Secretary General of the Anglican Communion, invited a small but diverse group of people involved in evangelism and church growth ministries, from around the Communion, to a short consultation from 9-11 February 2009 to discuss this proposal and make recommendations to ACC-14. The group began this meeting by sharing their personal faith experiences and the ways in which they have been involved in the ministry of evangelism and church growth.

Evangelism and Church Growth Initiative

Although the Joint Standing Committee's resolution was to set up a 'network' and affirming that the word 'Network' is commonly understood within the Communion, it was agreed that not all are comfortable with the use of this word. It was also noted that unlike the existing Anglican Networks, the Evangelism and Church Growth Initiative needs be staffed within the Mission Office.

The group therefore agreed that the word 'Initiative' rather than 'Network' would be more appropriate. In this regard 'Initiative' refers to the open association of people that would encourage maximum participation. 'Initiative' does not only imply the dynamic required to implement the mandate, to effectively develop vision and strategy, in a way that 'network' may not, but also implies a time-limited programme that will be reviewed from time to time, with a possibility of maturing into something even more dynamic! Thus, Evangelism and Church Growth Initiative (ECGI).

Purpose

The purpose of the Evangelism and Church Growth Initiative is to promote evangelism and church growth throughout the Anglican Communion.

This purpose needs to be seen in the context of the commitment to holistic mission outlined in the Anglican Communion's five marks of mission, and is intended to enhance collaborative work and mutual support in evangelism and church growth in parishes, dioceses and provinces of the Anglican Communion, in order to bring people to follow Jesus Christ as Lord and Saviour and become life long disciples within the community of God's people.

This purpose will be achieved by:

> Facilitating prayer and mutual encouragement
> Developing strategies to reach unreached peoples
> Recommending resources & sharing good practice
> Encouraging training in E&CG for the whole people of God
> Sharing stories, news and strategies
> Identifying key issues for specific consultation
> Building links with other E&CG networks within and beyond the Anglican Communion.

Stakeholders

It is anticipated that ECGI will aim for 'maximum participation' through an open network (facilitated by web-based, paper and oral communication) but with a small Core Group of **animators** to serve as an implementing group and to support the focal person (to be based at the ACO or elsewhere).

Therefore participants will include appropriate people in provinces, dioceses, mission agencies and other evangelism and church growth initiatives within the Communion, while noting that those on the ground who have stories are not always those who can make and drive strategy, or indeed have access to communication facilities.

It is expected that while relating to and working under the Anglican Communion Mission Desk and appropriate collaboration with other Communion networks, the ECGI, in pursuant with its vision, will need to work in collaboration with Anglican mission bodies such as, Alpha Programme, Anglican Frontier Mission, Anglimergent, Church Army, CMS, USPG, and also relate to ecumenical bodies such as World Evangelical Alliance (Mission Commission), WCC (Evangelism Desk), World Alliance of Reformed Churches (Mission & Unity), Lausanne Committee, 5015 Vision Network, Nigerian Evangelical Mission Alliance (NEMA), Faith2Share, Internet Evangelism, etc.

The group identified the sharing of stories and experiences as one of the major activities of the ECGI and recognised the internet as a major tool in facilitating this aim and need. It was therefore felt that the use of the internet will be key to achieving the purpose of the Evangelism and Church Growth Initiative, bearing in mind that there are many in the Communion for whom access to the internet is both costly and limited, the need to use other forms of communication is necessary.

Theological Basis

Within the rich diversity of the Communion a biblical and theological basis for Evangelism and Church Growth will need to be developed.

Way Forward
The Mission Desk is to:

- assess and identify evangelism and church growth initiatives and potential participants in the Communion;
- share information about this meeting;
- request the Secretary General to:
- ensure a theological basis for evangelism and church growth is developed;
- report to ACC 14 in May;
- make a press release about this meeting;
- appoint a Core Group of animators;
- appoint a focal person to be based at the ACO.

APPENDIX:
Consultation Attendance List

Mr John Clark	UK (Chair)
Bishop Moon Hing	West Malaysia (South East Asia)
Bishop Patrick Yu	Toronto (Canada)
Bishop Bill Godfrey	Peru (Southern Cone)
Revd Canon Mark Oxbrow	Faith2Share/CMS
Philip Johanson	Church Army International
Revd Canon Lovey Kisembo	SOMA (Uganda)
Dr Julian Linnel	Anglican Frontier Mission (USA)

Mr Stuart Buchanan   ACO Staff
Revd John Kafwanka   ACO Staff
Revd Canon Dr Kenneth Kearon ACO Secretary General

Anglican Relief and Development Alliance

This paper comprises three sections:

- The background to the concept of an Anglican Relief and Development Alliance;
- The report issued following the planning meeting of 15–16 January 2009;
- Questions for discussion at ACC-14.

A   BACKGROUND

Following the plans to restructure the Mission Office of the Anglican Communion, to better reflect holistic mission, and the request from the Bishops at the 2008 Lambeth Conference, for the 'Establishment of a global Anglican Relief and Development Agency' (p.19 Lambeth Reflections) in order to enhance a more collaborative approach to existing relief, development and advocacy activities in the Anglican Communion, the Archbishop of Canterbury invited a group of development practitioners and professionals from around the Communion to Lambeth Palace for a two-day consultation. The consultation was designed and led by Helen Stawski (Lambeth Palace) and John Kafwanka and Stuart Buchanan (Anglican Communion Office).

B   THE PLANNING MEETING 15 – 16 JANUARY 2009

ANGLICAN RELIEF AND DEVELOPMENT MEETING
LAMBETH PALACE – LONDON

The Five Marks of Mission clearly state the Anglican Communion's role in addressing issues of poverty, justice and care for the environment, as integral to God's mission.

Five Marks of Mission

To proclaim the Good News of the Kingdom
To teach, baptise and nurture new believers
To respond to human need by loving service
To seek to transform unjust structures of society
To strive to safeguard the integrity of creation and sustain and renew the life of the earth

During the Lambeth Conference in July and August of 2008, these issues featured prominently in the general discourse of the conference and explicitly in the 'indaba' groups on the 23rd July, where Bishops looked at the question of *Transforming Society – the bishop and social justice*. There was great enthusiasm amongst bishops, and their spouses, as they discussed the church's role in addressing the needs of the poor and marginalised in society. Participants shared stories of the daily work their dioceses and parishes engage in at local level, as well as the diverse range of experiences within the Communion of regional and international advocacy.

This enthusiasm and commitment 'To respond to human need with loving service' and 'To seek to transform unjust structures of society' was exemplified by the Walk of Witness, on 24 July. Over 1500 bishops and spouses marched through the centre of London, past the Houses of Parliament to stand with the UK Prime Minister and be a voice for the voiceless at the highest level. The UK Prime Minister called the event *'one of the greatest public demonstrations of faith that this great city has ever seen.'* Certainly the 'Walk of Witness' encouraged all who participated to believe that when we stand together as a Communion, to be a voice for the voiceless, we can become more than the sum of our parts, and that people will listen. The walk also clearly illustrated to those outside the Church the rich diversity of cultures and experiences of development we hold within the countries that are part of the Anglican Communion. As the third largest Christian grouping in the world, with structures that reach from the most remote village to the highest echelons of government, we have much to bring to the world of advocacy, relief and development, and are afforded great opportunity to speak.

The Lambeth Conference Reflections document sought to record something of the enthusiasm and aspirations of the Conference in this area, under Section C of Human and Social Justice. There was a clear desire not merely to talk, but to encourage action, and specifically to encourage better and more effective collaboration around the existing relief and development activities within the Communion. One suggestion was the formation of an Anglican Relief and Development Agency.

Following the Lambeth Conference, The Archbishop of Canterbury and the Anglican Communion Office have worked together to take forward many of the recommendations from the Reflections document. As part of this process and at the invitation of the Archbishop a select group of individuals working in the field of social development and community outreach met at Lambeth Palace on the 15 and 16 January 2009. These individuals were chosen because of their extensive experience in relief and development, all working within provinces and organisations within the worldwide Anglican Communion.

The purpose of the meeting was to discuss

The recommendation made by the bishops of the Lambeth Conference and propose ways to take this recommendation forward;

To engage in dialogue about how best the Anglican Communion may embark on a collaborative approach to existing Anglican relief, development and advocacy activities;

To deliberate about the possibilities for joint action within the Anglican Communion as it relates to social development and mission.

The consultation sought to build on existing successful models of practice and partnership and to draw out the energy and enthusiasm from the local church, while also working to develop a model that is workable for our Anglican Communion.

The group reached consensus on two key issues

A theological vision: The need to define and communicate an Anglican theological basis of understanding and practice of development that roots development work firmly within God's mission as understood within the Anglican Communion. To communicate this theology of development throughout the Communion, from parish level to national and international structures.

A strategic vision: To create an Anglican Alliance, in order to better coordinate and inform our development and advocacy work, and to share experiences of best practice. The Alliance would also serve to improve ownership of existing work throughout the global Anglican Communion and to improve visibility and communication of these activities, both within the Communion and to the wider world.

Next steps

To create a Foundational Document for an Anglican Alliance, which outlines how we plan to work more collaboratively together, *(with the expectation of a draft being presented to ACC-14 in May 2009.)*

To plan for the development of a theological document, seeking to draw in a diverse range of resources on mission and development from across the Communion.

The group also outlined risks and realities for any future process

The group had not tried to represent all provinces or all stakeholders in the Communion, but rather it had been composed of development experts with a wealth of practical and professional experience.

Therefore there is also a need to draw in others who were not at the meeting, into the wider process, in order that we do not miss expertise from other regions and organisations that were absent from this meeting.

The energy and enthusiasm of this group needs to be harnessed, by keeping momentum for this process, along with some consultation among other stakeholders.

It is crucial that the work evolving from this meeting begins to inform and engage with the Instruments of Communion (Archbishop of Canterbury, Primates and ACC), while establishing legitimacy to continue to take forward the development of the theological document and strategic alliance.

A great strength of this consultation was its ability to draw from parish, diocesan, provincial, regional and international experiences, and any resultant process must continue to draw expertise from all these forums, both for equity and for sustainability.

This meeting was incredibly successful and the group carried out the challenging task set before it with a high degree of expertise and commitment. That people from such diverse cultures and organisational structures could reach a consensus is a testament to their commitment to a vision for the Communion, and to the challenge of realising this vision in a truly collaborative and sustainable way. The hard work of realising this vision now begins and it will require continued commitment from all involved. Only by establishing a sustainable and equitable process will we hope to engage with the current challenges we face as a Communion, in the area of relief and development, as an integral part of God's mission.

Report by
Helen Stawski   *John Kafwanka*
Archbishop of Canterbury's   *Mission Office*
International Development   *Anglican Communion Office*
programme Director
                                                    January 2009

At their meeting in Alexandria in February 2009, the Primates of the Anglican Communion, supported efforts to improve the co-ordination and effectiveness of Anglican Relief and Development work outlined in the above report.

C   QUESTIONS FOR DISCUSSION

To assist in taking this work forward, we would welcome the response to the following questions from ACC members:

1. What is the most appropriate and effective mechanism for engaging provincial relief and development organisations and related community and Church bodies in the formation and establishment of Anglicans in Development?

2. More specifically, how might the Steering Committee best ensure that the rich diversity of experiences to be found across the Anglican Communion are faithfully captured and reflected in any foundational document?

3. Given that Anglicans in Development promises a significant realignment of the way that Anglicans and the Anglican Communion thinks about and does development, how do you think the relationship between Anglicans in Development and the Instruments of Communion best be structured or envisaged?

Ecumenical Affairs

The Vision Before Us – Inter-Anglican Standing Commission on Ecumenical Relations (IASCER)

Compiled and edited by Sarah Rowland Jones

The Vision Before Us is a volume which harvests the work of the Inter-Anglican Standing Commission on Ecumenical Relations (IASCER) between the years 2000 and 2008. In this period, the Commission was charged by the Instruments of Communion in the Anglican Communion with keeping an overview of ecumenical engagement and advising on the ecumenical work of the Communion and the Provinces.

The book offers an introduction and analysis of the entire breadth of ecumenical engagement in the Anglican Communion, as well as reproducing key texts: the Resolutions of IASCER, and other materials which they produced in their work, such as 'The Principles of Anglican Ecumenical Engagement' and 'Guidelines on Ecumenical Participation in Ordinations.'

This volume is intended as an introduction and handbook for all those concerned with Anglican participation in the ecumenical movement, and constitutes the Report of IASCER to ACC-14.

The volume will be available at ACC-14. In particular, the attention of members of ACC-14 will be drawn to the following sections:

In Part One, Chapter 2, the Report sets out 'The Principles of Ecumenical Engagement' developed by the current Director of Ecumenical Affairs, and adopted at the 2008 meeting of IASCER. They are commended to ACC-14 for adoption as principles that can undergird all Anglican ecumenical engagement, and to provide a short benchmark of Anglican ecumenical work in a parallel way to the 'Five Marks of Mission'.

In Chapters 4 and 11, resolutions of IASCER concerning Anglican discipline relating to Baptism and Eucharist are recorded. They are commended to ACC-14 for ratification as the accepted standard upheld by the Churches of the Anglican Communion in their ecumenical engagement.

In Part Three of the volume, the range of Anglican ecumenical dialogues and ecumenical agreements are reviewed. ACC-14 is invited to affirm the bilateral dialogues of the Anglican Communion, and to adopt the resolutions of IASCER concerning their conduct, direction and the reception of the work of the bilateral Commissions and the recent reports which have been published.

In Chapter 4 (in the document 'The Sacraments duly administered?') and in Chapter 6 (Reception of Ecumenical Documents), IASCER raises questions about the conduct of ecumenical relations. ACC-14 is invited to consider how the Anglican Communion responds to the discernment of ecumenical convergence or agreement, and to consider whether further work ought to be referred to the Inter-Anglican Standing Commission on Unity, Faith and Order, established by the Joint Standing Committee in November 2008.

The Report will be introduced at the meeting of the Anglican Consultative Council by Canon Gregory K Cameron, Director of Ecumenical Affairs

Theological Issues

Report on the Work of TEAC

(Theological Education in the Anglican Communion)

Report to ACC-14 and Request for Establishment of New Phase of the Working Party

'To equip the saints for the work of ministry, for building up the body of Christ, until all of us come to the unity of the faith and of the knowledge of the Son of God, to maturity, to the measure of the full stature of Christ.' *(Ephesians 4.12-13, foundational biblical text for TEAC)*

Theological Education in the Anglican Communion (TEAC) is a Working Party which was established by the Anglican Primates in 2002. Since then it has reported to each of the Primates' Meetings, and also made a presentation in June 2005 at Nottingham to the meeting of ACC-13. Additionally it has reported regularly to most meetings of the Joint Standing Committee of ACC and the Primates. The report to the Joint Standing Committee in March 2006 was particularly detailed and sought to set out TEAC's vision for theological education. Copies of that report will be available in Jamaica for those who have not yet seen it.

The current report therefore will focus on the work of TEAC since June 2005. It also introduces, and provides the background to, the request that will be made at ACC-14 for a resolution to be passed establishing a new phase of TEAC.

A. TEAC 2005-2009

During this period TEAC has held three major residential meetings, and several smaller meetings involving either members of the Steering Group and/or the Convenors of the Target Groups[1]. Other than that it worked by email correspondence among members of the Target Groups, which functioned better in some cases than in others. The three major meetings were:

- A meeting of the entire body of TEAC in Johannesburg, January 2006
- A meeting of the Anglican Way Target Group and invited consultants in Singapore, May 2007
- A meeting of Anglican Women Theological Educators held in Canterbury, UK, in February/March 2009. This particular meeting was organised by TEAC, and five members of the Working Party were present. However most of the participants at the meeting were women, from various parts of the Anglican Communion, who had not previously been involved with TEAC's work.

Work accomplished by TEAC or in progress includes:

1.   Statement of rationale, principles, structuring of TEAC's work
Material has been offered setting out in systematic form a rationale for the work of TEAC (and for the importance of theological education in the Anglican Communion). A description of TEAC's work as seeking to respond to three key questions has been developed, in order to communicate succinctly the importance of what the Working Party is seeking to achieve. *Why* is theological education important for Anglican Christians? *What* are the ideals, goals and outcomes that we should aiming for? And *how* can we help to enable such goals to be met, given the disparity in resources and other constraints which affect the life of the Anglican Communion?

2.   The outcomes based competency grids
These are a set of tables that have been produced which set out the 'competencies' that are ideally needed by those exercising various forms of ministry and/or discipleship in the Anglican context.   The grids are designed

---

[1] TEAC's current structure includes a Steering Group and five Target Groups. Each Target Group focuses on a particular aspect of theological education namely: Theological Education for Bishops; Theological Education for Priests; Theological Education for Vocational Deacons and Licensed Lay Ministers; Theological Education for the Laity; Theological Education in the Anglican Way. The Chair of the Steering Group is Most Revd Greg Venables (Southern Cone); the Vice-Chair is Rt Revd Robert Paterson (Wales/England); the Secretary is Mrs Clare Amos, who is the Director of Theological Studies in the Anglican Communion Office.

to highlight the different competencies needed at different stages of a person's vocation e.g. in the case of priests, competencies needed at the point of selection for training, at the time of ordination to the priesthood, and after a number of years in ministry. They are designed to make clear that theological education for Christians should not cease at the point of ordination or confirmation. The competencies suggested include spiritual, intellectual and practical experience and skills. Seven competency grids are available relating to Bishops; Priests; Vocational Deacons; Licensed Lay Ministers; the Laity; and two rather different grids relating to aspects of the Anglican Way. We have worked hard to ensure that these grids are distributed and 'owned' (with local adaptations as appropriate) by the Churches of the Anglican Communion. All the grids are available on TEAC's website at

http://www.anglicancommunion.org/ministry/theological/teac/grids/index.cfm .
Sample paper copies will be available at ACC 14.

3. The Anglican Way

A major focus of TEAC's work during the last two-three years has been on the importance of ensuring that 'the Anglican Way' is explored and communicated as part of a person's theological education for ministry or discipleship. To this end the following work has been achieved/is in progress.

a) Signposts statement

This ground-breaking statement, developed out of the work of TEAC and completed at the 2007 TEAC meeting in Singapore, seeks to set out in a concise form the key elements of 'the Anglican Way', particularly as they form part of theological education. One of the features of the statement is the way it seeks to show how different aspects of Anglican identity 'Formed by Scripture', 'Shaped by Worship', Ordered by Communion' and 'Directed by God's Mission flow into each other and inform each other. In this statement 'Mission' becomes both the goal and the inspiration for our self-understanding as Anglicans. The Signposts statement is available in English, French, Spanish and Swahili and can be found on the TEAC website at:
http://www.anglicancommunion.org/ministry/theological/signposts/english.cfm
It has been incorporated as Appendix One to this Report.

b) Signposts booklets

These are a series of booklets called the 'Signposts series' which seek to develop, expand upon, and present in an appropriate educational way, specific aspects of the 'Signposts statement'. The first two have been produced as printed booklets and electronically; three or four other booklets are already in the pipeline. Copies of the first two booklets, No. 1 – exploring the Signposts Statement as a whole No. 2 on an Anglican approach to Mission and Evangelism will be available in Jamaica. We would welcome specific suggestions for future booklets in the series. Our hope is (assuming that funds allow) to translate at least some of these booklets into languages other than English.

c) Supply of books on the Anglican Way to theological colleges

Supported by grants from the Compass Rose Society, TEAC is seeking to supply a set of key books on Anglican Studies to theological colleges around the Anglican Communion that request these books. These are books that we believe should be in the library of all colleges training people for ordination to the Anglican ministry. The bibliography can be found at:
www.anglicancommunion.org/ministry/theological/teac/anglicanway/keytexts.cfm
So far we have supplied 30 colleges – and have a list of 15-20 more who have requested the books when further funds allow.

d) Translation of Something in Common

The provision of the books referred to in (c) above was an important reminder to us that there were very few resources on Anglicanism available in languages other than English. With this in mind we selected one well regarded book on Anglicanism *Something in Common* by Adrian Chatfield and have organised the translation of this book into Spanish, Portuguese and Swahili. The French translation is in process. The Spanish and Portuguese translations are available on CD, the Swahili translation in hard copy. Copies will be available at ACC 14 both for inspection and for taking away – if the translation can be of use to you. We would welcome assistance to ensure that the availability of this resource is widely known throughout the Anglican Communion, and are also interested in working with Provinces if they wish to organise the translation of *Something in Common* into further languages.

e) Possible module on Anglican Studies
During the last couple of years we have considered whether or not to seek to provide a module on 'Anglican Studies' to be made available using distance learning resources via the Anglican Communion website. There are a number of questions that would need to be sorted out e.g. what 'level' would we be aiming at? How 'formal' would the module be? Should it be accredited? How (if at all) would any tutorial support be provided? Although these are significant questions we receive such regular comment about the need for such a study module, that we are wanting to take the issue further, and hope to work further on this in the year after ACC 14. Comments and suggestions relating to this aspect of TEAC's work would be particularly welcome.

4. TEAC website
As will already be clear from the web references given above, TEAC's website is already fairly substantial. We have a policy of seeking to make available on the website our 'work in progress' to invite comment from members of the Anglican Communion. We are also seeking to build up this Theological Studies/TEAC section of the Anglican Communion website to be a major resource for Anglicans engaged in any form of theological education. This is itself ongoing 'work in progress', but members of the AC might like to explore the website at the stage it is now, and make suggestions for further development. We suggest you start by going to:
http://www.anglicancommunion.org/ministry/theological/index.cfm

One website based project that we are hoping to activate as soon as possible after ACC 14 is the establishment of a database of Anglican theologians/theological educators with details of their particular skills and interests. There is also the question of the database of Anglican theological colleges, courses and training institutions. Until fairly recently this was administered by CUAC (Colleges and Universities of the Anglican Communion). CUAC have now suggested to us that we might take over work on this database, and updating it will be a major priority in the coming months.

5. Women theological educators consultation
The most recent major event in the life of TEAC has been a consultation for approximately 35 Anglican women theological educators. The choice of this professional group was due to the under representation of women in

theological education, both as teachers and as learners, in some parts of the Anglican Communion. It was an extremely fruitful week, 23 February–2 March 2009, and as well as sharing themes and experiences from the various contexts represented by the women, the consultation spent part of the week working in six task groups. The task groups agreed to take forward the following concerns:

a) Mentoring
Develop principles and protocols for the practice of mentoring potential theological educators, and guidelines both for those who could offer themselves as mentors and those who could benefit from such assistance.

b) Network
Establish a network for Anglican women who are theological educators to offer support and encouragement to each other, and to promote the role of women as theological educators.

c) Standards and Goals in theological education
Gather information from around the Provinces in order to educate ourselves on this topic and to stimulate thinking and response on the part of others. On the basis of the information received we will propose competencies needed by theological educators.

d) Pedagogical issues
In view of the marginal status of women in church and society in most parts of the Anglican Communion, seek to mainstream women's issues and perspectives in all theological education courses and encourage the development of specific courses in women's studies.

e) The Latin American region
Address specifically Latin American needs and concerns identified by members of the consultation from the Latin American region. As a consultation we affirm that this is a valuable part of our total work, and illustrates the importance of the contextual dimension in theological education.

f) Global Anglican Theological Academy for Women in Leadership
Establish a specific structure for helping in the development of a number of younger women from the two-thirds world as academic leaders for the future global Anglican Communion.

A number of the issues, particularly in c) and e) above, relate to theological education for both men and women.

The fruits of the consultation will provide a considerable agenda for TEAC to take forward in the immediate and medium term future.

6. TEAC and the Lambeth Conference

TEAC made a worthwhile contribution to the Lambeth Conference. As well as organising a number of self-select groups, it contributed to the documentation available in the Lambeth Reader. Perhaps most significantly the format for the Indaba exploration of 'The Bishop and the Anglican Way' was drawn from the TEAC 'Signposts' model, which has in turn been reflected in the Lambeth Conference Reflections document.

7. Staffing and Funding issues

The Director of Theological Studies, Clare Amos, acts as the Secretary to TEAC and spends about 60% of her working week on TEAC work (she is also responsible for inter faith concerns and works one day a week for USPG: Anglicans in World Mission). Her brief in the area of theological education is wider than purely TEAC work, for example she has been used as a consultant by the Church of Ireland as they restructured their theological education curriculum. As she is by training a biblical scholar she sometimes has a particular involvement in biblical studies concerns, for example being part of the team that wrote the Lambeth Conference Bible Studies and has, along with the Secretary-General and others, worked on the proposal for 'The Bible in the Life of the Church' project. She has been in the post in its current format since January 2006, although she was involved in the work of TEAC on a more part-time basis previous to that.

She works with three Regional Associates, who were appointed in May 2007. These are Rt Revd Michael Fape (Nigeria), Revd Sally Sue Hernandez Garcia (Mexico) and Revd Joo Yup Lee (Korea), who work for TEAC one day a week – helping in a variety of ways e.g. translation, course writing, distribution, to take forward the work of TEAC in their region. We still need to exploit the potential for the work of these Regional Associates more fully – however point 5e) above will certainly give Sally Sue Hernandez a substantial agenda to take forward over the coming two-three years.

102

As regards funding TEAC is not supported at present by the core Anglican Consultative Council budget. Instead, both for staffing and project costs it relies on the support of a number of funding agencies. These include: Trinity Church, Wall St; St Augustine's Foundation; St Boniface Trust; Compass Rose Society; the Archbishop of Canterbury's Anglican Communion Fund. Their considerable generosity has enabled us to carry out the work to date, and we believe that their willingness to continue support shows that the importance of theological education is widely realised.

B. The 'new' TEAC

It has become clear during the past year that TEAC in its present structure i.e. with 35 people in the specific Target Groups has probably come to the end of its natural life. This does not mean that Communion wide involvement in theological education issues should come to an end – far from it, we are proposing that a 'new TEAC' should be established to work more strategically particularly in the areas of the Anglican Way and supporting theological educators (the Women Theological Educators' Consultation was a foretaste of this) . Because the original TEAC was a Working Party accountable to the Anglican Primates, Bishop Greg Venables, Chair of TEAC, took to the recent meeting of the Primates in Alexandria the following suggestion, 'to draw the work of TEAC in its present form to a close, and to establish it in a new phase of its work. The formal establishment of this new phase (provisionally known as TEAC 2) would take place at ACC-14.' The Primates Meeting concurred with this suggestion, and we present to you a proposal for the structure and tasks of the new TEAC (to be called 'TEAC 2'). The Primates' Meeting have seen, and are content with, these suggestions as regards structure and tasks, though they also noted the importance of ensuring that the theological education of laity was not neglected.

Proposed Structure

1. TEAC 2 would be steered by an international group of 8-10 people, reflecting different regions of the Anglican Communion and different 'stakeholders' in terms of theological education (e.g. bishops, theological educators, lay people). They would meet once a year for a residential meeting. The Director of Theological Studies and the TEAC Regional Associates would be present at the meeting. The Director would act as

Secretary to it. The Chair of the body would be chosen by the Archbishop of Canterbury in consultation with the Secretary General; the members will be selected by the Secretary General in consultation with the Archbishop of Canterbury.

2. TEAC 2 would be accountable to the ACC.
3. Additionally the Director would seek to set up and keep in regular communication with a 'network' of Provincial theological education /Directors of Ministry.
4. It would be envisaged that particular foci of the work of TEAC 2 would be a) the relation to the Anglican Way b) in support of theological educators (understanding this term in a wide sense e.g. not simply college/course staff, but including those working as diocesan staff in the area of theological education for laity and clergy).

Proposed Tasks

1. To monitor, support and develop the work of the Director of Theological Studies and through him/her the work of the Regional Associates.
2. To sustain and continue ongoing projects developed by TEAC 1, e.g. the supply of textbooks to Anglican theological colleges, the translation of material into languages other than English; the distribution (and possible translation) of the ministry grids.
3. To develop and expand the 'Signposts' series.
4. To develop theological underpinning (e.g. reflection on the ordination vows) for practical work in the area of theological education.
5. To support the work of Anglican theological educators and theological education institutions as appropriate and realistic (e.g. by gathering people/consultations provision of resources).
6. To work with a network of other institutions and groups (e.g. the International Study Centre Canterbury, mission agencies, theological colleges) who are committed to supporting cross-regional theological education in the Anglican Communion
7. To consider establishing an internationally available module on Anglican Studies
8. To develop the theological education section of the Anglican Communion website with theological resources, a database of Anglican theological educators and an updated list of theological training institutions.

9. To offer consultancy to Provinces in the area of theological education as requested and as resources may be available.
10. To offer general support to 'The Bible in the Church' project (although dedicated groups to take this forward would be established.)
11. To nurture the network of Provincial Directors of Ministry/Training.
12. To accomplish other tasks in the area of theological studies/theological education that it is requested to undertake by the Archbishop of Canterbury, the Secretary General or the Joint Standing Committee.

At ACC-14, we will be inviting you to scrutinize this suggestion, soliciting discussion, and asking the meeting of ACC to approve the establishment of TEAC 2.

Clare Amos
Director of Theological Studies
23 March 2009

Appendix One

Theological Education for the Anglican Communion (TEAC)

The Anglican Way: Signposts on a Common Journey

This document has emerged as part of a four-year process in which church leaders, theologians and educators have come together from around the world to discuss the teaching of Anglican identity, life and practice. They clarified the characteristic ways in which Anglicans understand themselves and their mission in the world. These features, described as the 'Anglican Way', were intended to form the basis for how Anglicanism is taught at all levels of learning involving laity, clergy and bishops. This document is not intended as a comprehensive definition of Anglicanism, but it does set in place signposts which guide Anglicans on their journey of self-understanding and Christian discipleship. The journey is on-going because what it means to be Anglican will be influenced by context and history. Historically a number of different forms of being Anglican have emerged, all of which can be found in the rich diversity of present-day Anglicanism. But Anglicans also have their commonalities, and it is these which hold them together in communion through 'bonds of affection'. The signposts set out below are offered in the hope that they will point the way to a clearer understanding of Anglican identity and ministry, so that all Anglicans can be effectively taught and equipped for their service to God's mission in the world.

The Anglican Way is a particular expression of the Christian Way of being the One, Holy, Catholic and Apostolic Church of Jesus Christ. It is formed by and rooted in Scripture, shaped by its worship of the living God, ordered for communion, and directed in faithfulness to God's mission in the world. In diverse global situations Anglican life and ministry witnesses to the incarnate, crucified and risen Lord, and is empowered by the Holy Spirit. Together with all Christians, Anglicans hope, pray and work for the coming of the reign of God.

Formed by Scripture

1. As Anglicans we discern the voice of the living God in the Holy Scriptures, mediated by tradition and reason. We read the Bible together,

corporately and individually, with a grateful and critical sense of the past, a vigorous engagement with the present, and with patient hope for God's future.

2. We cherish the whole of Scripture for every aspect of our lives, and we value the many ways in which it teaches us to follow Christ faithfully in a variety of contexts. We pray and sing the Scriptures through liturgy and hymnody. Lectionaries connect us with the breadth of the Bible, and through preaching we interpret and apply the fullness of Scripture to our shared life in the world.

3. Accepting their authority, we listen to the Scriptures with open hearts and attentive minds. They have shaped our rich inheritance: for example, the ecumenical creeds of the early Church, the Book of Common Prayer, and Anglican formularies such as the Articles of Religion, catechisms and the Lambeth Quadrilateral.

4. In our proclamation and witness to the Word Incarnate we value the tradition of scholarly engagement with the Scriptures from earliest centuries to the present day. We desire to be a true learning community as we live out our faith, looking to one another for wisdom, strength and hope on our journey. We constantly discover that new situations call for fresh expressions of a scripturally informed faith and spiritual life.

Shaped through Worship

5. Our relationship with God is nurtured through our encounter with the Father, Son and Holy Spirit in word and sacrament. This experience enriches and shapes our understanding of God and our communion with one another.

6. As Anglicans we offer praise to the Triune Holy God, expressed through corporate worship, combining order with freedom. In penitence and thanksgiving we offer ourselves in service to God in the world.

7. Through our liturgies and forms of worship we seek to integrate the rich traditions of the past with the varied cultures of our diverse communities.

8. As broken and sinful persons and communities, aware of our need of God's mercy, we live by grace through faith and continually strive to offer holy lives to God. Forgiven through Christ and strengthened by word and sacrament, we are sent out into the world in the power of the Spirit.

Ordered for Communion

9. In our episcopally led and synodically governed dioceses and provinces, we rejoice in the diverse callings of all the baptized. As outlined in the ordinals, the threefold servant ministries of bishops, priests and deacons assist in the affirmation, coordination and development of these callings as discerned and exercised by the whole people of God.

10. As worldwide Anglicans we value our relationships with one another. We look to the Archbishop of Canterbury as a focus of unity and gather in communion with the See of Canterbury. In addition we are sustained through three formal instruments of communion: The Lambeth Conference, The Anglican Consultative Council and The Primates' Meeting. The Archbishop of Canterbury and these three instruments offer cohesion to global Anglicanism, yet limit the centralisation of authority. They rely on bonds of affection for effective functioning.

11. We recognise the contribution of the mission agencies and other international bodies such as the Mothers' Union. Our common life in the Body of Christ is also strengthened by commissions, task groups, networks of fellowship, regional activities, theological institutions and companion links.

Directed by God's Mission

12. As Anglicans we are called to participate in God's mission in the world, by embracing respectful evangelism, loving service and prophetic witness. As we do so in all our varied contexts, we bear witness to and follow Jesus Christ, the crucified and risen Saviour. We celebrate God's reconciling and life-giving mission through the creative, costly and faithful witness and ministry of men, women and children, past and present, across our Communion.

13. Nevertheless, as Anglicans we are keenly aware that our common life and engagement in God's mission are tainted with shortcomings and failure, such as negative aspects of colonial heritage, self-serving abuse of power and privilege, undervaluing of the contributions of laity and women, inequitable distribution of resources, and blindness to the experience of the poor and oppressed. As a result, we seek to follow the Lord with renewed humility so that we may freely and joyfully spread the good news of salvation in word and deed.

14. Confident in Christ, we join with all people of good will as we work for God's peace, justice and reconciling love. We recognise the immense challenges posed by secularisation, poverty, unbridled greed, violence, religious persecution, environmental degradation, and HIV/Aids. In response, we engage in prophetic critique of destructive political and religious ideologies, and we build on a heritage of care for human welfare expressed through education, health care and reconciliation.

15. In our relationships and dialogue with other faith communities we combine witness to the Lordship of Jesus Christ with a desire for peace, and mutual respect and understanding.

16. As Anglicans, baptized into Christ, we share in the mission of God with all Christians and are deeply committed to building ecumenical relationships. Our reformed catholic tradition has proved to be a gift we are able to bring to ecumenical endeavour. We invest in dialogue with other churches based on trust and a desire that the whole company of God's people may grow into the fullness of unity to which God calls us that the world may believe the gospel.

TEAC Anglican Way Consultation
Singapore, May 2007

The Bible in the Life of the Church

Based on a proposal drawn up by some Primates, meeting at Coventry Cathedral, England, there was initial discussion at the February 2007 (Dar es Salaam) meetings of the Joint Standing Committee and the Primates of the suggestion that a major three year project should be launched exploring the way or ways that the Bible is used in the life of the Anglican Communion. A more detailed proposal was then presented to the February/March 2008 meeting of the Joint Standing Committee, which agreed to 'welcome the initiative, and ask the Secretary General and Director of Theological Studies to develop the proposal in the light of the discussion at this meeting, and to commend it to the Lambeth Conference and ACC-14.'[1]

So the proposals being brought to the current meeting of the Anglican Consultative Council have been drawn up on the basis of previous discussion at both the Primates' Meeting and the Joint Standing Committee. Discussion about Scripture at the Lambeth Conference 2008 has also fed into the development of the proposal.

The essential question that needs to be addressed by 'The Bible in the Life of the Church' project is, 'What do we mean when we say that we are a Church that lives under Scripture?'

The following is a suggested structure for the project:

1. The project will be formally accountable to ACC, although it is expected that the Primates' Meetings will also be interested to hear of the progress of the work.

2. We envisage that the project will be of three years duration and will report to the next meeting of the ACC in 2012. This does not rule out further work that might develop out of the project, relating to other aspects of the Church's life in the modern world, but it is too early at this stage to make detailed proposals about such further work.

---

[1] Resolution 5 of JSC March 2008: *The Faith Of The Church And The Life Of The Modern World.* The project was also discussed and commended at the Primates' Meeting held in Alexandria in February 2009.

3. It will be essential to ensure that the project involves wide, regionally based, grass roots, participation from around the Communion, as well as drawing on the work of academic biblical scholars/theologians. It will also be important to find ways to take seriously the Anglican experience of diversity, as well as drawing on previous work done in this field by the Anglican Communion, by individual Anglican Churches and by some of our ecumenical partners.

4. There will be a Steering Group established containing approximately 10-12 members. The Chair of the Steering Group will be a person with credibility internationally, ecclesiastically and academically.

5. The majority of the work however will be done by 5-6 regionally based groups. These would seek as far as possible to use infrastructure which already exists e.g. theological educational institutions to develop the regional focuses.

6. The convenors of each of the regional groups will be members of the Steering Group, to ensure that regional insights are represented.

7. The project will be supported by the Department of Theological Studies. However, ideally, assuming that funds allow, there will be a part-time dedicated project manager who will have the particular responsibility of supporting and encouraging the work of the regional groups and their convenors. The project manager will also have the responsibility (along with the Steering Group as a whole) of ensuring that the outcomes of the project are made available and publicised in appropriate ways.

8. The project would operate in two or three phases (this would be a decision for the Steering Group). In each phase the regional groups would be asked to address how the Bible is used in relation to a specific issue. These might include e.g. Creation; Communion; Sexuality. It would be hoped that out of the exploration of such 'case studies' in the regional groups some principles about the way(s) Anglicans read scripture would emerge.

9. It is intended that the 'outcome' of the project would not be (simply) a formal report, but would include practical tools for the theological education of both clergy and laity. It may well also be that material from

the project could be presented to the newly established Faith and Order Commission.

10. While progress of the project is subject to the availability of funding, it is envisaged that an initial meeting of the Steering Group will happen before the end of 2009.

The members of ACC are invited to discuss the proposals for this project, and, if they are so minded, to pass the resolution which will formally establish it.

Clare Amos
Director of Theological Studies
20 March 2009

Report on the Work of NIFCON (Network for Inter Faith Concerns of the Anglican Communion)

This report seeks to draw together and report on the main aspects of the work of NIFCON (the Network for Inter Faith Concerns of the Anglican Communion) since the previous meeting of the ACC held in Nottingham, England, in June 2005. Over the last three-four years Christian-Muslim relations has been a key focus for our work, but we have tried to ensure that this has not been to the exclusion of engagement with other world faiths; we have also sought to reflect to reflect on theological and practical issues for Anglicans in relating to people of other faiths. 2005 was also the 40th anniversary of the Second Vatican Council's 'Declaration on the Relation of the Church to Non-Christian Religions', *Nostra Aetate* which is generally felt to have ushered in the modern era in respect of Christian engagement with people of other religions. Reflection on the impact of *Nostra Aetate* and response to the anniversary of its publication was also an underlying theme of our work during this period.

1. Consultation on 'Faith and Citizenship' in Kaduna, Nigeria

This was a significant regional event in the life of NIFCON which took place in Kaduna, Nigeria, at the invitation of Archbishop Josiah of Kaduna. We are extremely grateful to Archbishop Josiah Idowu-Fearon and the clergy of Kaduna Diocese for the helpful and hospitable way we were received. Participants in the consultation came from: Canada, Egypt, Germany, Ghana, Ireland, Jordan, Kenya, Liberia, Pakistan, Sudan, the United Kingdom, the United States, and Zambia, as well as a strong representation from the states comprising the Province of Kaduna and from other parts of Nigeria. We were grateful for the participation both of Canon Guy Wilkinson, the Archbishop of Canterbury's Secretary for Inter Faith Affairs, and of Archdeacon Dr Sola Igbari, who held responsibility for Inter Faith, Ecumenical and Inter Anglican Relations in the Church of Nigeria. During the consultation we had presentations describing Christian-Muslim relations in various countries, as well as in the continent of Africa as a whole. We worshipped and engaged in Bible study together, exploring key New Testament texts relating to the theme of 'Faith and Citizenship'. We experienced the situation on the grounds in Kaduna itself and were especially grateful to meet with Muslim members of the 'Bridge Builders' Association who work with Archbishop

Josiah in helping Christians and Muslims in the Kaduna region to relate to each other more effectively. The full report of the Kaduna consultation as well as substantial other documentation from the meeting is available on the NIFCON website at http://nifcon.anglicancommunion.org/work/consultations/kaduna/report.cfm . Particularly significant is a substantial report on the topic of Faith and Citizenship in Africa, given by Revd Dr Johnson Mbillah, Director of PROCMURA (Programme for Christian Muslim Relations in Africa) which is available at http://nifcon.anglicancommunion.org/work/consultations/kaduna/presentation s.cfm As a direct result of the consultation in Kaduna there was also NIFCON involvement in a training event organised by the Church of Sudan *(see below).*

2. Generous Love: The Truth of the Gospel and the Call to Dialogue.

This report, with the subtitle of *An Anglican theology of inter faith relations,* has been a ground-breaking piece of work undertaken by NIFCON throughout 2007 and early 2008. It is intended as a theology of inter faith relations rather than a theology of religions. It was produced as an initiative of NIFCON, and is commended by the Archbishop of Canterbury, who was consulted over its writing and production. It is intended as a 'marker' setting out certain Anglican principles in relation to engaging with people of other faiths at the beginning of the 21st century, drawing upon work done previously in this field eg *The Way of Dialogue* (produced for the Lambeth Conference in 1988). It was produced by a widely collaborative process that included correspondence with 50 people from around the Anglican Communion. Although produced partly with the Lambeth Conference in mind, it is intended to have a much wider audience (as indeed has proved to be the case). It is available in hard copy (we are on the 4th print run) as well as on the NIFCON website at: http://nifcon.anglicancommunion.org/resources/documents/generous_love_A 4_with_foreward.pdf

Printed copies will be available for members of the Anglican Consultative Council in Jamaica. French and Spanish versions of the document are also available. We are now in process of producing a web-based study guide for *Generous Love,* which is likely to form the basis of an interactive session at the ACC meeting.

3. The Lambeth Conference

NIFCON was asked to take responsibility for organising the 'Engaging with Other Faiths' element of the Lambeth Conference. This involved suggesting the input for the Indaba groups on the day that 'Engaging with Other Faiths' was the topic of the day, as well as organising a considerable number of self-select sessions. In relation to the Indaba groups a DVD was produced which featured six bishops from different parts of the Anglican Communion talking about their respective contexts – in relation to the issue of engaging with people of other faiths. The DVD also featured an introduction to the document *Generous Love: The Truth of the Gospel and the Call to Dialogue*, which was then discussed in the Indaba groups. The range of self-select sessions organised by NIFCON included a session on the Holy Land – Israel/Palestine with Jewish, Christian and Muslim involvement; sessions on engaging with Islam in Africa by Johnson Mbillah of PROCMURA, an exploration of religious fundamentalism, and groups concerned with issues such as the pastoral care of converts. In the Lambeth Conference Reflections document *Generous Love* was commended for study in the Anglican Communion.

4. The Al Azhar Dialogue and Study Exchange

Since 2003 NIFCON has administered the annual dialogue meeting between the Anglican Communion and Al Azhar Al Sharif, the historic Egyptian centre of Sunni Islam. This has continued with the meeting happening alternatively in Cairo and London. The most recent meeting of the dialogue, held in Cairo in November 2008, sought to take stock over where we had reached in the six years since the dialogue had begun, and suggested a list of topics that should be addressed over the coming three years. The communique from this most recent meeting can be found at http://nifcon.anglicancommunion.org/work/dialogues/al_ahzar/cairo2008.cfm.

However linked to the dialogue meeting there has also been an innovative study exchange developed of younger Christian and Muslim scholars, with the scholars spending a few weeks in the institution of the other faith. This exchange has now happened twice, with younger male scholars in 2006 and younger female scholars very recently in 2009. This has proved very worthwhile both for the individuals themselves and for the sending and receiving institutions.

Because of the restrictions relating to the way that the project is funded the exchanges have had to be to/from the United Kingdom and Egypt. If funding can be obtained it would be excellent to make such an 'exchange' process much more multi-lateral. The study exchange also facilitated the visit of the Grand Mufti of Egypt, Dr Ali Gomaa in November 2006, in which he spent a week at Cambridge University, as well as an earlier visit by Sheikh Fawzy el Zefzaf, then Chair of the Al Azhar Committee for Dialogue with the Monotheistic Faiths. .

5. Christian-Muslim Digest

In fulfilment of a mandate given to it at the 1998 Lambeth Conference to 'monitor Christian-Muslim relations' NIFCON has recently managed to establish a quarterly 'digest' which looks at how such relations are presented in the media – and analyses underlying trends. After a slow start on this project, the work was taken over at the end of 2008 by Dr John Chesworth who has now produced two substantial and informative issues, copies of which will be available in Jamaica. The January 2009 issues looks particularly at Tanzania and Kenya, the April 2009 issue will focus especially on Pakistan. It is hoped that eventually the issues of the digest will be collected together, and along with various country reports offered at NIFCON consultations form the basis of a substantial volume to be available at ACC-15. The digest is principally available in electronic form at http://nifcon.anglicancommunion.org/digest/index.cfm and copies are also emailed to a list of subscribers who have requested to receive it. We would be happy to include any members of ACC on this email list.

6. The NIFCON website

Mention has been made at several points above of the NIFCON website. This was substantially revamped and enlarged in the summer of 2007. It now contains a fairly comprehensive collection of documentation relating to Anglican involvement in inter faith work and is widely used as a resource both by members of the Communion and by ecumenical partners. The revision and enlargement of the website was largely the work of my colleague Susanne Mitchell.

7. Contact with correspondents around the world

As part of her career development Susanne moved on in September 2008 to another position linked to UK based inter faith relations. At the time of writing she has not yet been exactly replaced, although I have had some very helpful support from Suminder Duggal (who mainly works in Communication at the ACO). One of the tasks that Susanne undertook for NIFCON was the sustaining of the network of correspondents around the Anglican Communion. Since her departure it has not been possible to work proactively on this – although we have responded to enquiries etc, and publicised information about inter faith activities around the Communion that are sent to us for that purpose. When further assistance is available this is an area to re-develop, perhaps revising the way in which we approach this work.

8. The status of NIFCON; relations with colleagues on the Archbishop of Canterbury's staff

At the 2006 meeting of the Joint Standing Committee, NIFCON was given the status of a 'Working Party' in the Department of Theological Studies, the department of which I am the Director. This has allowed NIFCON (and where appropriate myself) to speak on behalf of and represent the Anglican Communion Office in the field of inter faith relations. One example of this has been our involvement in a consultation in October 2008 on Christian-Muslim relations that has been organised by the 'Christian World Communions', supported by the WCC. We facilitated the Anglican representation at that meeting. However NIFCON still remains in some important ways also a 'Network' of the Communion. Effectively the Management Group of NIFCON functions as the 'Working Party', supporting the wider Network extending through the Communion. The change of status to a 'Working Party' does not make any substantive difference to NIFCON's finances *i.e.* it does not receive funds from the core budget of the ACC.

Other aspects of NIFCON's structure have not altered: we still have three Presidents: Bishop Louis Tsui (Hong Kong); Bishop Michael Nazir-Ali (England); Bishop Josiah Idowu Fearon (Nigeria). Bishop Nazir-Ali and Bishop Fearon need, under NIFCON's constitution, to retire at the forthcoming meeting of the ACC, and we will be asking ACC 14 to approve the names of two Presidents to replace them (names and more details will be available at the meeting).

Since 2005 there has also been a development in the staff support that the Archbishop of Canterbury receives in this area, due to the fact that it is a clear priority for his ministry. I have enjoyed working closely with both Canon Guy Wilkinson and Canon Anthony Ball, the relevant staff members, and they have been very supportive of the work of NIFCON. There are of course some very significant initiatives that the Archbishop of Canterbury has taken in this field, such as *the Building Bridges* annual dialogue between a group of Christian and Muslim scholars, and the Archbishop's work in putting together a coordinated response to *A Common Word*, the letter of 138 Muslim scholars to Christian religious leaders. However as well as this work which is the direct responsibility of the Archbishop's staff at Lambeth Palace, there are some aspects of our work that involve both the Archbishop directly and the Anglican Communion structures. Primarily these are the dialogues between Anglicans and people of other faiths. The dialogue with Al Azhar was mentioned above; additionally there is a dialogue between the Archbishop and the Chief Rabbis of Israel and linked Anglican-Jewish Commission which was established in 2006; as a result of the Archbishop's recent visit to Libya there may also be a dialogue established with the World Islamic Call Society. The administration of such dialogues under the Archbishop is undertaken by Lambeth Palace along with staff of the Anglican Communion Office and it is hoped that this will be strengthened shortly by an additional Lambeth staff member managed through the ACO.

9. Wider involvement

Members of the NIFCON Management Group and myself have had a wide range of involvement with a number of inter faith activities around the Anglican Communion. Very recently (February 2009), there was been a training event organised by the Church of Sudan, and its Bishop for inter faith work, Bishop Andudu Elnail, to train clergy to minister more effectively in Muslim contexts. NIFCON raised some funding for this training event, and Bishop Michael Jackson of Clogher, Ireland, the Chair of NIFCON's Management Group, participated in the meeting and gave a number of the addresses. I myself will be speaking on Anglican inter faith work at a conference organised in April 2009 by the Bishop of Lahore. I also participated in a conference in March 2008 organised by Georgetown University at which I was asked to speak about Anglican approaches to engaging with Islam. Some members of NIFCON's Management Group also participate in the Church of England's 'Presence and Engagement Task Group' – which looks at how Anglican churches can witness and minister more effectively in contexts in which Christians are a minority. As part of its work the Task Group has put together some competency grids which look at the training needs for clergy and laity in such contexts. The Task Group has also produced a resource called *Encouraging Reading*, ten substantial and very useful Bible studies on Old Testament texts designed for use by Christians who are living and ministering in situations where issues like the relationship of the Abrahamic faiths, attitudes to the stranger, inter faith marriage, and conversion cannot be avoided. These are be found at http://www.presenceandengagement.org.uk/resources.php?1 and some copies will be available at the ACC meeting.

10. Priorities for the future

At the November 2008 meeting of the Management Group, as well as reflecting on our contribution to the Lambeth Conference, we sought to identify our priorities for the coming five years. In addition to continuing and developing most of the work referred to above, and in particular ensuring that the study guide for *Generous Love* is produced and made widely available, we have identified two areas to which we will be seeking to make a more substantial contribution. These are 'advocacy' and 'training'. We believe that NIFCON needs to develop ways to help the Anglican Communion speak and respond more effectively to the situation and needs of Christians in difficult contexts where they are a religious minority. We also believe that after finishing the study guide to *Generous Love* it will be appropriate to seek to provide other training resources for Anglican Christians relating to inter faith concerns, and, as in the recent case of the Sudan, be willing, as far as possible, to support training organised by Anglican Provinces. Alongside these priorities ideally we are hoping to hold a regional consultation in East Asia, given the region's particular inter faith profile, to complement those already held in Bangalore (2003) and Kaduna (2007)[1]. It is of course important to reiterate that NIFCON does not receive any direct funding from the ACC budget, so these priorities (and any other work that NIFCON undertakes) need to be funded by successful applications to grant-making bodies.

There is however another project that we hope to work towards. 2013 will be the 100th anniversary of the birth of Bishop Kenneth Cragg, an Anglican and global pioneer in the field of engaging with people of other faiths. He has been an inspiration for many who work in this field. We hope to plan a conference to take place before then, which will have as its subject matter Anglican engagement with other faiths over the last 100 years or so. The material from this conference will be published in a commemorative book intended to appear in 2013.

We invite ACC to endorse the ongoing work of NIFCON and these specific priorities, and to ratify the names put forward to be Presidents of NIFCON.

Clare Amos
Director of Theological Studies, Anglican Communion Office and
Coordinator of NIFCON, 23 March 2009

[1] There was additionally a consultation held in Oslo in December 2003, focusing on inter faith issues in Western Europe. There was NIFCON participation in this event, although it was organised by representatives of the Anglican and Lutheran (Porvoo) Churches involved.

Windsor Process

THE ANGLICAN COMMUNION COVENANT

The Third (Ridley Cambridge) Draft

Introduction to the Covenant Text

'This life is revealed, and we have seen it and testify to it, and declare to you the eternal life that was with the Father and was revealed to us – we declare to you what we have seen and heard so that you also may have communion with us; and truly our communion is with the Father and with his Son Jesus Christ. These things we write so that our joy may be complete.' (1 John 1.2-4).

1. God has called us into communion in Jesus Christ (1 Cor. 1.9). This communion has been 'revealed to us' by the Son as being the very divine life of God the Trinity. What is the life revealed to us? St John makes it clear that the communion of life in the Church participates in the communion which is the divine life itself, the life of the Trinity. This life is not a reality remote from us, but one that has been 'seen' and 'testified to' by the apostles and their followers: 'for in the communion of the Church we share in the divine life'[1]. This life of the One God, Father, Son, and Holy Spirit, shapes and displays itself through the very existence and ordering of the Church.

2. Our divine calling into communion is established in God's purposes for the whole of creation (Eph 1:10; 3:9ff.). It is extended to all humankind, so that, in our sharing of God's life as Father, Son, and Holy Spirit, God might restore in us the divine image. Through time, according to the Scriptures, God has furthered this calling through covenants made with Noah, Abraham, Israel, and David. The prophet Jeremiah looked forward to a new covenant not written on tablets of stone but upon the heart (Jer 31.31-34). In God's Son, Christ Jesus, a new covenant is given us, established in his 'blood ... poured out for the many for the forgiveness of sins' (Mt 26:28), secured through his resurrection from the dead (Eph 1:19-23), and sealed with the gift of the Holy Spirit poured into our hearts

---

[1] *The Church of the Triune God*, The Cyprus Statement of the International Commission for Anglican Orthodox Theological Dialogue, 2007, paragraph 1,2.

121

(Rom 5:5). Into this covenant of death to sin and of new life in Christ we are baptized, and empowered to share God's communion in Christ with all people, to the ends of the earth and of creation.

3. We humbly recognize that this calling and gift of communion entails responsibilities for our common life before God as we seek, through grace, to be faithful in our service of God's purposes for the world. Joined in one universal Church, which is Christ's Body, spread throughout the earth, we serve his gospel even as we are enabled to be made one across the dividing walls of human sin and estrangement (Eph 2.12-22). The forms of this life in the Church, caught up in the mystery of divine communion, reveal to the hostile and divisive power of the world the 'manifold wisdom of God' (Eph 3:9-10). Faithfulness, honesty, gentleness, humility, patience, forgiveness, and love itself, lived out in mutual deference and service (Mk 10.44-45) among the Church's people and through its ministries, contribute to building up the body of Christ as it grows to maturity (Eph 4.1-16; Col 3.8-17).

4. In the providence of God, which holds sway even over our divisions caused by sin, various families of churches have grown up within the universal Church in the course of history. Among these families is the Anglican Communion, which provides a particular charism and identity among the many followers and servants of Jesus. We recognise the wonder, beauty and challenge of maintaining communion in this family of churches, and the need for mutual commitment and discipline as a witness to God's promise in a world and time of instability, conflict, and fragmentation. Therefore, we covenant together as churches of this Anglican Communion to be faithful to God's promises through the historic faith we confess, our common worship, our participation in God's mission, and the way we live together.

5. To covenant together is not intended to change the character of this Anglican expression of Christian faith. Rather, we recognise the importance of renewing in a solemn way our commitment to one another, and to the common understanding of faith and order we have received, so that the bonds of affection which hold us together may be re-affirmed and intensified. We do this in order to reflect, in our relations with one another, God's own faithfulness and promises towards us in Christ (2 Cor 1.20-22).

6. We are a people who live, learn, and pray by and with the Scriptures as God's Word. We seek to adore God in thanks and praise and to make intercession for the needs of people everywhere through common prayer, united across many cultures and languages. We are privileged to share in the mission of the apostles to bring the gospel of Christ to all nations and peoples, not only in words but

also in deeds of compassion and justice that witness to God's character and the triumph of Christ over sin and death. We give ourselves as servants of a greater unity among the divided Christians of the world. May the Lord help us to 'preach not ourselves, but Jesus Christ as Lord, and ourselves as your servants for Jesus' sake' (2 Cor. 4.5).

7. Our faith embodies a coherent testimony to what we have received from God's Word and the Church's long-standing witness. Our life together reflects the blessings of God (even as it exposes our failures in faith, hope and love) in growing our Communion into a truly global family. The mission we pursue aims at serving the great promises of God in Christ that embrace the peoples and the world God so loves. This mission is carried out in shared responsibility and stewardship of resources, and in interdependence among ourselves and with the wider Church.

8. Our prayer is that God will redeem our struggles and weakness, renew and enrich our common life and use the Anglican Communion to witness effectively in all the world, working with all people of good will, to the new life and hope found in Christ Jesus.

The Anglican Communion Covenant

Preamble

We, as Churches of the Anglican Communion, under the Lordship of Jesus Christ, solemnly covenant together in these following affirmations and commitments. As people of God, drawn from 'every nation, tribe, people and language' (Rev 7.9), we do this in order to proclaim more effectively in our different contexts the grace of God revealed in the gospel, to offer God's love in responding to the needs of the world, to maintain the unity of the Spirit in the bond of peace, and together with all God's people to attain the full stature of Christ (Eph 4.3,13).

Section One: Our Inheritance of Faith

1.1   Each Church affirms:

(1.1.1) its communion in the one, holy, catholic, and apostolic Church, worshipping the one true God, Father, Son, and Holy Spirit.

(1.1.2) the catholic and apostolic faith uniquely revealed in the Holy Scriptures and set forth in the catholic creeds, which faith the Church is called upon to proclaim afresh in each generation[2]. The historic formularies of the Church of England [3], forged in the context of the European Reformation and acknowledged and appropriated in various ways in the Anglican Communion, bear authentic witness to this faith.

(1.1.3) the Holy Scriptures of the Old and New Testaments as containing all things necessary for salvation and as being the rule and ultimate standard of faith[4].

(1.1.4) the Apostles' Creed, as the baptismal symbol; and the Nicene Creed, as the sufficient statement of the Christian faith[5].

(1.1.5) the two sacraments ordained by Christ himself – Baptism and the Supper of the Lord – ministered with the unfailing use of Christ's words of institution, and of the elements ordained by him[6].

(1.1.6) the historic episcopate, locally adapted in the methods of its administration to the varying needs of the nations and peoples called of God into the unity of his Church[7].

(1.1.7) the shared patterns of our common prayer and liturgy which form, sustain and nourish our worship of God and our faith and life together.

---

[2] Cf. The Preface to the Declaration of Assent, Canon C15 of the Church of England.
[3] The Thirty-nine Articles of Religion, the 1662 Book of Common Prayer, and the Ordering of Bishops, Priests, and Deacons
[4] The Chicago-Lambeth Quadrilateral of 1886/1888
[5] The Chicago-Lambeth Quadrilateral of 1886/1888
[6] cf. The Chicago-Lambeth Quadrilateral 1886/1888, The Preface to the Declaration of Assent, Canon C15 of the Church of England.
[7] cf. The Chicago-Lambeth Quadrilateral 1886/1888

(1.1.8) its participation in the apostolic mission of the whole people of God, and that this mission is shared with other Churches and traditions beyond this Covenant.

1.2   In living out this inheritance of faith together in varying contexts, each Church, reliant on the Holy Spirit, commits itself:

(1.2.1) to teach and act in continuity and consonance with Scripture and the catholic and apostolic faith, order and tradition, as received by the Churches of the Anglican Communion, mindful of the common councils of the Communion and our ecumenical agreements.

(1.2.2) to uphold and proclaim a pattern of Christian theological and moral reasoning and discipline that is rooted in and answerable to the teaching of Holy Scripture and the catholic tradition.

(1.2.3) to witness, in this reasoning, to the renewal of humanity and the whole created order through the death and resurrection of Christ, and to reflect the holiness that in consequence God gives to, and requires from, his people.

(1.2.4) to hear, read, mark, learn and inwardly digest the Scriptures in our different contexts, informed by the attentive and communal reading of - and costly witness to - the Scriptures by all the faithful, by the teaching of bishops and synods, and by the results of rigorous study by lay and ordained scholars.

(1.2.5) to ensure that biblical texts are received, read and interpreted faithfully, respectfully, comprehensively and coherently, with the expectation that Scripture continues to illuminate and transform the Church and its members, and through them, individuals, cultures and societies.

(1.2.6) to encourage and be open to prophetic and faithful leadership in ministry and mission so as to enable God's people to respond in courageous witness to the power of the gospel in the world.

(1.2.7) to seek in all things to uphold the solemn obligation to nurture and sustain eucharistic communion, in accordance with existing canonical disciplines, as we strive under God for the fuller realisation of the communion of all Christians.

(1.2.8) to pursue a common pilgrimage with the whole Body of Christ continually to discern the fullness of truth into which the Spirit leads us, that peoples from all nations may be set free to receive new and abundant life in the Lord Jesus Christ.

Section Two: The Life We Share with Others: Our Anglican Vocation

2.1   Each Church affirms:

(2.1.1) communion as a gift of God given so that God's people from east and west, north and south, may together declare the glory of the Lord and be both a sign of God's reign in the Holy Spirit and the first fruits in the world of God's redemption in Christ.

(2.1.2) its gratitude for God's gracious providence extended to us down through the ages: our origins in the Church of the apostles; the ancient common traditions; the rich history of the Church in Britain and Ireland reshaped by the Reformation, and our growth into a global communion through the expanding missionary work of the Church; our ongoing refashioning by the Holy Spirit through the gifts and sacrificial witness of Anglicans from around the world; and our summons into a more fully developed communion life.

(2.1.3) in humility our call to constant repentance: for our failures in exercising patience and charity and in recognizing Christ in one another; our misuse of God's gracious gifts; our failure to heed God's call to serve; and our exploitation one of another.

(2.1.4) the imperative of God's mission into which the Communion is called, a vocation and blessing in which each Church is joined with others in Christ in the work of establishing God's reign. As the Communion continues to develop into a worldwide family of interdependent churches, we embrace challenges and opportunities for mission at local, regional, and international

126

levels. In this, we cherish our mission heritage as offering Anglicans distinctive opportunities for mission collaboration.

(2.1.5) that our common mission is a mission shared with other Churches and traditions beyond this Covenant. We embrace opportunities for the discovery of the life of the whole gospel, and for reconciliation and shared mission with the Church throughout the world. We affirm the ecumenical vocation of Anglicanism to the full visible unity of the Church in accordance with Christ's prayer that 'all may be one'. It is with all the saints in every place and time that we will comprehend the fuller dimensions of Christ's redemptive and immeasurable love.

2.2 In recognition of these affirmations, each Church, reliant on the Holy Spirit, commits itself:

(2.2.1) to answer God's call to undertake evangelisation and to share in the healing and reconciling mission 'for our blessed but broken, hurting and fallen world'[8], and, with mutual accountability, to share our God-given spiritual and material resources in this task.

(2.2.2) to undertake in this mission, which is the mission of God in Christ[9]:

(2.2.2.a)	'to proclaim the Good News of the Kingdom of God' and to bring all to repentance and faith;
(2.2.2.b)	'to teach, baptize and nurture new believers', making disciples of all nations (Mt 28.19) through the quickening power of the Holy Spirit[10] and drawing them into the one Body of Christ whose faith, calling and hope are one in the Lord (Eph 4.4-6);
(2.2.2.c)	'to respond to human need by loving service', disclosing God's reign through humble ministry to those most needy (Mk 10.42-45; Mt 18.4; 25.31-45);
(2.2.2.d)	'to seek to transform unjust structures of society' as the Church stands vigilantly with Christ proclaiming both

---

[8] IASCOME Report, ACC-13
[9] The five Marks of Mission are set out in the MISSIO Report of 1999, building on work at ACC-6 and ACC-8.
[10] *Church as Communion* n26

127

judgment and salvation to the nations of the world[11], and manifesting through our actions on behalf of God's righteousness the Spirit's transfiguring power[12];

(2.2.2.e)   'to strive to safeguard the integrity of creation and to sustain and renew the life of the earth' as essential aspects of our mission in communion[13].

(2.2.3) to engage in this mission with humility and an openness to our own ongoing conversion in the face of our unfaithfulness and failures in witness.

(2.2.4) to revive and renew structures for mission which will awaken and challenge the whole people of God to work, pray and give for the spread of the gospel.

(2.2.5) to order its mission in the joyful and reverent worship of God, thankful that in our eucharistic communion 'Christ is the source and goal of the unity of the Church and of the renewal of human community' [14].

Section Three: Our Unity and Common Life

3.1   Each Church affirms:

(3.1.1) that by our participation in Baptism and Eucharist, we are incorporated into the one body of the Church of Jesus Christ, and called by Christ to pursue all things that make for peace and build up our common life.

(3.1.2) its resolve to live in a Communion of Churches. Each Church, with its bishops in synod, orders and regulates its own affairs and its local responsibility for mission through its own system of government and law and is therefore described as living 'in communion with autonomy and accountability'[15]. Trusting in the Holy Spirit, who calls and enables us to dwell in a shared life of common worship and prayer for one another, in mutual affection, commitment and service, we seek to affirm our common

---

[11] WCC 1954 Evanston, *Christ the Hope of the World*
[12] Moscow Statement, 43
[13] IARCCUM, *Growing Together in Unity and Mission*,118
[14] Baptism, Eucharist and Ministry, WCC,
[15] A Letter from Alexandria, the Primates, March 2009

life through those Instruments of Communion by which our Churches are enabled to be conformed together to the mind of Christ. Churches of the Anglican Communion are bound together 'not by a central legislative and executive authority, but by mutual loyalty sustained through the common counsel of the bishops in conference'[16] and of the other instruments of Communion.

(3.1.3) the central role of bishops as guardians and teachers of faith, as leaders in mission, and as a visible sign of unity, representing the universal Church to the local, and the local Church to the universal and the local Churches to one another. This ministry is exercised personally, collegially and within and for the eucharistic community. We receive and maintain the historic threefold ministry of bishops, priests and deacons, ordained for service in the Church of God, as they call all the baptised into the mission of Christ.

(3.1.4) the importance of instruments in the Anglican Communion to assist in the discernment, articulation and exercise of our shared faith and common life and mission. The life of communion includes an ongoing engagement with the diverse expressions of apostolic authority, from synods and episcopal councils to local witness, in a way which continually interprets and articulates the common faith of the Church's members (consensus fidelium). In addition to the many and varied links which sustain our life together, we acknowledge four particular Instruments at the level of the Anglican Communion which express this co-operative service in the life of communion.

I. We accord the Archbishop of Canterbury, as the bishop of the See of Canterbury with which Anglicans have historically been in communion, a primacy of honour and respect among the college of bishops in the Anglican Communion as first among equals (primus inter pares). As a focus and means of unity, the Archbishop gathers and works with the Lambeth Conference and Primates' Meeting, and presides in the Anglican Consultative Council.

II. The Lambeth Conference expresses episcopal collegiality worldwide, and brings together the bishops for common worship, counsel,

---

[16] Lambeth Conference 1930

consultation and encouragement in their ministry of guarding the faith and unity of the Communion and equipping the saints for the work of ministry (Eph 4.12) and mission.

III. The Anglican Consultative Council is comprised of lay, clerical and episcopal representatives from our Churches[17]. It facilitates the co-operative work of the Churches of the Anglican Communion, co-ordinates aspects of international Anglican ecumenical and mission work, calls the Churches into mutual responsibility and interdependence, and advises on developing provincial structures[18].

IV. The Primates' Meeting is convened by the Archbishop of Canterbury for mutual support, prayer and counsel. The authority that primates bring to the meeting arises from their own positions as the senior bishops of their Provinces, and the fact that they are in conversation with their own Houses of Bishops and located within their own synodical structures[19]. In the Primates' Meeting, the Primates and Moderators are called to work as representatives of their Provinces in collaboration with one another in mission and in doctrinal, moral and pastoral matters that have Communion-wide implications.

It is the responsibility of each Instrument to consult with, respond to, and support each other Instrument and the Churches of the Communion[20]. Each Instrument may initiate and commend a process of discernment and a direction for the Communion and its Churches.

3.2 Acknowledging our interdependent life, each Church, reliant on the Holy Spirit, commits itself:

(3.2.1) to have regard for the common good of the Communion in the exercise of its autonomy, to support the work of the Instruments of Communion with the spiritual and material resources available to it, and to receive their work with a readiness to undertake reflection upon their counsels, and to endeavour to accommodate their recommendations.

---

[17] Constitution of the ACC, Article 3 and Schedule
[18] cf. the Objects of the ACC are set out in Article 2 of its Constitution.
[19] Report of the Windsor Continuation Group, 69.
[20] cf IATDC, Communion, Conflict and Hope, paragraph 113.

(3.2.2) to respect the constitutional autonomy of all of the Churches of the Anglican Communion, while upholding our mutual responsibility and interdependence in the Body of Christ[21], and the responsibility of each to the Communion as a whole[22].

(3.2.3) to spend time with openness and patience in matters of theological debate and reflection, to listen, pray and study with one another in order to discern the will of God. Such prayer, study and debate is an essential feature of the life of the Church as its seeks to be led by the Spirit into all truth and to proclaim the gospel afresh in each generation. Some issues, which are perceived as controversial or new when they arise, may well evoke a deeper understanding of the implications of God's revelation to us; others may prove to be distractions or even obstacles to the faith. All such matters therefore need to be tested by shared discernment in the life of the Church.

(3.2.4) to seek a shared mind with other Churches, through the Communion's councils, about matters of common concern, in a way consistent with the Scriptures, the common standards of faith, and the canon laws of our churches. Each Church will undertake wide consultation with the other Churches of the Anglican Communion and with the Instruments and Commissions of the Communion.

(3.2.5) to act with diligence, care and caution in respect of any action which may provoke controversy, which by its intensity, substance or extent could threaten the unity of the Communion and the effectiveness or credibility of its mission.

(3.2.6) in situations of conflict, to participate in mediated conversations, which involve face to face meetings, agreed parameters and a willingness to see such processes through.

(3.2.7) to have in mind that our bonds of affection and the love of Christ compel us always to uphold the highest degree of communion possible.

---

[21] Toronto Congress 1963, and the Ten Principles of Partnership.
[22] cf. the Schedule to the Dar es Salaam Communiqué of the Primates' Meeting, February 2007

Section Four: Our Covenanted Life Together

Each Church affirms the following procedures, and, reliant on the Holy Spirit, commits itself to their implementation.

4.1 Adoption of the Covenant

(4.1.1) Each Church adopting this Covenant affirms that it enters into the Covenant as a commitment to relationship in submission to God. Participation in the covenant expresses a loyalty grounded in mutuality that one Church freely offers to other Churches, in whom it recognises the bonds of a common faith and order, a common inheritance in worship, life and mission, and a readiness to live in an interdependent life, but does not represent submission to any external ecclesiastical jurisdiction.

(4.1.2) In adopting the Covenant for itself, each Church recognises in the preceding sections a statement of faith, mission and interdependence of life which is consistent with its own life and with the doctrine and practice of the Christian faith as it has received them.   It recognises these elements as fundamental to the life of the Anglican Communion and to the relationships among the covenanting Churches.

(4.1.3) The Covenant operates to express the common commitments which hold each Church in the relationship of communion one with another. Recognition of, and fidelity to, the text of this Covenant, enables mutual recognition and communion.   Nothing in this Covenant of itself shall be deemed to alter any provision of the Constitution and Canons of any Church of the Communion, or to limit its autonomy of governance.   Under the terms of this Covenant, no one Church, nor any agency of the Communion, can exercise control or direction over the internal life of any other covenanted Church.

(4.1.4) Every Church of the Anglican Communion, as recognised in accordance with the Constitution of the Anglican Consultative Council, is invited to adopt this Covenant in its life according to its own constitutional procedures.   Adoption of the Covenant by a Church does not in itself imply any change to its Constitution and Canons, but implies a recognition of those elements which must be maintained in its own life in order to sustain the relationship of covenanted communion established by this Covenant.

(4.1.5) It shall be open to other Churches to adopt the Covenant. Adoption of this Covenant does not bring any right of recognition by, or membership of, the Instruments of Communion. Such recognition and membership are dependent on the satisfaction of those conditions set out by each of the Instruments. However, adoption of the Covenant by a Church may be accompanied by a formal request to the Instruments for recognition and membership to be acted upon according to each Instrument's procedures.

(4.1.6) This Covenant becomes active for a Church when that Church adopts the Covenant.

4.2   The Maintenance of the Covenant and Dispute Resolution

(4.2.1) The Joint Standing Committee of the Anglican Consultative Council and of the Primates' Meeting, or any body that succeeds it, shall have the duty of overseeing the functioning of the Covenant in the life of the Anglican Communion. The Joint Standing Committee may nominate or appoint another committee or commission to assist in carrying out this function and to advise it on questions relating to the Covenant.

(4.2.2) If a question relating to the meaning of the Covenant, or of compatibility to the principles incorporated in it, should arise, the Joint Standing Committee may make a request to any covenanting Church to defer action until the processes set out below have been completed. It shall further take advice from such bodies as its feels appropriate on the nature and relational consequences of the matter and may make a recommendation to be referred for advice to both the Anglican Consultative Council and the Primates' Meeting.

(4.2.3) If a Church refuses to defer a controversial action, the Joint Standing Committee may recommend to any Instrument of Communion relational consequences which specify a provisional limitation of participation in, or suspension from, that Instrument until the completion of the process set out below.

(4.2.4) On the basis of advice received from the Anglican Consultative Council and the Primates' Meeting, the Joint Standing Committee may make a declaration concerning an action or decision of a covenanting Church that such an action or decision is or would be 'incompatible with the Covenant'. A declaration of incompatibility with the Covenant shall not have any force in the Constitution and Canons of any covenanting Church unless or until it is received by the canonical procedures of the Church in question.

(4.2.5) On the basis of the advice received, the Joint Standing Committee may make recommendations as to relational consequences to the Churches of the Anglican Communion or to the Instruments of the Communion. These recommendations may address the extent to which the decision of any covenanting Church to continue with an action or decision which has been found to be 'incompatible with the Covenant' impairs or limits the communion between that Church and the other Churches of the Communion. It may recommend whether such action or decision should have a consequence for participation in the life of the Communion and its Instruments. It shall be for each Church and each Instrument to determine its own response to such recommendations.

(4.2.6) Each Church undertakes to put into place such mechanisms, agencies or institutions, consistent with its own Constitution and Canons, as can undertake to oversee the maintenance of the affirmations and commitments of the Covenant in the life of that Church, and to relate to the Instruments of Communion on matters pertinent to the Covenant.

(4.2.7) Participation in the processes set out in this section .shall be limited to those members of the Instruments of Communion who are representatives of those churches who have adopted the Covenant, or who are still in the process of adoption.

4.3   Withdrawing from the Covenant

(4.3.1) Any covenanting Church may decide to withdraw from the Covenant. Although such withdrawal does not imply an automatic withdrawal from the Instruments or a repudiation of its Anglican character, it raises a question relating to the meaning of the Covenant, and of

134

compatibility with the principles incorporated within it, and it triggers the provisions set out in section 4.2.2 above.

4.4   The Covenant Text and its amendment

(4.4.1) The Covenant consists of the text set out in this document in the Preamble, Sections One to Four and the Declaration. The Introduction to the Covenant Text, which shall always be annexed to the Covenant text, is not part of the Covenant, but shall be accorded authority in understanding the purpose of the Covenant.

(4.4.2) Any covenanting Church or Instrument of Communion may submit a proposal to the Joint Standing Committee for the amendment of the Covenant. The Joint Standing Committee shall send the proposal to the Anglican Consultative Council, to the Primates' Meeting and any other body as it may consider appropriate for advice. The Joint Standing Committee shall make a recommendation on the proposal in the light of advice offered, and submit the proposal with any revisions to the constitutional bodies of the covenanting Churches. The amendment is operative when ratified by three quarters of such bodies. The Joint Standing Committee shall adopt a procedure for promulgation of the amendment.

Our Declaration

With joy and with firm resolve, we declare our Churches to be partakers in this Anglican Communion Covenant, offering ourselves for fruitful service and binding ourselves more closely in the truth and love of Christ, to whom with the Father and the Holy Spirit be glory for ever. Amen.

'Now may the God of Peace, who brought again from the dead our Lord Jesus, the great shepherd of the sheep, by the blood of the eternal covenant, make you complete in everything good so that you may do his will, working among us that which is pleasing in his sight, through Jesus Christ, to whom be the glory forever and ever. Amen.' (Hebrews 13.20, 21)

Windsor Continuation Group Report

A. Context: the Tradition we have received

1. Anglicanism is a tradition of Christian faith which affirms the revelation of God as Father, Son and Holy Spirit. It acknowledges the unique revelation of God in the incarnation, passion, death and resurrection of our Lord Jesus Christ. It affirms the primary authority of the Holy Scriptures; and - guided by the Holy Spirit - it acknowledges the interplay of scripture, tradition and reason in the continuing work of interpretation, understanding and discernment.

2. The Anglican Communion is a family of autonomous Churches. It finds its identity in the One Holy Catholic and Apostolic Church. The Churches of the Communion, which are self-governing, share something of a common history, and have traditionally set their faces against centralised government in favour of regional autonomy[1]. The Anglican tradition was fashioned in the turmoil of reformation in Western Europe in the sixteenth century. Its historic formularies acknowledge the circumstances in which its emerged as a distinctive church polity. The non-negotiable elements in any understanding of Anglicanism - the scriptures, the creeds, the gospel sacraments of baptism and eucharist, and the historic episcopate - are to be found in the Chicago-Lambeth Quadrilateral[2]; and the Instruments of Communion - the Archbishop of Canterbury, the Lambeth Conference, the Anglican Consultative Council and the Primates Meeting - provide an evolving framework within which discussion and discernment might take place. It remains to be seen if the circumstances in which the Communion finds itself today - externally and internally - might require over the years a shift of emphasis *from* 'autonomy with communion' *to* 'communion with autonomy and accountability'.

3. It is a primary concern of the Anglican Communion that its Churches and its congregations shall be 'formed by scripture, shaped by worship, ordered

---

[1] Cf the statements of the 1930 Lambeth Conference
[2] Originally fashioned as a basis for the reunion of Churches, the Quadrilateral has tended to become a statement of the irreducible minimum elements of the Anglican tradition.

for communion, and directed by God's mission[3]. It follows nonetheless that the Anglican way of being the Church, of doing theology, of exercising pastoral care, of engaging in evangelism, of voicing the prophetic priorities of God's Kingdom of righteousness recognise the wide variety of circumstances in which Christian people find themselves and the different insights and emphases within the Anglican tradition of faith and prayer and practice. It represents a discreet balance between authority and freedom, between the universal and the local, and between traditions of inter-dependence, autonomy and accountability.

4. The Anglican tradition attempts to be sensitive to the opportunities and the challenges presented in different places and at different times by the context and the culture in which we live. These challenges are addressed - and can only be addressed - in the light of our understanding of Scripture, the perceived guidance of the Holy Spirit, and the authority of shared experience and informed conscience.

5. It is an escapable consequence of living in the world that issues will arise from time to time where the conflict between continuity and change - *continuity* in doctrine and in pastoral practice and *change* in the discernment of new insights - raises urgent (and potentially divisive and destructive) questions concerning the received tradition, the *consensus fidelium*, and the limits of the diversity that can be sustained within the life of the Communion.

6. The Anglican Communion, which has evolved in recent generations, represents a model of reformed Catholicism which may yet make a distinctive and necessary contribution to the life of the wider church. It is unquestionably the case that the global context in which all institutions, all faith communities, are required to work demands appropriate structures, disciplines and traditions. It is necessary to recognise, however, that traditions of tolerance which are merely permissive, can so easily be abused; and yet a rediscovery of traditions of courtesy, patience and generosity, which are grounded in the scriptures and in the traditions of the church, will be required if the Communion in its entirety is to allow the Spirit of truth to lead us into a greater understanding of God's purposes for his church and for his world.

---

[3] See Lambeth Indaba §100-103 on the elements of "the Anglican Way", itself derived from the work of the Primates' Theological Education in the Anglican Communion Working Group (TEAC).

7. We believe that this tradition is now under threat to the grave disservice of our Communion and of the wider *oikumene*.

B. The Seriousness of the present Situation

8. The reality of our current life is complex; the divisions and differences are not always explicit in the presenting issues: doctrine, theology, ecclesiology, ethics, anthropology, culture, history, post-colonialism, post-modernity, post-denominationalism, political and global realities are all dimensions. There are competing value systems at work and a lack of clarity about a shared understanding of the nature and obligations of Communion. There is also a lack of mutual understanding about what is meant by 'authority'.

9. Much has been undertaken in the Communion through and in response to the Windsor Process, but as a Communion, we appear to remain at an impasse. There is inconsistency between what has been agreed, and what has, in the end, actually been done. This appears to create a gap between promise and follow through. The resolutions at General Convention (June 2006), the mutual Covenant of the House of Bishops of The Episcopal Church (TEC) at Camp Allen (March 2005), and the Bishop's Statement at New Orleans (September 2007) all point in the direction of accepting the recommendations of the Windsor Report (TWR), and yet some dioceses still proceed with the development of Rites of Blessing for same sex unions. There were serious undertakings and affirmations by the primates at their meetings in Dromantine (January 2005) and Dar es Salaam (February 2007) concerning interventions in other provinces, the spirit of which have not been honoured. There have been generous resolutions and responses by the House of Bishops and General Synod in Canada (2004, 2006, 2007) to the requests of the wider Communion, but still some dioceses and bishops feel that they can move in a contrary direction.

10. The gap is manifested in inconsistency between the stated intent and the reality – including the use and abuse of language, e.g. moratorium, 'initiating interventions'. The implications of requests and responses are either not fully thought through or they are disregarded. The consequences of actions have not always been adequately addressed, e.g. there appear to have been no consequences following the consecration of the Bishop of New Hampshire as

envisaged by the Primates' Statement of October 2003, or as a result of primatial interventions.

Breakdown of Trust

11. There are real fears of a wider agenda – over credal issues (the authority of scripture, the application of doctrine in life and ethics and even Christology and soteriology) and polity (comprehensiveness, autonomy and synodical government); other issues, such as lay presidency and theological statements that go far beyond the doctrinal definitions of the historic creeds, lie just over the horizon. Indeed, in recent months, the Diocese of Sydney has raised the issue of diaconal presidency at the Eucharist. Positions and arguments are becoming more extreme: not moving towards one another, relationships in the Communion continue to deteriorate; there is little sense of mutual accountability and a fear that vital issues are not being addressed in the most timely and effective manner.

12. Through modern technology, there has been active fear-mongering, deliberate distortion and demonising. Politicisation has overtaken Christian discernment. There is distrust of the Instruments of Communion and uncertainty about their capacity to respond to the situation. Polarisation of attitudes in the Churches of the Communion, not just in North America, but throughout the Communion, has developed, and the complexity of situations and attitudes caricatured.

13. There are growing patterns of congregationalism throughout the communion at parochial, diocesan and provincial level: for example, parishes feel free to choose from whom they will accept episcopal ministry; bishops feel free to make decisions of great controversy without reference to existing collegial structures. Primates make provision for episcopal leadership in territories outside their own Province. The symptoms of this breakdown of trust are common to all parties in the current situation – felt and expressed by conservative and liberal alike.

Turmoil in The Episcopal Church

14. There has been development from individual members leaving congregations, to congregations leaving parishes and dioceses, to dioceses seeking to leave provinces. Parties within The Episcopal Church have sought allies within the wider Communion, who are seen as only too willing to respond. Litigation and interventions have become locked into a vicious spiral – each side seeing the actions of the other as provoking and requiring response. At this time, it would appear that the divisions in the United States are playing out in the wider Communion, and already impacting in Canada.

15. All this amounts to a diminishing sense of Communion and impoverishing our witness to Christ, placing huge strains on the functioning of the Instruments of Communion. Such turmoil affects our relations with our ecumenical partners, many of whom face similar tensions. Some partners are beginning to raise questions about the identity of their Anglican partner. In the light of the ecumenical movement, there can no longer be tensions in one Communion that do not have wider repercussions across the whole Christian family.

The Lambeth Conference and Gafcon

16. The bishops who attended the Lambeth Conference overwhelmingly experienced an increase in mutual understanding and mutual loyalty, as noted in the Lambeth Indaba Document issued at the conclusion of the Conference. Of the twelve topics included in the agenda, the Reflections Group was able to report that the bishops found strong agreement in nine of the areas - on mission, the concern for human and social justice, the environment, ecumenism and inter-faith relations, on Anglican identity, scripture and addressing situations of injustice.

17. Areas of ongoing concern and with less agreement include Human Sexuality, the Windsor Process, and the proposed Anglican Covenant. Adding to the seriousness and tensions of the present time was the timing of the Global Anglicanism Future Conference (Gafcon) in June. While some bishops who attended Gafcon also attended Lambeth, many others did not. In fact, approximately 190 bishops of the Communion did not attend Lambeth either because of reasons of conscience or synodical

or primatial decision in their Provinces, a situation we regret both for their sakes and ours.

18. Anxieties have been expressed about the purpose, timing and outcomes of the Gafcon; there is some perplexity about the establishment of the Gafcon Primates' Council and of the Fellowship of Confessing Christians (FOCA) which, with withdrawal from participation at the Lambeth Conference, has further damaged trust.

19. For some time now therefore the issue of human sexuality has been the spark to the flame exposing tensions concerning the life of the Anglican Communion. The Instruments of Communion have sought to address these tensions through the Windsor Report and the process of reception of its ideas and recommendations. It has been the purpose of this group to assess where the Communion has arrived as a result of the Windsor Process, and to make recommendations about the next steps that could be taken to renew the Communion's life.

C. The Windsor Process

20. The Windsor Report 2004 responded to the developing situation by setting out a number of initiatives to address the tensions. While they remained recommendations of the Windsor Report, they carried only the authority of the members of the Commission. But many of these recommendations were picked up and adopted by the Primates, either in the Communiqué of the Dromantine Meeting (January 2005), or at the Dar es Salaam Meeting (February 2007). This does not entirely answer the question of their continuing authority in the Communion (see further the section below on *Ecclesial Deficit*) but it does at least give them purchase in the life of the Communion: these recommendations carry the weight of being the unanimous advice of the primates of our Churches - at the very least, the recommendations carry the authority of our chief pastors carrying back these recommendations to their own Church or Province with the voice of authority which they carry in that Province.

C(i). The Listening Process

21. The 1998 Lambeth Resolution 1.10 remains fundamental as the standard of teaching on matters of sexuality in the life of the Communion; but the Windsor Report also offered an acknowledgement that while there are divergent views on this, the discussion has to go on (TWR §146). Indeed, Lambeth 1.10 recognised this in the very terms of the resolution[4], echoing earlier resolutions at the 1978 and 1988 Conferences.

22. To enable this conversation to happen, space has to be created in which all sides can listen for the voice and leading of God; can listen to gay and lesbian Christians and learn of their experience; can listen to one another and the insights we bring to discernment on this issue. This was the end to which the *moratoria* recommended in the Windsor Report were shaped. They were conceived as a way of halting development in the situation while a conversation, together with an articulation of the purpose and ends of that conversation, could be undertaken.

23. The Listening Process has so far produced a significant amount of resources - an overview of the reflection on this issue taking place in each of the Provinces, which is set out on the Anglican Communion website[5], and a book of resources to encourage and inform the discussion[6]. Yet the listening process has not been totally embraced consistently across the Communion.

---

[4] Lambeth 1.10.3: We commit ourselves to listen to the experience of homosexual persons and we wish to assure them that they are loved by God and that all baptised, believing and faithful persons, regardless of sexual orientation, are full members of the Body of Christ. See also: Resolution 64 of the 1988 Conference: (1) Reaffirms the statement of the Lambeth Conference of 1978 on homosexuality, [Resolution 10] recognising the continuing need in the next decade for "deep and dispassionate study of the question of homosexuality, which would take seriously both the teaching of Scripture and the results of scientific and medical research." (2) Urges such study and reflection to take account of biological, genetic and psychological research being undertaken by other agencies, and the socio-cultural factors that lead to the different attitudes in the provinces of our Communion. (3) Calls each province to reassess, in the light of such study and because of our concern for human rights, its care for and attitude towards persons of homosexual orientation.

[5] http://www.anglicancommunion.org/listening/reports/index.cfm

[6] The Anglican Communion and Homosexuality – A resource to enable listening and dialogue (London, SPCK, 2008) Published June 2008

Recommendation

24. Only if the dialogue is seen to continue, and if there is an all-round readiness to engage in conversation and discernment on this issue, is there a hope of persuading the advocates of revision in the teaching of the Anglican Churches on this matter to remain committed to the period of 'gracious restraint', in which mutual conversation can take place. On both sides, we need to move from intransigence and the conviction that 'our' interpretation is the right one to a shared waiting upon God. There is something profoundly important about the Anglican way here - a readiness to acknowledge that Christian disciples discern God's truth by learning to wait upon one another, and that it takes the whole Church to know the whole truth.

25. We request that the Instruments of Communion commit themselves to a renewal of the Listening Process, and a real seeking of a common mind upon the issues which threaten to divide us.

C(ii). The Moratoria

26. The moratoria then arose from the necessity of gaining commitment to 'gracious restraint' all round in which conversation and discernment could take place. Such a season was also envisaged as a period in which the Covenant process (see below) could come to fruition. The Windsor Report identified three areas in which 'gracious restraint' would be necessary:

o   Consecration of Bishops living in a same gender union
o   Permission for Rites of Blessing for Same Sex unions
o   Interventions in Provinces

27. One of the most difficult areas of the life in the Communion at the moment arise from the differing extent to which the requests for such moratoria, recommended in the Windsor Report, and reflected in the requests of the Primates to their Churches in the Dromantine Communiqué (2005), have been adopted and are in force in the life of the Communion.

28. Nor do these moratoria rest on the authority of the Windsor Report or the requests of the Primates alone: it has been the unanimous advice of all four

Instruments of Communion[7] that the consecration of a bishop in a same gender union or permission or authorisation of Rites of Blessing for same sex unions are moves beyond what the Communion can, as a whole, approve or accept. They are therefore actions which 'tear the fabric of our Communion'[8].

29. It was the judgement of the Joint Standing Committee of the Anglican Consultative Council and the Primates and Moderators of the Anglican Communion (JSC)[9] that the first moratorium (*On the Consecration of Bishops*) is effectively in place in the communion. Although there continues to be some debate whether the wording of the resolution B033 of the 75th General Convention and its subsequent interpretation by the TEC House of Bishops at New Orleans in 2007 exactly meets the wording of the recommendation in the Windsor Report, such a moratorium does, in fact, exist; an interpretation agreed by both the strongest supporters and opponents of B033.

30. It is the judgement of WCG (Windsor Continuation Group) that the same is significantly, but not universally, true of the second moratorium on the authorisation of public Rites of Blessing of same sex unions. In The Episcopal Church up to a dozen dioceses out of the 110 dioceses of the Church are actively pursuing the exploration of such Rites within the life of the Church (10%). They do this with only the passive consent of General Convention[10], which has until now refused to take positive steps towards the recognition of such Rites. The remainder of the dioceses of TEC either explicitly or implicitly are living by the Windsor recommendation. While this situation cannot be characterised as a wholehearted embrace of the Windsor recommendation by TEC, neither should it be characterised as a

---

[7] Cf. "... the Lambeth resolution of 1998 declares clearly what is the mind of the overwhelming majority in the Communion, and what the Communion will and will not approve or authorise. I accept that any individual diocese or even province that officially overturns or repudiates this resolution poses a substantial problem for the sacramental unity of the Communion.", Letter to the Primates, Archbishop Rowan Williams, 23 July 2002, and subsequently; the statements of the Primates in May and October 2003; the 1998 Lambeth Resolution 1.10 and Resolution 10 of ACC-13 (2005).
[8] Cf. Statement of the Primates' Meeting at Lambeth, October 2003.
[9] The Report of the Joint Standing Committee to the Archbishop of Canterbury on the Response of The Episcopal Church to the Questions of the Primates articulated at their meeting in Dar es Salaam and related Pastoral Concerns, published October 2007.
[10] Resolution C051 of the 74th General Convention, sub-section 4: "we recognize that local faith communities are operating within the bounds of our common life as they explore and experience liturgies celebrating and blessing same-sex unions."

determined movement by the whole Church to carry forward the agenda to see such Rites firmly established in the life of the Church. It remains a pattern of isolated instances.

31. Of course, the situation could change with a Resolution of a future Convention - as indeed General Convention could decide to revoke B033 - but for the present WCG believe that TEC should receive some credit for substantially holding back from the development of such Rites. We note however that the structures of TEC have not shown any inclination to discipline those dioceses in which further steps have been taken.

32. This would seem to indicate that a differentiated approach towards the dioceses of TEC is necessary. Not all are acting contrary to the expressed wishes of the Instruments of Communion; action which penalises the whole Church would therefore appear to be inappropriate.

33. It is in respect to the third moratorium (on interventions) that there has been the least discernable response. As noted in the JSC Report of October 2007, there has apparently been an increase in interventions since the adoption of the Windsor/Dromantine recommendations by the unanimous voice of the primates. The adoption of dioceses into the Province of the Southern Cone, inconsistent with the Constitutions both of TEC and the Southern Cone; the consecration of bishops for ministry in various forms by different Provinces and the vocal support of such initiatives by the Primates associated with the Gafcon have all taken place, apparently in contradiction of the 2005 Dromantine Statement, although in each case, the primates involved would cite a conviction that their actions were provisional, born of necessity, and reactive rather than taking the initiative. From their perspective, some of the intervening primates have indicated that they will hand back those within their care as soon as the underlying causes have been resolved.

34. One of the aggravating factors in these circumstances has been the fact that a fourth moratorium requested by the unanimous voice of the Primates at

Dar es Salaam in 2007 - to see the end of litigation[11] - has also been ignored.

35. It has to be noted as well that the epicentre of the tensions arising out of the moratoria is located within North America, and largely within TEC. It is here that bishops and dioceses has shown themselves ready to set aside the entreaties of the Instruments of Communion with respect to Rites of Blessing. It is here that actions have been taken that exacerbate the sense of hostility and persecution perceived by some conservatives, including the recent action of the TEC House of Bishops to depose Bishop Bob Duncan of Pittsburgh. It is here that advocates of intervention have invited primates to initiate new forms of intervention.

36. In the Anglican Church of Canada the moratorium on the authorization of same sex blessings is being observed in the majority of the twenty-nine dioceses. While the Diocese of New Westminster has permitted the blessing of same sex unions using a rite authorized at the diocesan level since 2002, in six of its parishes, although the bishop has indicted that he would not authorise any further parishes to use the Rite. Three other diocesan bishops, following their attendance at Lambeth Conference 2008, have indicated their decision to proceed with the blessings of civilly married same sex couples in a small number of parishes. In the Diocese of Ottawa one parish only will be permitted to proceed with blessings of married same gender couples. In 2007, at the last General Synod of the Anglican Church of Canada, the House of Bishops presented new guidelines, which did not include the Blessing of Unions, for the pastoral care of gays and lesbians, and the reception by parishes of same gendered married couples. This continues to be upheld by the bishops as a whole in 2008.

37. The moratorium on the consecration of non-celibate gay and lesbian bishops is being observed.

38. Twenty-three parishes under the episcopal leadership of two formerly retired Canadian Anglican bishops have sought and received membership in

---

[11] "The Primates urge the representatives of The Episcopal Church and of those congregations in property disputes with it to suspend all actions in law arising in this situation. We also urge both parties to give assurances that no steps will be taken to alienate property from The Episcopal Church without its consent or to deny the use of that property to those congregations." - from the Key Principles set out in the Appendix to the Dar es Salaam Statement.

the Province of the Southern Cone and are now claiming membership in the newly proposed, but not recognized North American Anglican Province.

39.   The recent advent of the 'Anglican Church of North America' (ACNA) changes the context and the balance of any discussion about interventions. Those caught up in the various patterns of intervention are beginning to look to resource their protest and their identity from within an American ecclesial body. This development could bring to an end formal cases of intervention, but give rise to a new and equally intractable problem - parallel jurisdictions based on theological difference[12].

40.   Faced with the fact that despite several calls for observance of the moratoria requested by Windsor/Dromantine, rearticulated by the primates in Dar es Salaam in 2007, and winning a high degree of support at the Lambeth Conference[13], the moratoria have not received comprehensive support, WCG has to ask how to achieve genuine progress. Has the time come when it has to be recognised that the moratoria cannot be enforced absolutely in the life of the Communion? Does it therefore follow that the focus will have to be on holding the degree of restraint that can be achieved, while acknowledging that reversing some of the recent developments may not be possible?

41.   The inability of the Communion in recent years to be able to respond appropriately and effectively in a timely manner to a blatant disregard of the moratoria which had been called for gives rise to a degree of sadness, irritation, frustration and even anger which are unhelpful in the life of the Communion.   Such feelings and responses are probably responsible for the way in which more extreme reactions and measures have been generated. The disillusion has almost arrived at the point of cynicism about the effectiveness of the Instruments of Communion.

42.   If there is to be a situation where not all the moratoria are respected universally, the question arises as to how those bishops and provinces should be handled where there is a positive decision to live by another standard than that commended by the Communion as a whole. The Windsor Report had recommended that:

---

[12] There are instances of parallel jurisdictions in the life of the Anglican Communion - ministry to armed forces or ethnic minorities being the most obvious examples. What is distinctive in this new development is the theological and ideological difference with the geographical province in which they are situated.
[13] Lambeth Indaba Document, §145

'pending such expression of regret, those who took part as consecrators of Gene Robinson should be invited to consider in all conscience whether they should withdraw themselves from representative functions in the Anglican Communion. We urge this in order to create the space necessary to enable the healing of the Communion. We advise that in the formation of their consciences, those involved consider the common good of the Anglican Communion, and seek advice through their primate and the Archbishop of Canterbury. We urge all members of the Communion to accord appropriate respect to such conscientious decisions' (TWR §134)

43. Does this provide a way forward? It seems to the WCG that where a bishop elects to live in a way contrary to the morally authoritative discernment of the Communion, his or her actions damage Communion, and put a distance between the life of his or her see and the rest of the Communion. What, however, should be the relational consequences of such a decision?

44. Considering this question, the Covenant Design Group in their Lambeth Commentary offered these observations:

The language of 'teeth' and 'police' and even 'sanction' risks distorting the Covenant's overall purpose. A better way of approaching this matter is through the language of 'consequences' that devolve from assumed 'responsibilities', whether fulfilled or unfulfilled: covenantal responsibilities fulfilled lead to a deeper common life in Christ - an intensification; responsibilities left unfulfilled have as a consequence a thinning out of such common life, perhaps even a dissolving of it. But in either case, it is a matter of organic outcome, rather than juridical impositions, however these results are formally embodied or stated.

Within the scriptures, the divine covenants are always linked to consequences in their fulfilment or breaking (cf. Deut. 27-28). Even the covenant of baptism, though a gift from God, can be broken, and with it comes a radical loss (Heb. 6:4-8). In the service of the Gospel, Peter's reneging of the agreement made at Jerusalem with Paul results in a public confrontation and shaming (Gal. 2:11), while the Corinthians' fulfilment of their pledge will result in an overflowing gift of grace (2 Cor. 8-9). It is simply the case that those who choose to keep the promises they have made in love for one another in Christ take hold of the gifts of that deeper love, while those who choose to let go of these promises take hold of its lack or diminution, and live with its stunted fruit. Even this result is one that stands open to the hope for transformation and renewal of relationship (1 Cor. 5:4-5).

The language of 'sanction' does not adequately describe this reality of covenantal consequence, making it appear as an external law imposed upon us. Still, we should not mitigate the substance of this language: commitments are valued because of their fruit, and the declaration of such an outcome represents not only an honest appraisal of what is at stake in a commitment to another, but also points to the promise of its fulfilment. A covenant without consequences is, by definition, not a covenant at all, but an empty word. It is because our words matter, however, that we can testify to the power of God's faithfulness before the world (Mt. 5:37; 23:22)[14].

45. We agree with this model. A deliberate decision to act in a way which damages Communion of necessity carries consequences. This is quite distinct from the language of sanction or punishment, but acknowledges that the expression and experience of our Communion in Christ cannot be sustained so fully in such circumstances. A formal expression of the distance experienced would therefore seem to be appropriate.

46. The WCG spent some time discerning whether any such formal expression of impairment of communion should apply at the diocesan or provincial level. On one level, it is the local Church and its bishop who have acted to damage Communion; on another, it is the Province that bears responsibility if it does not act to restrain or discipline the bishop in question.

Recommendation

47. We recommend that the request for the moratoria expressed in Windsor/Dromantine be maintained in the life of the Communion, and that urgent conversations are facilitated with those Provinces where the application of the moratoria gives rise for concern.

---

[14] The Lambeth Commentary, Answer to Question 13, page 12

48. In cases where a see has, by its actions, impaired Communion, it has now become appropriate to explore what relational consequences should be formally expressed or put in place by the Instruments of Communion. The possible nature of such consequences are explored in relation to the Covenant in the Lambeth Commentary on pages 24 and 25. Further work remains to be done on who should take action to formalise any such consequences and whether they should be applied at the level of diocese or Province.

49. Although breaches of the three moratoria may not have moral or doctrinal equivalence, as acknowledged by the Primates at Dar es Salaam[15], yet the WCG agrees with the assessment of TWR that breaches of the moratoria are equal threats to our life in Communion, and that therefore there must be seen to be an equal and commensurate response in addressing breaches of all three moratoria.

D. Addressing the Ecclesial Deficit

D(i). An Ecclesial Deficit

50. The way in which the moratoria have been challenged or ignored in the life of the Communion raises a painful and sharp question: how can any decisions or recommendations be given authority or force in the life of the Communion?

51. Indeed, for some commentators, a central deficit in the life of the Communion is its inability to uphold structures which can make decisions which carry force in the life of the Churches of the Communion, or even give any definitive guidance to them. Other commentators will argue that such mechanisms are entirely unnecessary, but this touches upon the heart of what it is to live as a Communion of Churches.

52. To be a communion, as opposed to a federation or association, is fundamentally to acknowledge that the fellowship of Churches is not a human construct; it is the gracious gift of God. Churches are enabled to live in communion because they recognise one another as truly an expression of the One Church of Jesus Christ. If mutual recognition of faithful

---

[15] Dar es Salaam 2007 Communiqué, §10

discipleship, the preaching of the Word of God or the ordered administration of the Sacraments is threatened, then the entire foundation of the Communion is undermined. This is why although Anglicans remain committed to a generous accommodation of diversity, there must ultimately be some limit to the extent of the diversity which can be embraced. This limit is the point where the fellowship of Churches can no longer recognise in one of its members the faithfulness to Christ which flows from communion with the Father, in the Son, through the power of the Holy Spirit. If the recognition of one another as Churches is to be sustained, it implies a level of mutual accountability in the handling of the life of each Church.

53. The question of the limits of diversity becomes acute when major differences arise in the life of the communion of the Churches which concern the faith, order or moral life of the Communion. It is then that Anglicans need a common understanding of how together, in communion, they can, guided by the Spirit, discern and decide together. What are the sources that need to be brought to bear on any issue? What are the structures through which discernment takes place? What is the nature of their authority to guide discernment, to speak the mind of the Communion and even to request restraint while open reception takes place and the Churches of the Communion come to discover the mind of Christ for them?

54. Maintaining and nurturing communion between Churches, at whatever level, requires more than instruments of consultation. Guidance is at times required, and also decisions have to be made for the sake of unity. Organs of authority must be present and recognised as able to speak for and to the Churches of the Communion. In good times things will be easy - but when there is severe dispute within or between churches, the test of an authority's acceptance as an instrument of communion is whether its judgements are heeded, even when unwelcome; whether restraint is accepted while the matter is put to reception in the life of the Communion of churches.

55. The principle of autonomy-in-communion described in the *Windsor Report* makes clear that the principle of subsidiarity has always to be borne in mind. If the concern is with communion in a diocese, only diocesan authority is involved; if communion at a provincial level then only provincial decision. But if the matter concerns recognising one another as sharing one communion of faith and life, then some joint organs of discernment and

decision, which are recognised by all, are required. It is this necessity which led the WCG to articulate the move to 'communion with autonomy and accountability' as being a better articulation of the ecclesiology which is necessary to sustain Communion.

56. These are matters that have engaged Anglicans in their internal conversations and with their ecumenical partners particularly in the last 30 years. The discussions of the 1988 Lambeth Conference led to the *Virginia Report* with its sharp questions about the instruments of communion . The events following the 1998 Lambeth Conference led to the *Windsor Report* which raised many of the same issues.

57. The Commentary of the Covenant Design Group on the discussions on the Covenant at the Lambeth Conference 2008 reflects again on the ways in which the Instruments of Communion articulate and sustain the Communion: 'enabling the Churches to take counsel together, and to discern the responsibilities and obligations of interdependence.[16]'

58. The challenge remains for Anglicans to come to a common stance and acceptance of the authority which we will give to the instruments, structures and processes of the Communion which can lead to decisions that carry force in the life of the Churches of the Communion, regardless of circumstances.

59. To a certain extent, the Covenant is designed to address the expectations that one Province in the Communion can appropriately and legitimately expect in terms of mutual accountability and responsibility one for the other. But below this, there is a fundamental ecclesiological question: do the Churches of the Communion wish to live as a Communion?

D(ii).   The Instruments of Communion and the life of the Church

60. In order to make sense of the instruments of communion at the world level it is perhaps most instructive to consider first the role of the episcopate in an episcopally ordered church. Anglicans agree that bishops are a fundamental bond of unity linking the local to the universal and *vice versa*[17].

---

[16] The Lambeth Commentary, Question 13, page 12
[17] Cf The Virginia Report, "one who represents the part to the whole and the whole to the part, the particularity of each diocese to the whole Communion and the Communion to each diocese."

Bishops, as successors of the Apostles, are the ones who are charged with a special responsibility for the unity, mission, faithful teaching and governance of the Church.

61. But the ministry of bishops is never to be exercised apart from, but in, with and among the faithful. ARCIC[18] documents talk about episcopal ministry as enabling the symphony of the whole church, always helping to draw out and discover the *sensus fidelium*. Many ecumenical and Anglican texts talk of the ministry of oversight as having personal, collegial and communal dimensions. All of this has implications for understanding Anglican Instruments of Communion at the world level and as we consider how the present instruments can be developed to give authoritative leadership.

The Archbishop of Canterbury

62. The fact that resolution crafting was not part of the processes of the Lambeth Conference 2008 put massive weight upon the role of Archbishop of Canterbury as *primus inter pares* to articulate what was happening within the Conference, as marked by his three presidential addresses. His ministry to the Communion through these words have highlighted the extent to which there is scope for the ministry of a personal primacy at the level of the worldwide Communion.

63. The WCG understands this primacy as being exercised in personal, collegial, communal ways[19]. While ministry at the global level needs to be personal, it must also have collegial and communal dimensions . The collegial and communal dimensions of primatial ministry locate it firmly within the life of the whole Church and firmly within a specific community. The collegiality of a bishop is exercised from among his or her clergy, and in conjunction with the whole *laos* or people of God in that place. Primatial ministry is also collegial, in that the Archbishop's primacy should be exercised in conjunction with the college of bishops, a collegiality which is focused in the Lambeth Conference and also with other primates of the Anglican Communion. All primates are the first amongst the bishops of their

---

[18] Anglican Roman Catholic International Commission
[19] see Baptism, Eucharist, Ministry (The "Lima Text") Faith and Order Paper 111 of the WCC.

churches; together they can articulate the common counsel of the Churches of the Communion, informing and guiding discernment. It is communal, in that each bishop exercises the ministry of oversight in, with and among the faithful and so enables the *sensus fidelium* to be discerned. The communal dimension is reflected in synods and councils of the Church and is symbolised for Anglicans at the world level in the Anglican Consultative Council presided over by the Archbishop of Canterbury.

64.   We believe that ways of strengthening the collegial aspects of the Archbishop's ministry in a way that increases the links with the wider Communion. We believe that the Archbishop of Canterbury must have the freedom to draw round himself from time to time, as occasion requires, persons, sometimes on *ad hoc* basis, who can respond and act quickly. (This relates to the concept of Pastoral Visitors explored below).

Recommendation

65.   We recommend that a number of possibilities could be explored: the Archbishop might revisit the idea of a bishop, appointed from the wider Communion, to work closely with him and act on his behalf in Communion affairs. It may even be that a number of regional appointments from the local episcopate to represent the interests of the Communion along the lines of the *apokrisarioi* would be helpful. Exploration could be given to the idea of refocusing the position of Secretary General of the Anglican Communion as the executive officer of the communion who works alongside the Archbishop in carrying through the recommendations of the Instruments of Communion efficiently and rapidly; and to the formation of a small Executive Committee which could work with the Archbishop in responding to emerging situations.

The Lambeth Conference

66.   The Lambeth Conference expresses the collegiality of bishops. The bishops at Lambeth cannot make legally binding decisions. Nevertheless, the fact that it is a body composed of those who by their ordination to the episcopate have been given apostolic responsibility to govern means that the resolutions of a Lambeth Conference may be considered to have an intrinsic authority which is inherent in their members gathered together. It may be time for Anglicans to articulate the teaching role of the bishops gathered

around the Archbishop of Canterbury. Such recognition would still mean that decisions of a Conference would require the response and reception in the local Churches. It would mean that restraint might be required in a process of open reception. Some Lambeth Conference resolutions have been received by synodical action of individual member Churches other resolutions have not found such resonance and have been reversed by later conferences.

67. For collegiality to function most effectively in the Lambeth Conference then there are matters that require consideration such as the frequency of Conferences; the relationship of Lambeth Conferences to the Primates' meeting and the Anglican Consultative Council, how matters are dealt with in a conference, the preparation for a conference, the accountability from one conference to another for decisions taken, the mode of conference procedures following on the discovery of the immense value of indaba, the relation of indaba to formal decision making when required and other matters.

Recommendation

68. For a conference of bishops to provide the mutuality of counsel required of them, there is a need to ensure a high level of fellowship and sense of mutual responsibility. Quite simply, the bishops need to know one another. New patterns of Lambeth Conferences must therefore be considered: a shorter cycle of meetings, perhaps smaller meetings between plenary conferences, perhaps involving diocesan bishops only, or a system of regional or representative meetings.

The Primates' Meeting

69. Collegiality is also expressed in meetings of primates gathered together with the Archbishop of Canterbury where the primates offer support and advice to one another and in the life of the Communion. They have the potential to give some means of ongoing oversight between Conferences. The Primates' Meeting may be the most appropriate body to monitor the progress of resolutions and recommendations of Lambeth Conferences and to take note of and to guide the reception process. However, it has to be recognised that more than one model of primacy exists in the Anglican Communion and the diverse expressions of primatial authority can lead to some having concerns about the primates' meeting. The authority of the Primates arises

from the fact that they are in conversation with their own House of Bishops and located within their own synodical structures. They are, therefore, able to reflect the breadth and depth of the conversations and opinions of their episcopates and provinces. Because of this intrinsic relation with their episcopates and the faithful of their provinces, the Primates' Meeting may be thought to have a 'weight' - not from the individual primates but from their representative role.

Recommendation

70. The Primates' Meeting has sometimes been accused of overreaching its authority, and it is important to note the principle articulated in the Lambeth Indaba Document that the primates collectively should not exercise more authority than properly belongs to them in their own Provinces. However, the primates also have a high degree of responsibility as the chief pastors of their respective Provinces to articulate the concerns of that Church in the counsels of the Communion. When they speak collectively, or in a united or unanimous manner, then their advice - while it is no more than advice - nevertheless needs to be received with a readiness to undertake reflection and accommodation.

The Anglican Consultative Council

71. The great value of the Anglican Consultative Council (ACC), presided over by the Archbishop of Canterbury, is that it brings together at a world level bishops, clergy and laity thereby symbolising the communal dimension of the life of the Church. It is not understood as a synodical body, as its name indicates. It is consultative. The ACC tends to be accorded particular significance by those provinces whose liturgies emphasize the baptismal covenant and who therefore desire to find the contribution of the whole people of God in the life, mission and also governance of the Church at every level of the Church's life expressed in a conciliar gathering at the world level. However, there are questions about whether a body meeting every three years, with rapidly changing membership can fulfil adequately the tasks presently given to it. There may be other ways in which the involvement of the laity should be made effective in the discernment and guidance of the Communion and not only at the world level.

72. Related to the Anglican Consultative Council and the Primates' Meeting is the work of the Joint Standing Committee, which is the meeting together of the Standing Committee of the ACC with the Standing Committee of the Primates. It is not a separate Instrument of Communion, but it does contain representatives of all four Instruments - presided over by the Archbishop of Canterbury, with representatives of the Primates, of the bishops, and of the clergy and lay members of the Council. The crux is how the committee works and the various parts dovetail. In many senses, it is still in an early stage of development. As it develops, it will be important to stress the links to all four instruments so that it is not just seen as a branch of the ACC. It will also be important to ensure that the membership reflects the breadth of opinion in the Communion. If the membership becomes polarised, it will lose its ability to act effectively on behalf of the whole Communion. It would be strengthened by the Archbishop of Canterbury being present throughout the meeting.

Recommendation

73. A review should be commissioned of how the Anglican Consultative Council's effectiveness and confidence in its work can be enhanced. In particular, the WCG would like to see work done on exploring the effectiveness and role of the Joint Standing Committee in the life of the Communion. In order for it to be able to do this, questions need to be addressed about its membership and the extent to which Provinces are prepared to invest in its work. The JSC needs to be constituted in a way which is seen as fully representative; at which the primatial members are fully participating, and at which the Archbishop of Canterbury is fully present throughout its meetings.

The Instruments as a Whole

74. One of the great insights of the Anglican Communion may prove to be the way it holds to the Episcopal ordering of the Church and therefore an understanding of the distinctive role of bishops but within the context of the value it places on the *symphonia* of bishops, clergy and laity working together as the whole people of God. Anglicans struggle to express this in the instruments of Communion at a world level. What is needed now is a clear definition of the role of each instrument of the Communion. This should take

into account the specific gifts and responsibilities for governance as well as the representative functions entrusted to bishops and the how these might best work together with the whole body of the faithful. An important component of our present needs is also an articulation of the best ways in which the instruments can work together, each with its own specific tasks for the good of the Communion.

75. A deeper understanding of the Instruments of Communion at world level, their relationship to one another and to the other levels of the churches life should lead to a more coherent and inclusive functioning of oversight and authority in the service of the communion of the Church. The global nature of the Communion also needs to be grasped. The functioning of the Instruments must be adapted to accommodate global perspectives and participation.

Recommendation

76. IASCUFO (The Inter-Anglican Standing Commission for Unity, Faith and Order - for which, see below), as a priority, should be invited to produce a concise statement on the Instruments of Communion, their several roles and the authority inherent in them and to offer recommendations for developing the effectiveness of the instruments. This statement should be discussed by the Primates' Meeting and the ACC and sent jointly by them to the provinces for study and response. Although provincial responses could be collated by IASCUFO and brought to the next Lambeth Conference for expressing the mind of the Communion, it will be important to move to a common articulation of the role of the Instruments as swiftly as possible, and consideration should be given to whether these reflections could be incorporated into an ongoing development or revision of the text of the Covenant.

E. The Covenant

77. The Windsor Report made another recommendation: the production of an Anglican Covenant. If the 'bonds of affection' were not clearly articulated; if there was no clear and shared sense of the extent of true inheritance of common faith to be discerned in one another and what could be described as essential Anglicanism; of the rights and responsibilities of

'autonomy-on-communion', then TWR argued that the development of an agreed text to which the Anglican Churches explicitly bound themselves would go a long way to addressing this ecclesial deficit.

78. The covenant has been recognised as a development by which the Communion could be given a long term articulation of its identity and of the mutual responsibilities that arose from being a Communion of Churches: the Communion can only continue if we can continue to recognise the Church of Jesus Christ in one another. The Covenant has its value in seeking to articulate the essential elements of inheritance, mission and interdependence which can sustain our life in communion.

Recommendation

79. The WCG would like to affirm strongly that the covenant process is an essential element in rebuilding the confidence in our common life. We also recognise that ACC-14 will be a critical point in the process, since Provinces are being asked to give their 'in principle' response at this stage.

F. Other Initiatives

80. The WCG wishes to commend the ongoing work of other projects or bodies within the life of the Communion which can help to repair or strengthen our common life:

o   *The Bible in the Church Project*, which is being commended to ACC-14 next May.
o   *The Principles of Canon Law Project*, the first fruits of which were published at the Lambeth Conference. A process of study, education and reflection is now needed on this project so that it nature may be properly understood and its applicability to the life of the Communion correctly discerned.
o   The recent establishment of the *Inter-Anglican Standing Commission on Unity, Faith and Order* (IASCUFO) by the JSC as a body in succession to IASCER and IATDC to advise on ecumenical engagement and on key issues of faith and order within the life of the Communion. The agenda for such a body is already extensive and pressing.

G. Timely Processes of Response: Pastoral Forum and Pastoral Visitors

81. It is one of the realities of the current life of the communion that situations or matters are arising in the life of one or more of the provinces that affect the quality of the communion experienced between all the Churches of the Communion. In order to address the mechanisms which might be developed to assist the Churches to respond to such matters, several proposals or ideas have been raised or implemented in the recent past. The Windsor Report 2004 recommended the appointment of a *Council of Advice* to assist and support to the ministry of the Archbishop of Canterbury; the Primates Meeting in Dromantine (2005) advocated the establishment of a *Panel of Reference*; the Dar es Salaam Communiqué (2007) called for the establishment of a *Pastoral Council*. The TEC House of Bishops acknowledged the need for a mechanism of *informal consultation* with the other Provinces of the Communion, and indeed, the Presiding Bishop has recently moved forward with the appointment of a Deputy for Anglican Communion Affairs. We believe that this move closely parallels what we are proposing in terms of pastoral visitors.

82. Some of these ideas have found favour, some have not; those which have been established that have experienced varying degrees of success. The WCG wish to commend their proposal for a Pastoral Forum has some similarities with all of the foregoing, and yet it is distinct from them. Before describing what the Pastoral Forum could be therefore, it may be helpful to begin by saying what it is *not*:

- the Pastoral Forum is not envisaged as a juridical or quasi-juridical body in the life of the Anglican Communion with a constitutional or quasi-constitutional nature or authority;
- the Pastoral Forum would not have any jurisdiction;
- the Pastoral Forum would not act as a ' court of appeal';
- the Pastoral Forum could not override or supersede the Canons and Constitutions of any Province or the role of any of the Instruments of Communion.

83. The Pastoral Forum *is* conceived as an agency, which could be established with the co-operation of the lawful authorities of the Churches of the Communion to work with them in a pastoral, relational and advisory

capacity in the addressing particular issues of tension between them. As the Observations Document of the Windsor Continuation Group puts it, its aim would be 'to engage theologically and practically with situations of controversy as they arise or divisive actions that may be taken around the Communion'. There was a broad welcome to such an idea at the Lambeth Conference 2008.

84. The Forum would have a pastoral, relational and advisory role, working consultatively and collaboratively with the parties involved in situations of tension or disagreement around the Communion. It would aim to move parties 'towards reconciliation' through careful consultation and responsible accountability (cf. The Lambeth Indaba Document, §146) It could, however, with the co-operation of the parties, suggest, advance and, with their consent, develop models or mechanisms of pastoral care and relationship to assist in any situation.

85. There was a broad measure of support at the Lambeth Conference for this proposal.

'There is clear majority support for a Pastoral Forum along the lines advocated by the Windsor Group, and a desire to see it in place speedily. There is agreement that it should be pastoral and not legal and should be able to respond quickly. It was also clearly stated that this process should always be moving towards reconciliation. There is concern about mandate, membership, appointment process and authority. Some wondered whether the Pastoral Forum should have members from outside the Communion. Many felt strongly that the forum could operate in a Province only with the consent of that Province and in particular with the consent of the Primate or the appropriate body. It is essential that this should be properly funded and resourced if it has any chance of being productive. There was some support for an alternative suggestion: to appoint in any dispute a Pastoral Visitor, working with a professional arbitrator and to create in the Communion a 'pool' of such visitors.' (LI §146)

86. Since the establishment of such a Pastoral Forum would need authorisation and legitimacy within the Communion, and questions of 'mandate, membership, appointment process and authority' will have to be

addressed, it would seem appropriate that the proposal is given time for development by the Archbishop of Canterbury in consultation with the Joint Standing Committee and the Primates in preparation in advance of the fourteenth Meeting of the Anglican Consultative Council in May 2009.

87. However, the need for such a ministry of reconciliation is urgent in the life of the Communion. The WCG welcomes the fact that the Archbishop of Canterbury intends to move ahead with the appointment of a small number of 'Pastoral Visitors' as proposed by the bishops at the Lambeth Conference (see above), and who could be called upon 'in any dispute' or situation of tension between now and next May, as the proposal for a full Pastoral Forum is taken forward.

88. These Pastoral Visitors could be be:

- Appointed by the Archbishop of Canterbury for the limited period of twelve months in the first instance.
- Drawn from senior leaders of the Communion, present or retired, or other notable individuals with specific skills in mediation and arbitration.
- Available to the Archbishop to be commissioned as his emissary for specific work to assist in maintaining the highest degree of Communion possible in situations of disagreement or tension.
- Available as well to the Primates of the Anglican Communion to act on their behalf in situations of disagreement or tension as go-betweens, arbitrators or conciliators, as deemed appropriate by those primates.
- Available for appointment to particular positions or roles within the Anglican Communion which would be consistent with their work and the constitutional requirements or conventions of the body for which they are nominated.
- Required to act in a manner consistent with the Constitutions and Canons of those Provinces with which they relate in the pursuance of any matter referred to them.

89. The WCG affirms the decision of the Archbishop that it is an integral element in their ministry that Pastoral Visitors would **not** have any authority to make dispositions or proposals for structural solutions to any situation, unless expressly authorised to do so by the Primate or other lawful authority of the particular Provinces with which they have been asked to work.

90. The scope of the activity that the Pastoral Visitors will be able to undertake will depend on the availability of funding. In all matters referred to the Pastoral Visitors, it will be helpful if the Provinces concerned would be willing to nominate a colleague who would be committed to working alongside them.

Recommendation

91. The WCG wish to commend the proposals for a Pastoral Forum, and for Pastoral Visitors as an interim measure, in the form discussed above, and urges their adoption without further delay.

H. Parallel Jurisdictions

92. The advent of the ACNA is a serious and unprecedented development in the life of the Communion. It is proposed that eight different organisations - and different types of organisations - shall come together to create 'a network based Province' encompassing a variety of geographical and non-geographical associations. Its existence is predicated on the assumption that the current Anglican presences in North America - The Episcopal Church and Anglican Church of Canada - are no longer adequate to represent their understanding of faithful biblical Anglicanism, and this new association is intended to make such provision. Within ACNA are entities not formally part of the Anglican Communion or whose status within the Communion is disputed - the Reformed Episcopal Church, the Convocation of Anglicans in North America, the Anglican Mission in America and the Anglican Coalition in Canada - together with associations such as Forward in Faith in America and the American Anglican Council.

93. It is unclear to what extent this new body is seeking recognition within the Anglican Communion. On one level, the leaders of ACNA state that they seek a place within the Communion, but at the same time say that the approval of the Instruments of Communion or recognition by the Archbishop of Canterbury are unnecessary for them to proceed with the formation of the Province. They have sought recognition, however, from the Primates' Council of Gafcon. On the other hand, they include participants who clearly hold to their identity as Anglicans, and indeed, have only taken the steps they

have because they believe that this is the only way to be faithful to the Anglicanism which they inherited.

94. There will undoubtedly be Primates and Provinces, such as those involved with Gafcon, which will wish to give recognition to the new body. Equally, there will be primates and Provinces for whom even consideration of the request would be untoward, and involve the accommodation of schism.

95. If indeed it is the desire of the 'province-in-formation' to seek formal membership of the Anglican Communion, the WCG foresees formidable problems in the way ahead. They believe that such a proposal should only be entertained through the official channels which exist, namely according to the principles which were established and set out by ACC-9. Any move to recognise the new Province outside of these formal channels would further undermine our common life in Communion.

96. For such an approach to be successful, there would be very significant obstacles to be overcome. In the first place, the Communion would have to decide whether it could live with a parallel non-geographical Province based on theological ideology. This would be a significant change in the Catholic ecclesiological tradition upheld by the Communion throughout its history.

97. In the second place, the new Province-in-formation would have to reassure the Instruments of Communion that it does have the 'ecclesial density' appropriate to the life of a Province: that is, a Province is more than a loose confederation. Does the new Province-in-formation have a unified jurisdiction, a common canon law, and shared norms of worship and liturgy?

98. Thirdly, if it can be successfully argued that a new Province can be formed on doctrinal and ideological lines, what reassurances can be given about its relationship to the existing jurisdictions in North America, particularly in the life of those dioceses where bishops and synods have expressed their solidarity with the standards commended in the Windsor Report. TWR set its face against the concept of parallel jurisdictions[20]; it would be especially tragic if a generous accommodation of the new entity were to be seen as *carte blanche* for the new Province to establish a presence

---

[20] TWR §154

in localities where no cogent theological basis for differentiation could be advanced.

99. In reflecting upon the emerging situation, WCG is mindful of three of the principles articulated by the Primates at their Dar es Salaam Meeting in 2007:

- to encourage healing and reconciliation within The Episcopal Church, between The Episcopal Church and congregations alienated from it, and between The Episcopal Church and the rest of the Anglican Communion;
- to respect the proper constitutional autonomy of all of the Churches of the Anglican Communion, while upholding the interdependent life and mutual responsibility of the Churches, and the responsibility of each to the Communion as a whole;
- to respond pastorally and provide for those groups alienated by recent developments in the Episcopal Church.

and believe that these principles should continue to guide the thinking of the Instruments.

100. One way forward - although initially dismissed by some of the parties concerned - would be for ACNA to seek for some clear provisional recognition which seeks to keep it in relation to the Communion, but which acknowledges its provisional and anomalous nature. WCG has explored on previous occasions the idea of 'escrow' - the creation of a body which could take on the oversight of these groups on behalf of the Communion, but which recognises the provisionality of such bodies. The group wonders whether there is any mileage in the model of extra-Provincial jurisdictions? In at least one case, such jurisdictions have been recognised as provisional - e.g. in Sri Lanka Such a provision is fraught with difficulties. Such a scheme could not guarantee any particular outcome, the nature of which would be dependent on many factors, including the progress of the Covenant process. The provision would have to be hedged around with all sorts of restrictions, to avoid such a scheme becoming a haven for discontented groups, and institutionalising schism in the life of the Communion. Who would be the metropolitical authority? If all other obstacles were overcome, the WCG would favour a Metropolitical Council similar to that which operates for Cuba rather than linking the new entity to the Archbishop of Canterbury.

Recommendation

101. The WCG therefore recommends that the Archbishop of Canterbury, in consultation with the Primates, establish at the earliest opportunity a professionally mediated conversation at which all the significant parties could be gathered. The aim would be to find a provisional holding arrangement which will enable dialogue to take place and which will be revisited on the conclusion of the Covenant Process, or the achievement of long term reconciliation in the Communion. Such a conversation would have to proceed on the basis of a number of principles:

o   There must be an ordered approach to the new proposal within, or part of a natural development of, current rules.
o   It is not for individual groups to claim the terms on which they will relate to the Communion.
o   The leadership of the Communion needs to stand together, and find an approach to which they are all committed.
o   Any scheme developed would rely on an undertaking from the present partners to ACNA that they would not seek to recruit and expand their membership by means of proselytisation. WCG believes that the advent of schemes such as the Communion Partners Fellowship and the Episcopal Visitors scheme instituted by the Presiding Bishop in the United States should be sufficient to provide for the care of those alienated within the Episcopal Church from recent developments.

I. The Life of the Communion

102. Throughout its work, the WCG were undergirded by a deep sense of the value of the Anglican Communion as a particular expression of the providence of God's grace, and of its value to the proclamation of the Gospel and the life of the *oikumene*. We believe that the life of the Anglican Communion must not be allowed to falter. We call upon all Anglicans to look again to the value of the existing fellowship into which God has called us all; to embrace again the charity and forgiveness to which Our Lord entreats us in our dealings with one another; to be joined in working together for the healing of the Communion and the service of God's mission. We do not believe that the moment for division or excommunication has come, although we recognise that a critical point in the life of the Communion has

been reached. We urge the Archbishop of Canterbury to be bold in gathering the leaders of the Communion for prayer and common discernment. We urge all those, from the Primates to the bishops, clergy and faithful of the Communion, to be ready to think afresh, and to seek in Christ to be One so that the world might believe.

Bishop Clive Handford, former Primate, Jerusalem & the Middle East, *Chair*
Archbishop John Chew, Primate of South East Asia
Bishop Gary Lillibridge, Bishop of West Texas
Bishop Victoria Matthews, Bishop of Christchurch
Dean Emeritus John Moses, former Dean of St. Paul's, London
Bishop Donald Mtetemela, Bishop of Ruaha, former Primate of Tanzania

The Windsor Continuation Group was supported in its work by
Canon Gregory K Cameron, *Secretary*
Canon Andrew Norman
Dame Mary Tanner

Mustang Island, 17th December 2008

Report of the Listening Process on Human Sexuality

The Anglican Consultative Council XIII Nottingham 2005
Resolution 12 - Listening Process

In response to the request of the bishops attending the Lambeth Conference in 1998 in Resolution 1.10 to establish 'a means of monitoring the work done on the subject of human sexuality in the Communion' and to honour the process of *mutual* listening, including 'listening to the experience of homosexual persons' and the experience of local churches around the world in reflecting on these matters in the light of Scripture, Tradition and Reason, the Anglican Consultative Council encourages such listening in each Province and requests the Secretary General:

1. to collate relevant research studies, statements, resolutions and other material on these matters from the various Provinces and other interested bodies within those Provinces
2. to make such material available for study, discussion and reflection within each member Church of the Communion
3. to identify and allocate adequate resources for this work, and to report progress on it to the Archbishop of Canterbury, to the next Lambeth Conference and the next meeting of this Council, and to copy such reports to the Provinces.

Revd Canon Phil Groves was appointed Facilitator from January 2006.

1. Collation of Materials

Each province was requested to send any materials relating to human sexuality and specifically to Lambeth Conference resolutions concerning homosexuality. Materials were collated and summarised and the draft summary for each province was given to the primate for them to amend and endorse. These draft summaries were presented to the Joint Standing Committee (JSC) and to the Primates at their respective meetings in 2007. A further process of editing resulted in the publication of the summaries on the Anglican Communion website.

They are available at:
http://www.anglicancommunion.org/listening/reports/provinces.cfm

Many articles and books published by interested bodies have been presented to the office. They have been of great use, especially in developing materials for study, discussion and reflection.

2. Making Material Available

The publication of the Summaries was one way of making material available. Anglicans are able to better understand the thought and engagement of the provinces of the Communion on human sexuality.

Shorter submissions from provinces, interested bodies and individuals on human sexuality and mutual listening have been published separately on the Anglican Communion website.

The publication of *The Anglican Communion and Homosexuality* and its distribution to every bishop in the Communion has been the major achievement in this area. Thought, prayer and energy went into the method behind the writing of the book. The JSC and the Primates Meeting were asked to consider the method proposed and the Archbishop of Canterbury gave his approval. The Primates emphasised their desire for the work to take seriously the results of scientific research called for by the 1978 and 1988 Lambeth Conferences. The resulting work initially focuses on the mission context for listening and sets patterns of mutual listening. There are then three foundational chapters. These focus on a commitment to the authority of the Scriptures and the biblical witness, the traditions of the church and the handling of reason and to the relationship between culture and Christianity. Space is then given to 'listen to the experience of homosexual persons' directly both in a chapter on identity and in a chapter on spirituality. The book ends with the scientific study – which should not be seen as a conclusion – but rather as additional information. The scientists concerned were keen to stress that science in this matter is open to interpretation. The writers involved in the book are men and women, gay and straight, lay and ordained, from the diversity of cultures and theological traditions of the Communion. Articles submitted and utilised in the publication are available on the website and form an extensive source of resources.

In addition, the Facilitator has also assisted as a consultant others in developing resources for listening. For example, he has worked closely with The Mothers' Union in the publication of *We are Created By God*. He was consulted concerning the formation of the House of Bishops theological

Commission on the blessing of same sex relationships in TEC (USA) and has advised some dioceses and provinces as they contemplate formal and informal listening processes.

3. Identifying Resources and Reporting

Anglicans from around the world, who have offered their time and talents to listening processes, are the most significant resource for process throughout the Communion. Many are participating in processes of listening in formal and informal settings. Many have written articles and contributed to the book. Some have offered gifts of money to the task of the process. No strings have been attached to any of the donations.

The Facilitator report to the JSC. In addition, a report was distributed to bishops on request at the Lambeth Conference and the bishops were offered a variety of self-select sessions on human sexuality.

Significant Developments

1. Mission Focus

A key focus of the work has been to emphasise on the need for us all to discover the good news we share with gay and lesbian people as an articulation of the good news for all people. Good news is both the open inclusive welcome of all and the call to discipleship and obedience. This has offered a common ground basis on which we can examine difference and created safe space for conversations to develop.

2. Relationship Building

The developing of good relationships with people from the full diversity of the Communion has been the absolute priority. Opportunities to meet with significant people visiting the UK have enabled relationships to develop. Limited budgets have allowed for visits to East Africa, the USA and Canada and meetings with LGBT[1] advocacy groups, post-gay groups[2] and advocates for the diversity of theological and pastoral responses. The Facilitator has not only developed good relationships with people but also fostered building relationships between individuals and groups.

---

[1] 'LGBT' – a recognised shorthand way of saying Lesbian, Gay, Bisexual and Transgender
[2] 'Post gay' includes those who might define themselves as having same sex attraction and living in singleness and those who once had same sex attraction, but are now ex-gay.

3. Don't Throw Stones

One positive result of the building of relationships between diverse groups, including gay and lesbian people of widely differing theological perspectives, is the **Don't Throw Stones** initiative. A consensus approach has led to the publication of joint declaration in support of the statement from the 2005 Primates meeting that 'the victimisation or diminishment of human beings whose affections happen to be ordered towards people of the same sex is anathema to us'. The aim is to provide a means of encouraging and equipping individual believers and Christian communities to be faithful in bearing practical witness to the truth of the Primates' statement. Don't Throw Stones was presented to the Primates Meeting in 2007, adopted at the JSC and presented to the bishops at the Lambeth Conference 2008.

Currently there is a website with the declaration and some resources available at http://www.dontthrowstones.info/

The **Don't Throw Stones** statement is a secure basis on which to build safe space for assertive, but not aggressive, dialogue.

Mutual Listening – Continuing Indaba

The Windsor Continuation Group made the following observations and recommendations:

C(i). The Listening Process

21. The 1998 Lambeth Resolution 1.10 remains fundamental as the standard of teaching on matters of sexuality in the life of the Communion; but the Windsor Report also offered an acknowledgement that while there are divergent views on this, the discussion has to go on (TWR §146). Indeed, Lambeth 1.10 recognised this in the very terms of the resolution, echoing earlier resolutions at the 1978 and 1988 Conferences.

22. To enable this conversation to happen, space has to be created in which all sides can listen for the voice and leading of God; can listen to gay and lesbian Christians and learn of their experience; can listen to one another and the insights we bring to discernment on this issue. This was the end to which the moratoria recommended in the Windsor Report were shaped. They were

conceived as a way of halting development in the situation while a conversation, together with an articulation of the purpose and ends of that conversation, could be undertaken.

23. The Listening Process has so far produced a significant amount of resources - an overview of the reflection on this issue taking place in each of the Provinces, which is set out on the Anglican Communion website, and a book of resources to encourage and inform the discussion. Yet the listening process has not been totally embraced consistently across the Communion.

Recommendation

24. Only if the dialogue is seen to continue, and if there is an all-round readiness to engage in conversation and discernment on this issue, is there a hope of persuading the advocates of revision in the teaching of the Anglican Churches on this matter to remain committed to the period of 'gracious restraint', in which mutual conversation can take place. On both sides, we need to move from intransigence and the conviction that 'our' interpretation is the right one to a shared waiting upon God. There is something profoundly important about the Anglican way here - a readiness to acknowledge that Christian disciples discern God's truth by learning to wait upon one another, and that it takes the whole Church to know the whole truth.

25. We request that the Instruments of Communion commit themselves to a renewal of the Listening Process, and a real seeking of a common mind upon the issues which threaten to divide us.

An emphasis over the coming three years will need to be on mutual listening and listening to God. This may be achieved by continuing the Indaba process begun at the Lambeth Conference and extending Indaba with both lay and clergy participation. The aim of seeking a common mind goes beyond the desire to enforce a majority decision and requires consideration of methodologies that are both biblical and that reflect the diverse cultures of the peoples of the Communion - not just western cultural models.

Revd Canon Phil Groves

Facilitator for the Listening Process

Report from the Anglican Observer at the United Nations

Submitted by Mrs Hellen Grace Wangusa, Anglican Observer at the United Nations

The Anglican Mission at and to the United Nations

Mission is a word we have in common with the United Nations (UN). In its simplest definition, we do understand when mission is used for example to mean:

* an organisation (which in this case could be the Church or the UN) sends out missionaries or delegates to a foreign land to carry on religious or UN work
* an operation that is assigned by a higher headquarters
* a special assignment that is given to a person or group which could be confidential or to deliver a sensitive message
* the organised work of a religious missionary or the UN
* deputation: a group of representatives or delegates.

With that convergence in purpose, the Communion obtained a credible, legitimate, legal and effective presence in the world's intergovernmental body.

This mission grew out of a collective awareness that the mission of the Communion was in more than one preoccupation of the intergovernmental body. It was mostly in the areas of refugees, development and human rights.

At the time, this affiliation was seen as an opportunity for:

* sharing of studies and documents
* making a link with premier international organisations concerned with basic human rights.

Relevance and Legitimacy

One way the United Nations legitimises the work on any entity is first by examining its credentials.

In 1985, the delegate from Libya moved the acceptance of the ACC application by recognising the Communion, '...for its well known dedication to humanitarian work, for its global perspectives and universal inclusiveness, for its organisation which brings representatives from all continents into its decision making process...', an application that was approved without dissent!

That was our invitation to take our mission to the UN. Thanks to The Episcopal Church for the office space, we have maintained a voice, presence, legitimacy and relevance at the UN and from time to time send delegates to key and strategic events and conference. As a result, the profile of the Communion is high at the UN.

A lot has happened in the world in 21 years. In 2006, therefore it became clear to the Secretary General of the ACC that the Observer was under-resourced yet implementing an 'ambitious program'. He further noted that the office lacked support and in his opinion was weak, particularly in policy identification and implementation.

Now only three years on, we continue to:

- be a voice, an effective presence at the UN
- be ably representing the Communion at the UN and related forums
- serve as an advocate for the Communion on issues of justice, equity, ecology and development
- facilitate and develop forums which discuss major global issues and the work of the office to create awareness within the Communion
- respond to emergencies and urgent issues including security (case in point is the Democratic Republic of Congo)
- establish contact with the different programs of the UN and serve as a liaison between the UN, the Provinces and the dioceses of the Anglican Communion
- collaborate with other religious and non-governmental organisations at the UN, where appropriate
- provide pastoral ministry together with ecumenical partners, to members of the UN community

However, though the mission field has changed, the response of the Communion has not evolved in tandem with this change.

It is important that the Communion was admitted to the UN on the strength of its robust Mission Driven Goals. We have now added to that an easier UN MDG tool to work with because it is targeted, specific, achievable and time bound. But because of the current crises, it is clear that even the modest gains made towards the UN-MDGs are in danger of being wiped away by the compounded nature of crises. This is particularly because the UN-MDGs were not designed to address directly causes of poverty and inequity, and it was not an instrument that could be used to predict the crisis we are in now!

What does the UN expect of us?

In general we continue to keep up the pressure in government and the UN. We must examine the ideological and systemic positions of the Bretton Woods Institutions and the World Trade Organization to ensure that this financial situation is not seen as an alibi[1] for not doing anything about development-MDGs, debt cancellation, climate change and sustainable development.[2] It also means working towards eliminating the inward trend of protectionism especially if the poor countries have to generate wealth through trade or trade their way out of poverty!

Specifically we are called to:

1. Support the work of the United Nations.[3] We take part in appropriate intergovernmental forums and these are, for example, in the form of Commissions, high level events, summits and side events.

At the moment the Communion needs to take part in the discussions and debates about the financial crisis through both the high level meetings and the UN Summit to be held in this June. It is interesting that we have had a food and commodity crisis longer that the a banking crisis, the credit crisis, but it is the money related ones that have sent out shock waves to the 'right places'. This is clearly the moment to shape our response to energy, climate

---

[1]   Archbishop of Canterbury, Dr Rowan Williams
[2]   Archbishop of Canterbury, Dr Rowan Williams
[3]   ECOSOC RESOLUTION 1996/31, paragraph 61(c): Guidelines for NGOs in special consultative status with ECOSOC for submission of quadrennial report.

and environment through the UN Commission on Sustainable Development (CSD), and Financing for Development (FfD).

The urgency of these crises calls for us to make eco-linkages in order to have a comprehensive and sustainable solution needed to address them now! It is time for us to generate messages with ethical and moral arguments that go beyond tinkering with impact only and begin to confront root causes. This may call for an active engagement with economic policy analysis, research based advocacy and understanding the systematic as well as ideological challenges that the international financial and trade institutions have contributed.

For the Communion, this shall also need to include a theologically informed argument that enhances the quality and dignity of all life forms as issues of justice and equity. It is time to point out how the current financial crisis is also a result of sustaining an immoral and unrealistic set of economic and trade practices, and a surfeit of injustices, and to correct mistakes that the 'Market and Capital' have made.

We need to be seen as responding justly to these issues on behalf of those who have no voice of their own.[4]

Perhaps this is the time to call for a new world order and to change theological education to inform this process of re-creation. And to recognise that this time the big answers are going to come from the grass roots![5]

2. To take part in the appropriate intergovernmental forums so that the work of ECOSOC and the UN at large might benefit from our specialised input. The UN has made resolutions and developed instruments that, if they do not conflict with our values, can be used for awareness creation and advocacy in our own countries, Provinces and other constituencies. There are tools that our own government may have signed on to. But even those that they have not signed are a legitimate basis for advocacy. You will be shocked to learn that some of the developing countries have made progress in areas that you would have thought come naturally to developed governments. One of those is environment, the other is equal pay for equal work, the other is

---

4 Archbishop of Canterbury, Dr Rowan Williams
5 Rev Theodora Brooks, Rector Episcopal Church in the Bronx, USA

equal representation in decision-making bodies where, for example, Rwanda leads on parity. One can also use campaign materials developed by UN agencies such as the Millennium Campaign, UNIFEM's 50/50, and the UNICEF score card on the girl child, to list a few.

3. To participate in a wide variety of UN-sponsored meetings and activities. In this particular case we are expected to undertake specific activities to advance the achievement of the MDGs. The greatest difficulty is to have an Anglican delegate at key UN events. This is one reason the Walk of Witness in London during the Lambeth Conference, and the one held in New York, plus the 'Education for All' event at the UN made such a mark in the global scene. The main reason though is that a lot is expected of the Communion because we are, according to the World Bank's Assessment, a trusted presence on the ground, and a dependable development partner especially in the social service delivery and community mobilising, as witnessed in the Jubilee Campaign against External Debt.

Under Economic Issues, the UN organises forums and special events to discuss trade, external debt aid/overseas development assistance, and innovative ways of generating wealth. It is the moral duty of the Church to draw attention to the unimaginable wealth that has been generated by equally unimaginable levels of fiction, paper transactions with no concrete outcomes beyond profit for traders.[6] This profit has not been used to meet human needs or even conserve life. The financial world today needs open scrutiny and positive regulation. It also needs a basis for some common prosperity built on social stability and reliable institutions. The key question is how to identify the points and practices where social risk becomes unacceptably high and how to remove the concentration of wealth and power into a few hands.

'For example, any wealthy individual can go to a broker these days and put down $1 million, and then leverage this amount 3 times. The resulting $4 million ($1 million equity, $3 million debt) can be invested in a fund of funds that will in turn leverage this $4 million another 3 or 4 times and invest them in a hedge fund',[7] and so forth.

---

6 Archbishop of Canterbury, Dr Rowan Williams, UK, on Financial Crisis
7 www.sovereignsociety.com/portals/0/svs/fullpromo_WSVSK202.html

4. To contribute to the furthering of the development aims of the Economic Social Council and the UN at large. The development aims of the UN include Sustainable Development issues. Under Commission on Sustainable Development (CSD) the UN is focusing on themes such as Africa, desertification, drought and agriculture. In these debates and discussions, the crucial and basic need for food is central. We know what it means to pray for our daily bread. It is important to add action to this prayer especially for the 10,000 children who die daily due to food insufficiency.

Most International Financial Institutions (IFIs) and national institutions do not finance agriculture although 'a good number of clients 43.4% especially in the rural areas do actually invest in agriculture related activities'.[8] Local financial institutions do not have sufficient branch networks and have not developed specific products and financial services for the poor rural clientele.

For example for one ton of fertiliser, it costs the USA US $50 to transport it from Iowa to Mombasa but the same ton of fertiliser will cost US $100 to transport it from Mombasa to Kampala, Uganda! How can the poor farmers in Uganda afford this fertiliser?

5. To make our activities to the member states more widely known to member states. We have done this through Mission visits during the Commission on the Status of Women (CSW). The mission visits provide us with quality time to present our concerns and needs as well as an opportunity to recognise and support what governments are doing right.

6. To receive valuable feedback on their program of work and official acknowledgement of their contribution as partners to global development. We received feedback from the UK government on our work on the MDGs. A copy of that is available in print and in DVD form.

The deeper moral issue according to Dr Williams, is that capital and the markets have been made into 'individuals', with purposes and strategies, making choices, deliberating reasonably about how to achieve aims. The 'invisible hand of the market' gives it a body and divine attributes! Put that way, it makes it impossible to 'turn the tables' or change the governance and

---

[8]   SEDU, NCUSBO, 2003

policy development systems of the traders and money lenders especially in Wall Street, the World Band, IMF and the WTO because they are 'invisible' and have acquired divine attributes. In addition, these institutions have been closed to developing countries.

Perhaps one of the difficulties with financial and economic issues in that the tables have moved from the back of the Synagogue to Wall Street where they are beyond our reach or 'invisible'!

The other issue is that emergency response remains a challenge despite the successful evacuation of the 135 Synod members of the Democratic Republic of Congo (DRC). That is why Chad, the Middle East, Zimbabwe, Pakistan, Sri Lanka seem like 'silent' advocacy issues that only gain prominence when the UN Security Council puts them on its agenda.

Conclusion

I welcome the resolutions you have made. They are instruments that mandate the Observer office to operate as the centre of advocacy. It legitimises the programs and is a basis for effective partnership with UN member states and agencies. This will make it an efficient Centre for Advocacy.

The resolution on Indigenous Peoples is to be welcomed because of the vast knowledge they bring to the climate, environments and health discussions.

The resolution to Eliminate All Forms of Violence provides the needed room to deal with the status of women in situations of conflict and to advocate against rape as a weapon of war.

The co-ordinated work of the Anglican Development Agencies is going to increase the ability of the Communion to showcase collective action as best practice in development. It will eliminate duplication thus releasing resources for more programs. This is a prudent measure in these times of financial crisis.

Co-ordination shall also add value to our work in the UN. It will be a platform for building a case of an organisation that indeed brings specialised input to the UN in MDGs, development, human rights, the innovative peer-education on HIV/AIDS; education and health services; environmental work and sustainable energy issues; the reconciliatory work using water; distributing bed nets; restoring Indigenous peoples' land rights; and the campaign against human trafficking especially girl children.

If for nothing else than that, the Communion must remain engaged at all levels of life of the UN because: 'We run the danger of promoting the 'privatisation of morality'.'[9]

---

[9]   H E Kaire Mbuende: Namibia Permanent Mission to the United Nations, March 2007

Report on the International Anglican Liturgical Consultation

A Report to the Fourteenth Meeting of the Anglican Consultative Council
May, 2009

Chair: The Rt. Revd George Connor, Aotearoa New Zealand

Steering Committee Members: The Rt. Revd Ezekiel Condo, The Sudan; The Revd Juan Quevedo Bosch, The Episcopal Church (USA); The Most Revd Ellison Pogo, representing the Meeting of Primates; Dr Eileen Scully, Canada

Staff: The Revd Canon Cynthia Botha, Southern Africa

Background

The International Anglican Liturgical Consultations (IALCs) are the official network for liturgy of the Anglican Communion, recognized by the ACC and the Primates' Meeting, and holding first responsibility in the Communion to resource and communicate about liturgy on a communion-wide basis. Historically, the Consultations developed as Anglicans met alongside the congress of the international and ecumenical society Societas Liturgica. The Consultations are held at least every four years, and each Consultation appoints a steering committee in accordance with the guidelines that follow to hold responsibility for arrangements between those meetings.

IALCs were served from 1993 to 2007 by the Revd Paul Gibson, now retired, as staff on secondment (on a limited part-time basis) from the Anglican Church of Canada. The Revd Canon Cynthia Botha was appointed in 2008 on a part time basis to serve as the secretariat for the IALC supported financially by the Communion Office.

Participation/Membership

The IALCs strive to maintain a wide set of categories for membership, with the view that a mixture of scholars and members of Provincial liturgical commissions, as well as official representatives of Provinces provide a healthy basis for conversations and the advancement of the Consultation's work. Invitations are sent to every Province of the

Anglican Communion to encourage participation from the following categories of persons:

- Anglican members of Societas Liturgica;
- members of Provincial liturgical commissions (or their parallel)
- Those particularly appointed to represent their Province

This combination of categories for participation ensures that Provinces have representation in the setting of agenda and creation of the outcomes of the IALCs, and that a potentially wide basis of scholarship, theological views, cultural and ecclesial experience can be brought to the table.

Participation in the IALCs is funded by the sending Provinces or bodies within Provinces who wish to support individual members. It s not uncommon for participants to fund their own participation personally. In addition, the IALC Steering Committee has created a bursary fund to support participation from as wide a range of Provinces as possible, and communicate the availability of this fund particularly to the financially less independent Provinces.

In addition to those from the categories above, the IALC steering committee also makes special invitation to an Ecumenical Partner to serve as a 'reflector' during the meetings, and from time to time invites other special guests whose contribution to the theme under study is helpful to the advancement of the work.

Setting the Agenda

The business of the IALCs is directed by the steering committee and includes, but is not limited to:

- items or themes determined by the steering committee;
- matters referred by the ACC or the Primates' meeting;
- matters referred by Provinces

The IALCs and the steering committee normally proceed by consensus, except in the case of regular electoral processes to set the Chair and Steering Committee in place.

182

Details related to the ordering of IALCs can be found on the Anglican Communion website, Liturgy section, in the document entitled 'Guidelines adopted at Berkeley'.

At the Consultation

Once a topic for consultation has been determined, often following upon extensive consultation, the steering committee invites individuals to prepare papers in advance of the meeting. Provincial representatives from across the Communion are invited to plan worship throughout the meeting, so that there is a true sense of the Communion gathered, as the liturgical gifts of many parts of the Anglican world are lifted up. Worship, from opening and closing eucharists and through daily offices, ground the Consultations.
In recent years, the style of working has involved a combination of plenary talks and small group reflections. Membership in each working group is intentionally organized to allow for the greatest diversity within small groups for the best possible situations in which all voices can be heard, and cross-cultural engagement thrive. Often these working groups turn into drafting groups.

English has been the working language of the IALCs. However, more and more there are present at the Consultations those whose first language is not English, and increasingly efforts have been made to accommodate translation and interpretation needs. These efforts have very much been on voluntary and ad hoc bases, as funding has not been available for the translation necessary to ensuring a more fully culturally and linguistically appropriate environment. However, it is fair to say that the efforts are extremely well intentioned, and that the experiences of multilingual worship in particular have been extraordinarily rich.

One of the real Communion-building fruits of such meetings is that members of different Provinces are able to engage with each other, share each other's liturgical texts, discuss commonalities and differences, contribute to each other's insights and share wisdom. Provinces' liturgical books published since the beginnings of the IALCs exhibit the fruits of Communion-wide consultation.

Brief Overview of IALC work

IALC Reports received by previous meetings of the Anglican Consultative Council have detailed the work of the Consultations on matters related to the sacraments of the church in their contexts – from Christian initiation to the shape and form of the Eucharist and ordination rites, to questions related to the inculturation of Christian worship across the many contexts of the Anglican Communion. The IALC statements on the **Eucharist** (Dublin, 1997), particularly in its explication of the shape and form of eucharistic worship, and on the **Ordinal,** (Berkeley 2001) have been widely recognized for their contribution in real and important ways to the liturgical development of Provinces in the Communion.

In more recent years, the Consultations have turned to examine matters related to pastoral rites and formation.

Recent Work by the International Anglican Liturgical Consultations
2009 (upcoming, August of 2009) Auckland, Aotearoa New Zealand

Official Liturgies of Marriage in the Member Churches of the Anglican Communion

2007 Palermo, Sicily, Italy

Rites related to Death and Funerals – publication pending

2005 Prague, Czech Republic

Anglican Identity and Worship – Paper published in *Anglican World* and on Communion Website

2003 Cuddesdon, England

Liturgical Formation of the People of God – publication pending

For an overview of the origins and work of the IALCs through the 1980s and 1990s, see: *International Anglican Liturgical Consultations: A Review,* by the Rev'd Paul Gibson, on the Liturgy section of the Anglican Communion Website

Moving Forward

The IALC has entered into a period of examining matters related to the various pastoral rites of the church. Beginning with the focus on rites related to death, at Palermo, in 2007, and moving to examine the official liturgies of marriage of the member churches of the Communion t Auckland this coming summer (2009), this work will not only allow for concentrated examination of existing rites across our various cultures and contexts, but also build on the insights gained by previous IALCs in their work both on sacraments and inculturation.

Respectfully submitted by Eileen Scully. Canada

Appendices

Appendix A   Anglican Identity and Worship (The Prague Statement, 2005)

Appendix B   IALC Guidelines Adopted at Berkeley 2001

Appendix A

Liturgy and Anglican Identity A Statement and Study Guide by the International Anglican Liturgical Consultation Prague 2005

Contents

- **Overview**

- **Anglican Ethos, Elements, what we value in worship**

- **Some Anglican emphases, trends and aspirations**

    - Bernard Mizeki Anglican Church   - South Africa

    - St Mary's Anglican Church   - England

    - St Mark's Anglican Church   - Australia

    - St John's Anglican Church   -Japan

- **Suggestions for Study**

Overview

     We believe that Anglican identity is expressed and formed through our liturgical tradition of corporate worship and private prayer, holding in balance both word and sacramental celebration. Specifically, our tradition is located within the broad and largely western stream of Christian liturgical development but has been influenced by eastern liturgical forms as well. The importance of the eucharist and the pattern of daily prayer were re-focused through the lens of the Reformation, making both accessible to the people of God through simplification of structure and text and the use of vernacular language. Through the exchanges and relationships between the Provinces of the Anglican Communion the legacy of these historic principles continues to inform the on-going revision of our rites and their enactment in the offering to God of our worship. Each Province of the Anglican Communion has its own story to tell, and although within the Communion we are bound together by a common history, what really unites us, as with all Christians, is our one-ness in Christ through baptism and the eucharist. Our unity in baptism and at the table of the Lord is both a gift and a task. We celebrate our unity in Christ and seek to realize that unity through the diversity of backgrounds and cultures within the compass of the world-wide Anglican Communion.

Recognizing the role of the bishop as a symbol of unity and the partnership of ordained and lay, clergy and people, we value a leadership which is competent and liturgically formed and seeks to engage local culture, language and custom within a vision of what holds us together as part of the one, holy, catholic and apostolic church. We value a view of leadership which sees the leader of worship as a servant who enables people to worship in a way that has integrity within their own experience, customs, and gifts.

We value and celebrate the ways in which we have been formed by and within our customs to attend to the grace of God, invoked and celebrated in our public prayer, and active in our lives and in the world around us.

Ethos/Elements

We value...

- Worship that includes and honours the proclamation of the word and celebrates the sacraments of baptism and eucharist.

- An inherited tradition that holds together both catholic and reformed.

- The fact that we have texts which are authorized.

- Freedom for varieties of expression.

- The aesthetic potential of environment, music, art, and movement, offered as appropriate to the culture.

- The symbiotic relationship between corporate worship and individual piety.

- Worship in an ordered liturgical space.

- The liturgical ministry of bishops, priests and deacons.

We value the following characteristics in our rites

- Shape (see the *Toronto Statement of the IALC, 'Walk in Newness of Life'*, for its treatment of the structure of the baptismal rite, and the *Findings of the Fifth IALC, Dublin*, for descriptive notes on the structure of the eucharistic rite).

- Extensive reading of scripture.

- Lectionary.

- Rhythms of year, week, day.

- Regular celebration of Holy Communion.

- Baptism in public worship.

- Prayers which include thanksgiving, (general) confession, intercessions.

- Extensive intercessions—focusing on the world, those in authority and the world church before local concerns, and including concern for those who lives as shadowed by poverty, sickness, rejection, war, and natural disaster.

- Use of the Lord's Prayer.

- Use of responsive texts.

- Knowing words, music, and actions by heart.

- Common prayers.

- Corporate and participatory worship.

- Use of Creeds in worship.

- The openness and accessibility of our worship.

Some Anglican emphases, trends and aspirations.

In worship, we are drawn into a living relationship with the Triune God in patterns of prayer that are in themselves Trinitarian in form and content, and invite us to enter more deeply into God's life and love as those who are called to be 'partakers of the divine nature' (2 Peter 1.4). In our coming before God in adoration and thanksgiving, penitence and prayer, we recognize that liturgical celebration is both our corporate action, our work, words and ritual gestures, and also an occasion when God, through the Holy Spirit, is active and at work making and re-making our lives.

Our worship is rooted in God's work of creation, incarnation and redemption and so needs to be embodied and enacted in ways that engage all the senses. Thus we honour the goodness of creation, pray for its healing, and come to delight in splendour as we celebrate both the beauty of holiness and the holiness of beauty.

We recognize that God's creation is often disfigured by sin, by human greed and violence and we seek that healing grace which flows from the cross of Christ. As we commemorate Christ's saving death and transfiguring resurrection in the celebration of the eucharist we are again made one in him and strengthened to witness to his reconciling love in our broken world.

We invoke the Holy Spirit, seeking to be open to God's future, and to orient ourselves to the fulfilling of God's purposes. Recognizing this essential eschatological dimension of Christian worship, we seek to attend to the various relationships that transcend both space and time: our sharing in the Communion of Saints, with our Anglican brothers and sisters around the globe, and with the whole *oikoumene*. Through our conversations and engagement with each other in the work of Christ we seek to realize more fully the unity that God has given us and to which Christ calls us.

We believe that our worship conveys and carries the historic faith of the Church, and recognize that as we are blessed with reason, memory and skill we are called to use our gifts in crafting liturgy that honours our received and living faith in this time and context.

We believe that the rhythm of worship, our gathering and our being 'sent out' mirrors the *missio* of God, of God's engagement with the world and the claims of God's Kingdom of justice, righteousness and peace. We therefore commend again the inseparable relation between worship and mission. (cf. the 'marks of mission' preamble IASCOME statement.)

I Ways of Worship

Here are four stories of Sunday mornings around the Anglican world. None of them is quite a documentary, and none is entirely imaginary. Each of them captures something of a local expression of Anglicanism. How do the people in the stories experience their Anglican identity in and around their liturgical celebrations? And how do we, when we read about these Anglican brothers and sisters, grow in our understanding of what it means for us to be part of the Anglican Communion?

1 Bernard Mizeki Anglican Church

Mary and Tsepo are going to Sunday church together. It's Bernard Mizeki Church, named after a local martyr, in the village where Mary lives and where Tsepo, her grandson, comes back to visit. (Tsepo works in the city, where he attends St. Francis' Anglican Church, Parkview.)

The service starts at eight, but they arrive early because Mary helps to prepare the altar. The Churchwardens are there, unlocking everything. Mary collects the altar cloths and all the paraphernalia—candles, chalices and so on—and sets the altar. Tsepo is catching up on village news with one of the Churchwardens. People are trickling in. The priest hasn't arrived yet—he's on the road from somewhere else. This is the Sunday he comes to Bernard Mizeki.

There are no music books and no prayer books in the pews, but people who have books at home bring them along. As people arrive, singing starts: choruses, with bodies swaying. It won't be quiet, though, as people continue to arrive and greet each other. The men sit on the right hand side of the church, facing the altar, the women on the left. The Mothers' Union members are easily identified by their white tops and black skirts and Mothers' Union badges. Though Tsepo can sit with his girlfriend in the city church, he can't even sit with his grandmother in the village. The choir and the lay ministers are robing and heading for the room at the back. Hopefully by now the priest has arrived—they'd rather not start without him.

When the priest is robed and ready a signal is given and the chorus-singing stops. A hymn is announced from three different hymn books: English, isiXhosa and seTswana, all translations of 'Ancient and Modern'. The singing starts, unaccompanied, and the ministers and the choir process in from the main entrance.

The priest and lay ministers lead the service from 'An Anglican Prayer Book' in seTswana, and most of the people respond in seTswana, though the page numbers are the same for the English and isiXhosa versions of the book. The bible readings are taken from the Lectionary for the day, and are read in seTswana. A chorus is sung as the priest prepares to read the gospel. Although the church is small, the priest still carries the bible closer to the people for the gospel reading. Just before the sermon, the children go outside for Sunday School, where they are taught by teenagers and a couple of older people. They will come back in for their blessing at Communion time. The sermon is in seTswana, but is translated into isiXhosa by someone from the congregation or one of the lay ministers, complete with gestures imitated from the preacher. It could be quite a long sermon—the preacher hasn't been there for a month, and this is his big opportunity to teach the people.

The prayers are chosen from one of the four forms the Prayer Book offers, with more singing before and after the prayers. There are lots of local community concerns in the prayers: Mama Rose who's not well, the school books that need to arrive in time, the bishop who's coming to do confirmations in a fortnight, and the confirmation candidates. Tsepo notices that it will be the same bishop who visited Parkview a month or so back.

After the prayers, the notices are given: about the confirmation and the bishop's visit and the special meal to be held on that day, about money needed for flowers, and a reminder about Thursday's Mothers' Union meeting. Then there is the greeting of peace, and people are moving around everywhere with handshakes and hugs.

At the offertory, one of the Churchwardens puts the collection plate at the front and people come singing and dancing down the aisle to make their offerings. Mama Mary and Tsepo, because he is visiting, bring up the bread and wine for the eucharist.

The priest sings the eucharistic Great Thanksgiving, with lots of gestures and signs of the cross. People sing the responses and the Lord's Prayer. The women come up first for Communion, though Tsepo's cousin,

Patience, stays back with her baby. The men follow, then all the children come up for a blessing at the end of Communion.

Then there is more singing, a blessing and the dismissal, and a procession of all the ministers out of the church door. When the priest has said a final prayer with the lay ministers and the choir, the choir members go back into the church, still singing, to disrobe, while the priest greets the members of the congregation. Of course everyone has tea: the mothers go into the vestry to boil the kettle, set up tables outside, and bring out the cakes they have brought to share. Everyone is busy, catching up on news, drinking tea, paying funeral dues, asking Tsepo what he has been up to in the city.

2 St Mary's Anglican Church

Chris and Sophie arrive in plenty of time for High Mass, as it says on the notice board outside, at 11.00 am. On entering the church they notice the familiar smell of charcoal being lit for the incense. The notice board beside the door has posters advertising a big event at the Cathedral, and the forthcoming parish Pentecost pilgrimage.

Two congregation members are giving out hymn books and service booklets and a single sheet of paper with music and notices. The visitors take theirs and sit down at the back between a man in casual clothes and a woman with two young children. She is kneeling, holding a rosary in her hand, and the children are making sure they have all the same books as the adults, along with photocopied sheets with illustrations about the day's bible readings. Just to the side is a beautiful chapel with a statue of *Mary* holding the child Jesus, and several people are lighting candles on the stand in front of it. At the front of the church, three people in red cassocks and white cottas are setting up the chalices and lighting the candles in a highly ritualised way, bowing to the altar whenever they pass it.

At 11.00 am a bell sounds from the back and everyone stands as the organ plays the introduction to the hymn and everyone starts to sing as the choir and clergy process in, led by people carrying incense, cross and candles. People bow as the cross and priest pass. It all seems very dignified and formal. So far no announcement has been made, no words have been spoken, yet everyone seems to know what to expect and what to do. There are three clergy wearing matching vestment, and the priest presiding is a woman.

The words of the service are very familiar 'Almighty God, to whom all hearts are open....' People are very comfortable with making gestures, standing and kneeling, and Chris and Sophie take their cues from the rest. They sit for the first reading, and a woman makes her way to the lectern carrying her own Bible. When she announces the reading and that she is using the Moffat translation, people smile as if they recognize a familiar eccentricity of hers. There is a splendid procession for the reading of the gospel. The priest preaches from the pulpit for 10 minutes, a challenging and humorous message based on the Gospel reading. After the Creed, which is sung, prayers of intercession are led by members of the congregation from the back of the church. There is plenty of silence, which Sophie and Chris use to add their own thoughts; and the prayers finish with the Hail Mary.

Then they stand up for the Peace, which the priest leads from the front. People turn only to their immediate neighbour with a handshake, and the children solemnly greet the visitors with just the right words. Another hymn starts without announcement and the sidespeople come round and take up the collection. Then a group of people process up to the altar carrying the wafer bread and wine. More incense is used, and the congregation is censed as well as the priest. All the servers seemed to know exactly what they are doing. The priest sings the first part of the Eucharistic Prayer and everyone responds. As the prayer progresses, bells are rung and there is an atmosphere of reverence and attentiveness in the church.

After the Lord's Prayer, which everyone sings, the sidespeople make sure the visitors know they are invited to the sanctuary for Communion. People genuflect, bow and cross themselves very unselfconsciously. The children receive communion too, carefully making the sign of the cross as they kneel. After Communion, back in their seats, there is quite a long silence and everyone seems very comfortable with it. Before the blessing, the priest invites everyone to a 'Refreshment Sunday Party' in the vicarage after the service, with canapés and pink champagne. Everyone stands to sing 'Guide me, O thou great Redeemer', which Chris thinks a bit rousing for Lent, and the choir and clergy process out again during a lively voluntary on the organ. The woman with the children escorts Sophie and Chris across to the vicarage for the party.

3 St Mark's Anglican Church

At 10.30 on Sunday morning, a crowd of university students have arrived at St Mark's for the main morning service. The notice board outside the building shows that there has already been an early morning service of Holy Communion here, according to the Book of Common Prayer of 1662, and there will be a youth service at 8.00. There are little black books on shelves at the back of the church that have clearly been in use earlier in the day. The floor is carpeted and there are banners with scripture texts on them adorning the walls. Helpers are busy moving the chairs into a semi-circle from the earlier rows, so that everyone will be able to see the screen at the front. As people arrive they are given a leaflet with the week's coming events and prayer points, but for this service, no books are needed.

Before the service, images of inner-city streetscapes and close-ups of children's faces are projected on the large screen, which soon comes into use for the words of the songs and some of the prayers. Towards the front of the building is a communion table that's not the centre of attention at present, as the music stands of the band are in front of it. The music will be provided by this group of very talented people who spent most of Saturday afternoon rehearsing. The music is loud, and while the words praise God, the musical idiom ranges from heavy rock to ballad style.

The service moves from a block of energetic and repetitive opening songs and choruses into a quieter mode, with prayers from a leader calling the congregation to be aware of God's presence and to prepare to hear God's word. It's all moving towards the centrepiece of the service: a substantial sermon. A ;good number of the congregation are checking references in their pew Bibles as the minister preaches. Some of the congregation seem to be taking notes. Key points and relevant scripture texts, and the occasional video clip, appear on the big screen as the sermon progresses. The sermon is part of a series looking at St Paul's letter to the Romans. After the sermon, there is plenty of time for unscripted prayer and testimony from a range of young adults.The shifts in focus are managed by another leader who may well be ordained, but who is wearing casual clothes like all the others present.

The prayers mention the local bishop, and the imminent visit of an African bishop who is being sponsored by the diocese to lead a local mission. In the notices, there is an appeal for additional prayer support for the family the parish has sent to run a children's home in Romania, and for accommodation that needs to be found locally for students from out of town.

After the service, there is excellent coffee, and an offer of pizza for those who want to stay and work on planning next week's service. There is a bookstall and Fair Trade craft stall, and someone is collecting signatures for a petition to cancel debt in the developing world.

4 St John's Anglican Church

In Japanese society, the Christian population is very small. Many Japanese people pay homage at a Shinto shrine, but only once a year, on New Year's Day. In such a society, it is not easy for many people to visit a Christian Church. For many, the distinction between Roman Catholic and Protestant churches is not clear. Still fewer people know about the Anglican Church. When people hear the name 'Nippon Sei Ko Kai— Anglican Church☐they wonder whether it is Roman Catholic or Protestant. So an Anglican pastor or church member can only answer by saying, 'We are catholic, but not Roman Catholic. Please come and see. If you attend the Sunday service, you can find out.'

Akiko is a junior high school student. Her first impression is of the church building, and she is also attracted by the beautiful resonance of hymns and organ music. She has been standing outside the small country church, near the window, listening to the music flowing from inside. When she decides to enter the church and attend the Sunday 10.30 a.m. service, everything is a new experience for her. As she enters, she is impressed by the solemn, quiet atmosphere inside.

A church member who also stands near the door greets her. 'Hello, welcome. Is this you first time in a church?' An old man hands her three books, the Book of Common Prayer, a Hymnal, and the Lectionary for Year A, as well as a leaflet headed 'today's programme.' Akiko is a bit confused, but the old man kindly leads her to a seat and says, 'Please relax! People stand when they are singing, and sit to listen. They sometimes kneel when they pray. But please feel free to do as you wish.'

At 10.30, when the worship begins, people around her suddenly stand up and begin to sing. Ministers wearing unusual dress come in, and process to the front. During the service, everything is completely new to her. Sometimes she feels strange, because the ministers and people say prayers together, and act corporately.

After the service, the pastor introduces her to the congregation and says, 'Welcome to this church.' One lady—not so old—approaches Akiko, asks her impressions, and says, 'If you have time, please join us. We'll have lunch, it's Japanese noodles today.' Two or three young women, almost the same age as Akiko, also come up and welcome her and invite her to come along with them.

A few months have passed since Akiko's first visit. Now she participates in the church's Sunday service almost every week. Sometimes she can sit inside the church, very quietly. Little by little, she learns the pray, not only for herself, but for her family and friends and for people in distress. She has seen how, every Sunday, people pray for others who are ill and in trouble, and for peace for the world.

At the beginning, Akiko thought that religious faith was a very private matter, just for her personal rest and relief. But now she is gradually realizing that the Christian faith is not only an individual matter. Through the worship, and through encounters with members of the church, she now feels that she is accepted as a member of a family, the family of God. Akiko is beginning to think of being baptized, and belonging to the church formally. She thinks that she wants to share the bread and wine like the other members. She feels a kind of mystery is there. It is not easy to express, but she feels her life is strengthened by the mysterious power of God.

Suggestions for Study

Read the story. In a group, have someone read slowly aloud. Try to let your imagination visualize the events described. Take a few minutes to reflect on the story, letting it play in your mind. As you reflect on each story you might ask yourself the following questions, taking time to form your reply. In a group, members may first reflect in silence and then share their responses with each other, in smaller groups of five or six if there are many participants.

1. How much of the story reflects your own experience of worship?

2. Would you feel comfortable in this worship setting? If not, why not?

3. What elements in the story would you recognize as being particularly Anglican? What elements would be foreign to you as an Anglican?

4. Do the styles of worship reflected in these stories contribute to or detract from Anglican unity?

5. In the light of these stories what would you seek to change in your own pattern of worship?The four vignettes were intended to illustrate the diversity of worship in the Anglican Communion. Please write a description of Anglican worship which would express the hope of our calling to be one in Christ.

Appendix B

Guidelines adopted at Berkeley 2001

Amended at Berkeley, California, August 2001

1.   The International Anglican Liturgical Consultations (IALCs) are the official network for liturgy of the Anglican Communion, recognized by the ACC and the Primates' Meeting, and holding first responsibility in the Communion to resource and communicate about liturgy on a communion-wide basis. Historically, the Consultations developed as Anglicans met alongside the congress of the international and ecumenical society Societas Liturgica. The Consultations are held at least every four years, and each Consultation appoints a steering committee in accordance with the guidelines that follow to hold responsibility for arrangements between those meetings.

2.   Attendance at an IALC shall consist of:

    a.   those whom Provinces and Regional Churches choose to nominate and send;

    b.   Anglican members of Societas Liturgica;

    c.   members of provincial liturgical commissions;

    d.   others whom the steering committee may invite.

3.   The business of the IALCs shall be directed by the steering committee and should include (but not be limited to):

    a)   items or themes determined by the steering committee;

    b)   matters referred by the ACC or the Primates' meeting;

    c)   matters referred by particular Provinces or Regional Churches.

The IALCs and the steering committee shall normally proceed by consensus.

4.   The steering committee may arrange other meetings between Consultations as required or appropriate. Such meetings do not have the standing of Consultations, do not qualify for IALC bursry grants to participants, have no power to issue statements as though from a Consultation in the name of IALC, and have no power to change these Guidelines or to instruct or appoint the steering committee. Provinces and regions shall be given due notice of such meetings.

5.   IALCs are empowered to respond to matters referred by the ACC, the Primates' meeting, and the Provinces and Regions.

Procedures for an IALC shall include:

a.   The steering committee shall notify each province or region of the date of the Consultation at least one year in advance.;

b.   The steering committee shall arrange for a summary of relevant work done at any prior meeting to be circulated in advance. Additional papers may be solicited in advance by the steering committee

6.   The responsibilities of the steering committee shall include:

a.   planning IALCs and any other meetings.;

b.   responding to matters referred by the ACC, the Primates' meeting, or Provinces or Regions that cannot wait until the next IALC.

c.   preparing a budget for its own work, and for IALCs and preparatory meetings and submitting a financial report to each IALC.

The steering committee should normally meet yearly.

7.   The steering committee shall consist of:

a.   two members elected at an IALC for a term of one Consultation;

b.   two members elected at successive IALCs for terms of two Consultations;

c.   one liaison person appointed by the Primates' Meeting.

This committee will elect from its own number a chairperson.
The ACC-appointed Coordinator participates fully in the work of the steering committee and normally serves as its Secretary.

8.   The procedure for electing the steering committee shall be:

a. A nominating group of three people shall be elected at each IALC. Agreement to serve on this group shall disqualify a person from being nominated to the steering committee.

b. The nominating group shall invite nominations for membership in the steering committee and then present three names to the IALC for election. It shall take into account the diversity of regions and traditions of the Anglican Communion, as well as practical considerations.

c. The IALC will have the right to make further nominations and will conduct a direct election.

d. At each election the person obtaining the most votes shall be elected for two Consultations and the others for one Consultation.

e. If a vacancy occurs, the steering committee shall appoint a person to fill the office until the next IALC.

The Consultation adopted these guidelines by vote.
27 August 2001

Reports of the Anglican Communion Networks

Colleges and Universities
of the Anglican Communion

Report submitted by the Revd Canon Dr Don Thompson, CUAC General Secretary

Background

The Colleges and Universities of the Anglican Communion (CUAC), founded at Canterbury, England in 1993, is a Network of the Anglican Communion consisting of over 130 institutions of higher education around the world that were founded by and/or retain ties to a church or branch of the Anglican Communion. With institutions on all five continents, CUAC was founded for the exchange of ideas, for the development of programs among member institutions, and for mutual member-collaboration through which they might better serve students, faculty and staff of these institutions in educational ministry to their societies and the world at-large.

CUAC functions as a communication and collaboration network that links all the Anglican-related higher-education (post-secondary) colleges and universities world-wide. It is autonomous in governance and self-supporting in finance, sustained through subscriptions by participating colleges and universities (fees based on student numbers and adjusted to currency and economy). CUAC provides for its members forms of communication through the Internet (web-site: www.cuac.org), Newsletters (Compass Points and eNEWS). Key to the association is an international conference for all members held every three years (the Triennial), and then national/regional 'Chapters' (British Chapter, Chapter of the Americas, India Chapter, Asian Chapter, and Australian Chapter) which meet in their regions once or twice between Triennial Conferences. All these activities help CUAC institutional and individual members to discover and pursue opportunities in global education, faculty and student exchanges. CUAC colleges and universities create joint programmes and projects in cross-cultural education, in service-learning and community service, and in educational and cultural aid for developing nations. Exchange of students, faculty and administrators is a constant activity of member institutions, to support but also to enrich and broaden each college or university. CUAC strives to promote the ideals of Christian education in the global world through the dialogues, exchanges and joint projects among its members. It pays special attention to the role of Chaplains in the settings of a contemporary university or college.

A qualifying member institution is any college or university that is associated by history and tradition with the Anglican Communion and maintains an active relationship with its local diocese or province. Membership is made up of institutions of higher learning, which can provide teaching and research in any field. CUAC is not an organization of theological colleges, but there are some colleges which find the association beneficial to them. As an inter-Communion service, CUAC does maintain on its web-site a list of those known Anglican theological colleges, seminaries and programmes. Regular membership assumes payment of an annual subscription as set by the Board of Trustees of CUAC. Each institution has one vote at the Triennial Meeting of the association. Each institution designates which of its administration, faculty, or staff are to serve as delegates and who is to vote on behalf of the institution. The Archbishop of Canterbury, The Most Revd Rowan Williams, is the Patron of CUAC, as was the Most Revd George Carey before him. The organization functions through an elected international Board of Trustees, most of whom are college/university heads and some of whom are bishops of dioceses which have an active college/university that is a member of CUAC. The organization is a registered non-profit corporation in the State of Connecticut, but maintains an office in New York provided by The Episcopal Church. CUAC has a small endowment that was gifted to it by its founding organization, the Association of Episcopal Colleges, which also requires that the CUAC staff person also carries on some functions specifically for those U.S. Episcopal-related colleges in the US and abroad.

Recent and Current Activities

- In May 2008, CUAC held its **6th International Triennial Conference at Chung Chi College of the Chinese University of Hong Kong**. The conference explored what the Asian Chapter identified as, for them, the three 'marks' of an Anglican-shaped university/college education:

Excellence 卓越
Character 德性
Service 服務

- While held in Hong Kong, the Conference delegates traveled to mainland China over two days to visit and meet with leaders and students at Lingnan College, Sun Yat-sen University, Union Theological Seminary, as well as churches in Guangzhou and Shenzen. The vitality of these communities and their dedication to learning were as apparent as their enthusiasm for ecumenical inclusion and liturgical practice. The experience itself provided direct evidence of thriving and growing communities committed to education and Christian faith together and living in a working relationship within the People's Republic of China. Contacts were made between CUAC members and some of that leadership, which is the primary function of CUAC as a 'Network'.

- After the visit of the conference to the mainland, the keynote address by Archbishop Njongonkulu Ndungane, 'The Anglican Way in Higher Education,' set out the nature of the strengths that the Anglican Communion brings to the pluralism that is increasingly the environment of faith:

> Anglicanism is not 'one size fits all.' It provides God's tailor-made coat of many colours for every one of us! One of the strengths of the Anglican way of being Christian is precisely this enrichment that comes from legitimate diversity, and of the resources it gives us to deal with diversity - whether we face it within Anglicanism, within the ecumenical life of the difference Christian churches, or within the widely varying cultures of our world, into which we, and our young people, are called to be salt and light.

Archbishop Ndungane also reported on the Historic Schools Restoration Project in South Africa, which seeks to bring back educational centers that had been deliberately run down during the period of Apartheid. As he said, 'The Historic Schools Restoration Project is not specifically Christian, but I hope you can see how Christian values and aspirations are mirrored within it.' This principle of joining in action in the service of

201

Christ, whether or not Christianity is specifically invoked, proved to be another key emphasis of the conference.

- Finally the 'business' meeting mapped out the way ahead for CUAC until the next Triennial at University of the South (Sewanee, Tennessee, USA) in May 2011. Two themes that inform present and future CUAC activity were identified:

  1. There are different cultural varieties of ways in which 'service' has been and is being integrated into university curriculum, and members accepted such diversity in CUAC.

  2. Anglican higher education is to encourage the basic educational and moral goals of the Anglican tradition, even while the Communion is in the midst of difference. Cultural differences are not seen as a barrier to the common mission of the colleges and universities.

- The Conference decided that it was important for CUAC to be present at the **Lambeth Conference in July 2008**. The General Secretary of CUAC – the Revd Dr Donald Thompson – was present at the Conference as 'staff' along with other Communion networks, and participated in several presentations. A Reception was held at the nearby CUAC institution, Christ Church Canterbury University, for all bishops who have a CUAC institution in their midst. Several bishops had not appreciated that their colleges or universities participated in the educational ministry of CUAC. An important initiative that took place at Lambeth was the inauguration of a possible health network of the Anglican Communion. There are several CUAC institutions which are medical colleges or nursing colleges and have clinics attached to them. These were very interested in a healthcare network along the lines of CUAC. The General Secretary remains active in that initiative. It may be that, should the network is developed, that the office support for it could be provided by CUAC, since the entire internet, publishing, and communications skills are already assembled for the educational network.

- The new **CUAC Trustees for 2008-11 met January 10/11 2009 in New York City**. A complete review was undertaken of CUAC: its historical mandate, its current membership and member expectations. It was noted that the chief new characteristic of CUAC is the establishment of national and/or regional chapters. Currently, there is a British Chapter, an Americas Chapter, an India Chapter, an Asia Chapter, and possibly an Australia Chapter. The Chapters are the key arenas for much of CUAC's programmatic and cooperative work between members. CUAC also functions as the network of information and cross-Communion encounter, primarily through the Triennial meeting and also Internet exchanges, by which institutions become aware of each other and can initiate projects and exchanges amongst themselves as opportunities arise. The current budget was reviewed, revealing an expected deficit. Some of the servicing (income-producing) operations of the New York office have ended, meaning that CUAC now has to rely totally on the subscriptions/dues and the small endowment provided for it by the primarily United States-based Association of Episcopal Colleges. In light of these restraints, it was decided to suspend publication of the journal, *Prologue*, and also to move the one office assistant position in New York from full-time to part-time. The dates for the next Triennial are Saturday, May 21 to Thursday May 26, 2011. One theme it may explore is the impact of race on educational institutions.

The Anglican Communion
Environmental Network

Report submitted by Bishop George Browning, ACEN Chair

As a network we are relatively new; we had our beginning at the Global Anglican Congress on the stewardship of creation in Johannesburg in 2002, where a declaration and resolution were passed calling for our creation. This resolution was taken by the Anglican UN Observer to the 12th meeting of the ACC in Hong Kong in 2002 where it was passed. This resolution established the Anglican Communion Environmental Network (ACEN) as an official instrument in the Anglican Communion and it calls upon churches in the Anglican Communion to respond urgently to our fifth mark of mission. Three years later, in 2005 I hosted our first meeting in Canberra Australia; the meeting was devoted to climate change and received reports from Provincial representatives. The meeting made its own declaration in relation to climate change and renewable energy. As an Australian representative I was able to speak of the already present features of climate change on the Australian continent which are experienced in more frequent and prolonged droughts, the general decline of fresh water for urban areas, much reduced water for irrigation and a drastic decline in the health of the river systems. More recently the terrible February 2009 bushfires exploded because of the convergence of extreme heat, tinder dry conditions, and very strong winds.

Despite our relative youth and the extreme importance of our portfolio, since the last report the Environment Network has struggled to gain traction. This is due to three factors:

1. No financial resources have been made available to enable representatives from the less resourced areas of the Communion to participate. There has been no face to face meeting since the Canberra meeting in 2005. The network most urgently needs financial resourcing to enable people from the two thirds world to be active and influential contributors.

2. Despite our best efforts it has been very difficult to enlist significant representation from across the Provinces.

3. Climate change has become so globally significant and urgent that it is literally impossible for a group of busy volunteers with absolutely no allocated resources to be anything other than marginally effective.

However during this time there have been important ways in which the Environment agenda has been pursued across the Communion by members of the network.

2007 Millennium Development Goals meeting in Johannesburg.
This meeting with delegates from across the globe was an extremely important vehicle for the furthering of these most important justice goals and the heightening of their awareness across the Communion. The environment received significant profile at the meeting and was strongly represented in the resolutions emanating from it. It became clear to all delegates that the environment agenda undergirds almost all the other agendas. (For example, deteriorating access to water means that many women and children fill their day collecting water over long distances, negating attempts to build primary education and improve women's health and well being). Delegates went

204

away from this meeting with a clearer understanding that environmental stewardship is a core Christian commitment and that the fifth mark of mission is as significant as the other four.

2008 Lambeth Conference. The Lambeth Conference met in an atmosphere of internal tension within the Communion; however despite this, the conference gave very considerable attention to the various marks of mission, the fifth mark of mission receiving perhaps the highest profile. It was encouraging that the vast majority of Bishops seemed to leave the conference convinced that they ought to take significant leadership in ensuring that the fifth mark of mission is effectively pursued. The Bishops were painfully aware that this is urgent, that time is not on our side, that it is no longer satisfactory to simply talk about the issue; genuine and substantial goals need to be set by the Church as well as by the wider community. From the Conference about 40 bishops across the entire spectrum of the Anglican Communion indicated they would like to be proactive in an ongoing network. The voice of bishops from countries like Bangladesh, where the effects of climate change are immediate and potentially quite disastrous was profound.

The Network is aware that on the ground there have been some wonderfully creative and bold initiatives emanating from the local Church. These initiatives have come from as diverse a range of countries as Kenya, Bangladesh, Sri Lanka the US and Britain. In some cases proponents of these initiatives have won local and international recognition.

The Network is also very grateful for the leadership shown by some of our most influential leaders and especially from Archbishop Rowan.

In the last 12 months the political and scientific ground has shifted significantly. We are more aware than ever that environmental degradation generally, and climate change in particular, is connected to, and exacerbated by, the human footprint. We are also aware that time is not on our side. Very significant global conferences are being held later this year, it is vitally important that the voice of the Church is clearly heard.

The world economy must move away from its reliance on a carbon base to an economy thriving on the energy the sun brings to us daily (in its various forms). We must also balance the inexorable movement into globalisation with a recovery of sustainable local and regional communities.

Forward movement with the clarity passion and speed that is required will not come without a vision for what the future can be, and without a sense of profound gratitude for the gift of creation itself. The Church is well placed to provide the lubrication for the wheels of change.

Because this is one of perhaps the two most pressing issues facing the planet today clearly the whole Church from its leadership to its membership must be energetic, committed, informed and passionate about our involvement in a solution, for the sake of the worlds' most vulnerable, for the sake of our children and grandchildren and above all for the sake of the integrity of the Gospel. This is not a situation of opt in or opt out. Only the ignorant, the fool hardy or the self interested will want to stay out of a movement so vital to us all.

The Network is somewhat at the cross roads of its existence. The contribution of a few is enormous and without their efforts the network would have failed. In particular I want to acknowledge the work of the Revd Ken Gray of Canada who almost single handedly keeps the network alive.

In this context the future of the network and its effectiveness is dependent on several factors.

- We need the assistance of the Anglican Communion Office, the Office of the Anglican Observer at the United Nations and of Provincial leaders to not simply help the network, but to be the network.

- We need every Province to make the appointment of a network representative of the highest priority.

- We need the executive of the network, which has been in place for sometime to be renewed with new ideas and leadership.

Speaking for myself, I do believe the time has come for me to relinquish the reins as convener; I am no longer in a position which enables me to regularly and easily communicate with the Church's leadership. I will not step aside however and leave the network rudderless, but I encourage the Anglican Consultative Council to see that the appointment of an effective and resourced person in this role is a very high priority.

The Environment and Sustainable Development

Report submitted by the Anglican Observer at the United Nations, Ms Hellen Grace Akwii Wangusa, and the Revd Canon Jeff Golliher Ph D, Environmental Consultant to the Anglican Observer

Program Areas

The core of our program encompasses the fundamentals of survival in terms of air, food, and water, and how they are organised economically, socially, and politically.

In the past, we have also focused on issues involving biodiversity, and still do, although the overall concern of our efforts today is in keeping with the Millennium Development Goals. These program areas and their extreme urgency are briefly outlined below.

1. Climate Change and Renewable Energy

The scientific consensus on climate change is not difficult to describe. According to James Hansen of NASA, probably the best spokesperson in this field, the number we need to watch is 350 parts per million (of carbon dioxide in the atmosphere). That is the number beyond which we cannot go without significantly changing the biosphere -- the ecological conditions of the earth to which life as adapted. We have already gone well beyond it -- to 387 parts per million. According to Hansen and many others, unless we bring the number down to 350 by 2030, changes in the biosphere now underway (e.g., the melting of the Arctic) will be irreversible. Hence, the necessity of making the transition to renewable energy immediately. The Intergovernmental Panel to Climate Change (IPCC) estimates that the transition must be significantly underway by 2012. This is probably accurate.

2. Food and Agriculture

A central tenet of the UN's work in the environmental and sustainable development is that solutions to the environmental crisis cannot be separated from the elimination of poverty. This puts the local community at the heart of any viable sustainable development strategy. With regard to food and hunger, we have two courses of action. We can invest further in the globalised, corporate strategy for producing food at the expense of local communities, or we can complement the corporate strategy by strengthening community-based agriculture and supporting local farmers. In most areas of the world, small and medium-sized farmers need financial help and technical assistance with depleted soils, water management, and the replacement of harmful pesticides with organic methods. The second approach, which builds sustainable communities, has the advantage of not only preserving biodiversity and the health of watersheds, forests and soils, but also drawing upon local knowledge and decreasing reliance on uncertain overseas markets. Unless policies are adopted in poverty-stricken areas to actively support the livelihoods of small farmers, especially women, then vulnerability to hunger and malnutrition will markedly increase in the years ahead.

3. Water

1.1 billion people worldwide lack access to clean water; while global consumption doubles every 20 years -- twice the rate of human population growth. To help solve these problems, we work in accordance with the 1999 Dublin Conference on Water and the Environment, which advocates participatory strategies involving users, planners and policy makers at every level -- especially women -- as well as proclamations made at the 2001 Water for Peace and Nature Summit that affirm the intrinsic value of water (over and above its commercial value). This approach establishes water as a fundamental human right and collective responsibility, rather than a private commodity.

4. Community Development and Corporate Responsibility

In 2008, the Advisory Council voted unanimously to become a member of the Interfaith Center for Corporate Responsibility (ICCR). The intent was to raise issues and questions which might help the church move in the direction of greater human rights, environmental stewardship, and sustainable development. This decision was made with the understanding that the environmental crisis threatens, even destroys, all kinds of communities, including human communities. At the same time, the current global economy may bring material comfort to a minority, but it seriously undermines the functional integrity of most local communities. Thus, the solutions we must seek require the creation of environmentally sustainable and just human communities and the adoption of strategies for economic development that help them thrive.

The Current Context of our Work

At least since the Rio Summit in 1992, the overall strategy for sustainable development adopted by the UN (here 'the UN' means its member nations, departments and programs) has been largely based on assumptions rooted in the neo-liberal economic system. The implementation of Agenda 21, for example, has depended on technology transfers to developing and least-developed nations and large amounts of development assistance. It was assumed that profits gleaned from economic growth in developed nations would produce funds needed to make sustainable development happen everywhere. Although this system had some marginal success, the current global economic meltdown calls these assumptions into serious question -- which, to be blunt, means that we (humankind) are in deep trouble.

Furthermore, the political and social structures on which these assumptions were based have been shaken on almost every level. This applies as much to the church and NGOs as it does to nations and multinational economic organisations.

The result is that we must redouble our efforts to create viable, workable structures relating to our work - structures that keep communication and collaboration open across the Communion, both to and from our Office, so we can advocate effectively on their behalf at the UN.

CURRENT GOALS: Forming stronger linkages with the Anglican Environmental Network and the creation of a thematic working group to assist us in our work

Given these circumstances, one of our immediate goals is primarily organisational; that is, we are in the process of reorganising how we go about doing our work. We already know that we need more committed involvement from the Provinces in connection with the environment and sustainable development. However, this is not to say that the involvement and enthusiasm demonstrated by the Provinces so far has not been substantial, because it has been substantial. ACC resolutions and declarations that had their origin at the Global Anglican Congress on the Stewardship of Creation in 2002 and others made at the first meeting of the Anglican Environmental Network in Canberra in 2004 have been significant. They have given us the authority to speak and advocate at the UN on behalf of the Provincial representatives who made them. Nevertheless, this kind of involvement, important as it is, is still not enough given the world's current condition -- when local conditions are rapidly changing and the need for even greater participation is essential.

For that reason, among others, adequate, effective participation from Provincial representatives in a Thematic Working Group for the UN Office is also an immediate, timely, and urgent goal. This Working Group will be composed of Anglicans with special interest and/or expertise in our major program areas (climate change/renewables, food and agriculture, water, community development and corporate responsibility). The accomplishment of this goal depends, in large part, on developing an ongoing working relationship with the Anglican Environmental Network. We hope to form this Working Group from key members of the Network, who will help us advocate on all issues at UN meetings, including, for example, the Commission on Sustainable Development and a variety of other meetings and conferences related to our program areas. Overall, our goal is to create a vital link with all the Provinces, through the Environmental Network, so we can advocate at the UN on behalf of the Anglican Communion in the most effective way.

Finally, an important meeting of the UN Intergovernmental Panel on Climate Change will take place later this year in Copenhagen. We will be at that meeting, and will work in whatever way required to make the Network's presence there timely and worthwhile. Archbishop Rowan Williams has shown great support for all our efforts in this area of our work, and we offer him our sincere gratitude.

International Anglican Family Network

Report submitted by Dr Sally Thompson, IAFN Co-ordinator

The International Anglican Family Network (IAFN), one of the official Networks of the Anglican Communion, has been in existence for over 20 years. Its work has been welcomed by three Lambeth Conferences and described by a recent meeting of the Joint Standing Committee of Primates and ACC as 'a valuable instrument of unity' within the Anglican Communion. The Network publishes regular Newsletters on issues important to families, circulating these world-wide and sending them free of charge to the Two Thirds World.

The Family Network's aims are three fold:

- To develop mutual understanding about the impact of forces such as poverty, HIV/AIDS, globalisation, migration and violence in and on families in both the developed and the developing world.
- By publishing articles - written by women and men, lay and clerical - about practical work being done to help families, to provide encouragement to workers in family ministries and the Christian community.
- By telling of practical projects, often from small beginnings and scarce resources, to draw on and share experience and expertise within the Communion and encourage further action by Churches.

Much of the work featured in the Newsletters is unsung and unknown to the rest of the Communion. It is often carried out by women whose voices are not always heard in the Church.

From 1996 – 2007 the IAFN newsletters were published as an insert in *Anglican Episcopal World*. The recent suspension of this publication because of its cost, poses new challenges for the Family Network. The Management Committee are clear that, while electronic means of communication should be used to the full, the printed Newsletters have a particular value as they are accessible to those without easy access to the web, and the developmental content can be shared by many and made available in institutions such as church offices and theological colleges. Through the generosity of a small number of Provinces and Church Leaders, funding has been found to enable IAFN to print and mail out the 2009 Newsletters. Some funding is already pledged for 2010 – 2011 and it is hoped the necessary additional resources can be found to enable the Network's planned contribution to continue.

Current priorities

- Build up a targeted mailing list of those who wish to receive the printed Newsletters and who will also contribute articles about work being done.
- Produce three specialist–topic Newsletters each year, with colour illustrations. The current newsletter on *Investing in Childhood* has recently been published and copies are available for this meeting. Work is underway on the next publication, on the theme of *Valuing Our Elders*.
- If funding can be found, IAFN plans to hold a regional consultation in 2010 in Oceania on issues of V*iolence and the Family,* following the successful gatherings held in Nairobi (2003) and Seoul (2007).

How can ACC members help?

- By informing others in their Diocese about the work of IAFN, its website and the printed Newsletters.
- By suggesting names of people who might like to receive the Newsletters and contribute information.
- By suggesting topics for future Newsletters.
- By encouraging those who can afford it to pay an annual subscription of £10, or US$ equivalent, for the three issues of the printed Newsletter (cheques payable to *ACC (IAFN)*).
- By helping identify other possible sources of financial support.

The Anglican Communion has been described as a family. Like most families it needs to know about its members, and value the contribution of the different parts – especially those, as St Paul said, which are often undervalued. Our hope is that the Family Network, by linking the developed and the developing world on matters which affect us all, can deepen our understanding and knowledge of each other and the priorities of God's mission, helping us embrace the Millennium Development Goals in tackling poverty, HIV/AIDS and the suffering of many families.

Réseau Francophone de la Communion Anglicane[1]

Rapport soumis par le président du Réseau, Mgr Pierre Whalon

Communiqué du Réseau francophone, Aylesford, Angleterre

La sixième réunion du Réseau francophone de la Communion anglicane a eu lieu à Aylesford, Angleterre, du 1er au 4 Juillet, 2008. Le groupe comprenait des représentants du Canada, d'Europe, d''Haïti, et de sept diocèses africains. D'autres participants ont été empêchés d'y assister à cause de problèmes de visa.

Les évêques et membres du clergé présents ont prié ensemble, partagé et échangé.

Ils ont ressenti un désir profond de réaffirmer l'importance primordiale de l'Unité de l'Église surtout dans le contexte des difficultés que vit présentement la Communion anglicane.

Il s'est avéré que malgré les différences culturelles et les divergences sur certaines questions importantes, ce n'est que par le dialogue et la concertation que l'on peut reconnaître et jouir des richesses que chacun apporte à la Communion et à l'accomplissement de la Mission de Dieu.

Le Réseau francophone, qui relie plus que 4 millions de personnes qui célèbrent en français à travers le monde, est un organisme officiel de la Communion anglicane; il est sous l'égide de l'Archevêque de Cantorbéry. À la fin de cette conférence, les participants ont réaffirmé leur reconnaissance de sa direction pastorale.

Le groupe a aussi reconnu la contribution des provinces et diocèses d'expression française en matière de liturgie et culte. (Une province dans la tradition anglicane est souvent reliée à un pays, et inclus plusieurs diocèses.)

Plusieurs résolutions ont été avalisées lors de cette réunion. Le Comité exécutif a reçu le mandat :

---

[1] See below for the English translation of this report

213

- d'aider les provinces à trouver des moyens pour former des formateurs en éducation théologique, suivant le document « Balises » (*Signposts*) et les schémas présentés par le comité de *Theological Education in the Anglican Communion*
- de former une équipe pour appuyer les provinces et diocèses dans ce travail
- de recommander aux autorités appropriées de la Communion de constituer un fonds pour l'éducation théologique à l'intention de toutes les provinces, en particulier celles qui ne sont pas anglophones
- de trouver des partenaires afin d'établir un fonds de $250.000 US destiné à alimenter un programme de microcrédit dans l'Église anglicane du Congo
- de faire des partenariats pour aider les femmes victimes de violences sexuelles lors de conflits en Afrique.

En plus, les membres présents à la réunion ont décidé de faire un appel d'offre aux provinces francophones pour l'établissement d'un ou deux centres de traduction, afin de pouvoir fournir aux membres du Réseau des traductions rapides et ponctuelles de documents importants, ainsi que d'ouvrages courts destinés au grand public. Le comité exécutif se chargera d'émettre des appels d'offre, et s'engage à trouver un financement pour ces centres.

Un nouvel exécutif a été élu : président, Mgr. Pierre Whalon, France; vice-présidents, Mgr. Zacharie Masimango Katanda, Congo, et le Vénérable Pierre Voyer, Canada; secrétaire, la Rév. Mary Ellen Dolan, Allemagne; trésorier, le Rév. Chanoine David Oliver, Canada; conseillers, Mgr. Ian Ernest, Île Maurice, et la Rév. Muhindo Tsongo Joyce, Congo.

Le Réseau a tenu à remercier de façon officielle l'ancienne équipe en particulier le président sortant, le Très Révérend Ogé Beauvoir et le secrétaire sortant, le Rév. Bernard Vignot. Ceux-ci continueront à travailler pour le Réseau en tant que conseiller et archiviste respectivement.

Anglican Francophone Network

Report submitted by Bishop Pierre Whalon, Network President.

Communiqué of the Anglican Francophone Network, Aylesford, England

The sixth meeting of the Francophone Network took place in Aylesford, England, 1 to 4 July, 2008. The group included representatives from Canada, Europe, Haiti, and five African dioceses. Other representatives were prevented from attendance due to problems with visas.

The bishops and clergy in attendance prayed together, shared their stories, and exchanged ideas.

They experienced a profound desire to reaffirm the primordial importance of the Unity of the Church, especially in the context of the difficulties that the Anglican Communion is currently facing.

It became clear that, despite cultural differences and disagreements on certain important questions, it is only through dialogue and working together that the riches that each brings to the Communion and the accomplishment of the Mission of God can be recognised and enjoyed.

The Francophone Network, which connects four million people throughout the world who celebrate in the French language, is an official body of the Anglican Communion, under the aegis of the Archbishop of Canterbury. At the close of their meeting, the participants reaffirmed their gratitude for his pastoral leadership.

The group also gave recognition to the contribution of those provinces and dioceses of French language in the areas of liturgy and worship.

Several resolutions were passed during the meeting. The Executive Committee received the mandate to:

- help francophone provinces to find the means to train professors of theological education, using the 'Signposts' document and 'grids' proposed by Theological Education in the Anglican Communion (TEAC)
- gather a team to support the provinces and dioceses in this work
- recommend to the appropriate authorities of the Communion that a fund for theological education for all provinces be raised, in particular for those provinces which are not anglophone
- find partners in order to develop a fund of US$250,000 for a microcredit program in the Anglican Church of Congo
- develop partnerships to help women victims of sexual violence in recent African conflicts.

Also, the meeting decided that a request for proposals should be sent to all the francophone provinces, calling for the establishment of one or two translation centres, so as to furnish timely translations of important documents, as well as short items intended for the general public. The Executive Committee will be in charge of the requests for proposals, and will commit to help find funding.

A new executive committee was elected : President, Bishop Pierre Whalon, France; Vice Presidents, Bishop Zacharie Masimango Katanda, Congo, and the Ven Pierre Voyer, Canada; Secretary, the Revd Mary Ellen Dolan, Germany; Treasurer, the Revd Canon David Oliver; Advisers, Archbishop Ian Ernest, Mauritius, and Joyce Muhindo Tsongo, Congo.

The Network wishes to thank officially the former committee, especially the former President, the Very Revd Ogé Beauvoir, and Secretary, the Revd Bernard Vignot. They will continue to work for the Network as Adviser and Archivist, respectively.

Anglican Health Network

Renewing the Commitment to Anglican Health Care: The case for an Anglican Health Network

Report submitted by the Revd Paul Holley, Anglican UN Representative, Geneva

Background

The established tradition in which the Church offered health care services to the communities of which it was a part has diminished in the face of modern comprehensive health systems. Many Anglican and Episcopal hospitals have been sold to private or public providers in the developed world. In the developing world hospitals and clinics have been closed due to cost constraints. There has been little reflection on the impact of this retreat, but an underlying assumption that it is no longer the responsibility of the Church to provide medical care except in a vacuum of provision in the poorest communities.

At the same time, the practice of evidence-based medicine offered by scientifically trained physicians has assumed prominence over the healing arts practised by religious communities. As scientific understanding has taken centre stage, the practice of 'faith healing' has remained vibrant in many settings, but mostly disconnected from modern medical disciplines.

These trends no longer seem to serve the Church or the wider society well. There is a widespread renewed interest in holistic approaches to medicine, and a positive policy shift towards the contribution of faith-based medical services to national health systems. Along with global health development donors, the World Health Organization is seeking to utilise church health programmes in a pragmatic step to maximise health impacts through a mixed economy of public, private and civil society delivery partners. Moreover, the remaining Episcopal hospitals in the United States have resisted proposals from the health care industry to buy their facilities on the basis that their spiritual and pastoral approach adds value to the clinical setting. Anglican health programmes find that the medical establishment is showing renewed interest in the multiple elements of their work.

Perhaps the most significant driver of this renewed interest in faith-based health care has been the spread of the HIV/AIDS virus, which has in some countries reached pandemic proportions. At a time when the global health community continues to fail those most vulnerable to the disease, the churches have reflected both on their preventative messages and on their ability to treat the sick and dying. In conversation with various global health agencies, they have recognised that they have a great deal more they can offer to begin to halt the progress of the virus. And it has been in assessing the opportunities and needs of HIV service provision that the agencies have begun to recognise that there is a more sustained and permanent place for church medical programmes in national health systems.

At a plenary session of the World Health Assembly held in Geneva in May 2008, Archbishop Desmond Tutu gave the headline address. He suggested that God looked at the medical establishment as a partner in the holy quest to bring life and health. This message was warmly received, especially in the context of a renewed commitment to the primary health care model. Following a series of interactions within the Anglican Communion, it seems timely that an Anglican Health Network should form to foster and guide a renewed commitment to God's mission for health and wholeness.

Lambeth Conference: interests coincide

The proposal to form an Anglican Health Network emerged during the Lambeth Conference at two self-select sessions. The following people had been considering independently the value of some Anglican collaboration, and came together at the sessions to share their ideas:

- Bishop John Gladstone of the Church of South India, who has engaged in a major renewal of the province's mission hospitals
- Bishop Rayford High of the Diocese of Texas, where the St Luke's Episcopal hospital system offers a significant proportion of health care in the Houston area.
- Revd Paul Holley of the Anglican UN Representation in Geneva, following his work with the World Health Organization, the Global Fund and the Council of Anglican Provinces in Africa on HIV/AIDS.

- Revd Dr Don Thompson of the Colleges and Universities of the Anglican Communion, following an interest shown by some of the member medical colleges in linking with Anglican hospitals.

In addition, 15 bishops from dioceses throughout Africa registered their interest in being supported in health care projects. Bishop David Beetge of Southern Africa and his development colleague Dr Robert Lee of Fresh Ministries offered their support, as did Bishop John Pritchard of Oxford.

Anglican Health Assets study

During August 2008 an intern at the Anglican UN office in Geneva carried out a desk-based review to begin to pull together an Anglican health care database. This built on a previous study of the response of the Anglican provinces of Kenya, Tanzania and Zambia to HIV/AIDS, which revealed a significant spread of medical work (see http://www.aco.org/un/resources/working_together.pdf). The database study garnered information about Anglican health facilities where web-based information was available, identifying 145 facilities in 96 dioceses. This covered a limited number of Provinces, and the information on it has not been independently verified, but it gives an indication that Anglicans are sufficiently active in health care delivery to warrant greater attention.

Episcopal Health Ministries Conference 13-15 January 2009

Following the Lambeth Conference, Bishop High invited a range of participants to the St Luke's Episcopal Health System conference centre in Houston to consider further the value of Anglican/Episcopal collaboration. Delegates included health managers, medics and chaplaincy staff from within the Episcopal Church, including representatives from Haiti and Puerto Rico, plus others from the wider communion including Bishop Gladstone, Revd Paul Holley and the medical director of the Diocese of Jerusalem. Following this, Revd Paul Holley took the initiative to form an email distribution list of those present under the banner of an Anglican Health Network, and is now leading the development of the ideas and structures that will form the basis of the network. One immediate project was to facilitate a transfer of some used medical equipment from US Episcopal hospitals to those in the developing world.

An Anglican Health Network rationale

The following points have emerged in discussion at the two conferences: Why should Anglicans and Episcopalians form a health network?

1. To renew the Church's gospel calling to go out and heal the sick.
2. To utilise the strengths of a common Anglican identity in mobilising resources and expertise.
3. To facilitate the Communion's commitment to the MDGs; recognising that Anglican and Episcopal health ministries are in a position to deliver health improvements to the poor.

Proposed outcome

Increased scope and quality of Anglican health activity leading to substantial gains in the health of the communities served, particularly amongst the poor.

Potential practical outputs

1. Establish a web-based portal for communication and interaction. Produce a regular newsletter and animate specialised email discussions.
2. Organise a programme of conferences to facilitate learning and relationships.
3. Facilitate the shipping of used medical equipment from hospitals in the developed world to those in the developing world.
4. Establish a system of exchange visits for medical and management staff amongst Anglican/Episcopal hospitals and other health-related projects.
5. Enable the funding of professional development for medics in the developing world.
6. Facilitate effective political relationships with global, national and local health authorities and develop partnerships.
7. Develop relationships with donors to bid for increased investment in the Anglican capacity to deliver health gains targets amongst the poor.
8. Build the capacity to provide technical assistance to those seeking to develop existing or new health activity.
9. Pioneer some new approaches to health funding through social business and insurance models.

10. Animate a broad discourse on the theological, pastoral, political and economic aspects of modern health and well-being.
11. Provide a forum where medical ethics can be debated.
12. Create a dynamic database of health activity in the Communion.
13. Compile the learning and publish.

Next steps

An interim steering group meeting will be gathered to consider the operation of individual and institutional membership of the network. This group can be drawn from the following interests: the hospitals of the Episcopal Church; the Church of South India; the Council of Anglican Provinces in Africa; the Diocese of Jerusalem; the Church of England; National Episcopal Health Ministries; Church Pension Fund; Anglican Aids South Africa; Anglican UN Office Geneva.

The governing mission principle of this initiative is found in the simple instructions of Jesus to his disciples: 'He sent them out to proclaim the kingdom of God and to heal the sick'. *Luke 9.2*

Anglican Indigenous Network

Report submitted by Malcolm Naea Chun, AIN Secretary-General

A Cry In the Wilderness: A Statement from the 11th Gathering of the Anglican Indigenous Network

We, the delegates attending the 11th Gathering of the Anglican Indigenous Network (AIN) are indigenous peoples who are minorities living in our own homelands. We come from Aotearoa, Australia, Canada, Hawai'i, and the United States of America. We are committed to the Anglican faith tradition while at the same time we affirm our traditional spiritualities shaped by our understanding of the interdependence of ecology, theology, spirituality and morality. We share many things in common. We believe that God is leading us to a turning point in our histories, toward full partnership between indigenous minorities living in our respective homelands.

We have pledged to work together to exercise our leadership in contributing our vision and gifts to transform the life of the Anglican Communion. We celebrate the trajectory of God's living Word in Creation and we further celebrate the continual incarnation and fulfilment of that Word in the life of our peoples.

As indigenous peoples from countries that have experienced and continue to experience the effects of colonialism, we claim our authority to live into God's future for us based upon our values, teachings, and communal self-understandings. As Indigenous minority Anglicans, we believe it is time for national churches whose borders are based upon colonial conquest, to respectfully and formally acknowledge the reality of our existence and its implications for their on-going life and governance.

Resolutions to ACC-14

Draft resolutions will be submitted to ACC-14 for consideration, concerning the United Nations Declaration on Indigenous Rights; access for indigenous members of Anglican churches to all levels of theological education and training appropriate to cultural context and traditions; the contribution of elders to planning and development processes in respect of climate change; the healing of indigenous families and the protection of women and children from violence and trafficking.

We also commend to you our statement from the ninth gathering at Pala 2005. (see below)

A Letter from the Secretary-General of AIN

The Indaba Reflections document of the bishops who met in Lambeth particularly named the Anglican Indigenous Network in paragraph 62. It says, 'Indigenous peoples have traditional understandings of the earth as a gift of the Creator and of their relationship to it and its creatures being one of interconnectedness and responsible caring. The Indigenous peoples have reminded us that we are not aliens in a wilderness to be conquered, but integral parts of the created order, as are plants and animals, which are to be cherished and nurtured. The Anglican Indigenous Network could provide good resources for the Communion to develop these ideas more fully.'

Concurrently as we met in Hawai'i, a summit was held in Alaska under the United Nations gathering indigenous peoples to consider the issues of climate change. I commend their 'Anchorage Declaration of April 24, 2009' to be adopted by the Communion for serious actions to be taken by a non-governmental organisation. Our gathering in Hawai'i affirmed their fundamental beliefs and states, as we should as indigenous peoples of the land and sea, that we both call out for the upholding of 'the inherent rights of Indigenous Peoples, affirmed by the United Nations Declaration on the Rights of Indigenous Peoples (UNDRIP)' and that they 'must be fully respected in all decision-making processes and activities related to climate change.'

The gifts the Indaba document refers to are 'our knowledge, spirituality, sciences, practices, experiences and relationships with our traditional lands, territories, waters, air, forests, oceans, sea ice, other natural resources and all life.' These are gifts that the Anchorage Declaration says, 'We offer to share with humanity our Traditional Knowledge, innovations, and practices relevant to climate change, provided our fundamental rights as intergenerational guardians of this knowledge are fully recognized and respected.' It is priceless, it is precious, and it is sacred. It is a gift we have been trying to offer to the church since 400 years ago, but it has been rejected or been made token in our presence. If these gifts are to be respected then as we state in AIN's mission statement and affirmed in the Anchorage Declaration, there must be 'full and effective participation of Indigenous Peoples ... in formulating, implementing, and monitoring activities, mitigation, and adaptation relating to impacts of climate change'. A change of climate change is a change in our attitude to our only home, this earth, and to the way we live with the earth. Our real gift is that we as indigenous peoples have survived as peoples for so long while great civilisations have come and gone. It is our way of living and how we make decisions that affect our relationship with this island home called earth.

'Ask and you shall receive ... Seek and you shall find.' The man and the woman on the road to Emmaus invited the stranger to eat together at the table as full partners in Christ, not as children, nor servants, or as the Australian Constitution has categorised, as flora and fauna, but as Peoples. We have only been asking for the same treatment. Faithfully, yours in Christ

223

A Brief History of AIN

During the 1991 General Convention of the Episcopal Church in Phoenix, Arizona the first step was taken toward forming a network of indigenous Anglicans. It was here that the Anglican observer to the United Nations, the Rt Revd Sir Paul Reeves, convened a meeting of indigenous Anglicans and/or their representatives: Dr Owanah Anderson, the Revd Dr Martin Brokenleg, Bishop Steven Charleston and Dr Carol Hampton of the Episcopal Council of Indian Ministries; Bishop Wakahuihui and Doris Vercoe from Aotearoa; the Revd Charles G K Hopkins from Hawai'i; Archbishop Michael Pierce representing native Canadians. The idea of an indigenous network to coincide with the United Nation's International Year of the World's Indigenous People was presented and the countries represented at the meeting agreed to participate in it. It was further decided that one person from each country meet as a steering committee with Sir Paul Reeves to develop a plan for networking among American Indians and Alaska Natives, Canadian Natives, Native Hawaiians and Maori.

At the seventh gathering since Phoenix, ACC member Dr Winiata was asked to seek formal recognition for this network as the voice of indigenous Anglicans who are minorities in their own homelands. At the following gathering in Cairns, Australia, the network established the office of a Secretary-General to help co-ordinate future gatherings, to ensure the continuance of the network between gatherings and to represent it. Also established were programme groups that would also be reflected in the make of the delegations: Women, Youth, Clergy, Theological Educators and Elders.

Some of the results of being a network have been the establishment of an indigenous theological training institute in the United State, the publication of an indigenous theological journal, greater exchanges of peoples at respective events, the support of the exchange of theological students and faculty, the development and support for the office of the national indigenous bishop of Canada and the covenant for Aboriginal and Torres Strait Islanders in the Anglican church of Australia.

Members continue to gather once every two years with a rotating hosting of the gathering. The host member affords all ground arrangements for the gathering while others are responsible for their airfare. AIN had not dues or budget until some of the members were able to contribute for the first time after the 2007 Vancouver gathering.

The network realises that its present membership reflects an area around the Pacific of English speaking peoples and has set out a means for other Anglican indigenous minorities to become full members. Prospective members are asked to send a representative to the next gathering as an observer so to determine if the network is something they really would like to participant in. If so, then at the following gathering they would send a full delegation. If they are not English speaking then they would need to provide their own translators, either as part of the delegation or accompanying them. With the new budget it may be possible for the network to hire the technology to assist with simultaneous translation costs.

Pala Statement 2005

We believe that the following will enrich our traditions and relationship with the Trinitarian aspects of a 'Living God' who was, and is, always among us:

- The development of a living pedagogical model that will enable indigenous communities to articulate the diverse theologies that are grounded within those communities; develop these tools and or models that enable indigenous communities to create liturgies that express their unique spiritualities; develop a 'gospel lens' that is appropriate to each of our indigenous languages, cultures and life experiences; strongly urge the non-indigenous church to also develop a 'gospel lens'.

- The development through the text and traditions of the Anglican Communion of a post-colonial and post-modern critique, that transforms the colonial legacy that has been imposed upon us; to believe that we have a responsibility and obligation to the future, to those generations who are children now and those yet to be born, not to repeat the destruction, damage and cultural genocide of our colonial past.

- The increased sensitivity of the wider church to the pressures upon indigenous leaders, both lay and ordained, who walk the path between the two worlds, i.e. the world of the church and their own respective worlds; to urge the Anglican Communion, in all of its Anglican ministry units throughout the world, to establish clearly defined and accessible resource, including finance from national churches, to undertake effective professional and curriculum development and to enable appropriate exchanges of indigenous educators and students within the Anglican Communion, and to urge the Anglican Communion to honestly and seriously engage in cross-cultural exchange with their respective indigenous communities.

Anglican Communion Legal Advisers' Network

Report submitted by Canon John Rees, ACLAN Convenor

The Anglican Communion Legal Advisers' Network (ACLAN) was established in 2002, as an initiative of the then Archbishop of Canterbury, Lord Carey. Its initial meeting took place in the Education Centre at Canterbury and attracted 30 representatives drawn from 17 Provinces. Its initial work was reported to both the Primates' Meeting and the ACC Meeting in 2002, and an editorial group was established to take forward a suggestion by Professor Norman Doe that work be undertaken to identify *Principles of Canon Law Common to the Churches of the Anglican Communion.*

The editorial group met subsequently in Toronto (2005) and Nassau (2006). It consisted of representatives from each continental region of the Communion, assisted by Professor Doe, and after final approval by e-mail correspondence, its work was published, with a foreword by the Archbishop of Canterbury, in time for the Lambeth Conference 2008. Copies of the *Principles of Canon Law Common to the Churches of the Anglican Communion* were made available to all bishops attending the Conference (courtesy of funding from Westminster Abbey and another charity with which the Convenor is associated).

Several members of the editorial group attended the Conference, and organised a seminar and reception chaired by the Archbishop of Wales (as the trustee liaison with the Network). The seminar was one of the 'self select' seminars arranged at the Conference, and was one of the best-attended: over

60 bishops were present, and the *Principles* became a significant discussion item both in the Press and amongst the larger number of bishops attending the Conference. The Press briefing given by the Convenor remains available on You-Tube!

Looking ahead, ACLAN is working towards the following:

1   Promulgation of the *Principles*, in responding to enquiries from interested individuals and Provinces, and through wider acquaintance with them by further lectures and seminars.

2   A further plenary meeting of the Network during the next twelve months. However, as most of the members are practising lawyers, it is difficult to make adequate professional time available in busy practices for adequate reflection to take place in an environment that encourages mutual understanding.

3   Ongoing use of the Network as a 'clearing house' for sharing canon law issues across the Communion. Ecclesiastical issues go far beyond the controversial theological and ethical questions which have preoccupied so much of the Communion's attention in recent years, and come in all shapes and sizes, though with largely common themes: examples include Child Protection policies, Clergy Discipline issues, and appropriate means of safeguarding Church property.

We invite your continuing support for the Network's activities, and trust that you will enjoy reading the copy of the *Principles* supplied to each member of the Council.

Anglican Peace & Justice Network

Submitted by Canon Margaret Larom, APJN Secretary

In early 2009, published copies of the 2008 Anglican Peace and Justice Network (APJN) report 'Community Transformation: Violence and the Church's Response' were mailed to all ACC-14 members in advance of their May meeting. This is available on-line at http://apjn.anglicancommunion.org/reports/index.cfm. A summary report follows.

Representatives of 17 Provinces travelled to the Great Lakes region of Africa for the triennial meeting of the Anglican Peace and Justice Network in 2007. The gathering, from 25 September to 3 October in Rwanda and Burundi, was focused on conflict resolution, exploring the role of violence and civil unrest in societies and considering how best the church might respond.

The Provinces represented were: Aotearoa/New Zealand and Polynesia, Burundi, Canada, Central Africa, Central America, Congo, England, Japan, Korea, North India, Philippines, Rwanda, Scotland, Southern Africa, Sudan, Uganda, United States. The International Anglican Women's Network convenor (from the Indian Ocean), also participated.

APJN issued a substantial communiqué to the Communion through ACNS4327(www.anglicancommunion.org/acns/news.cfm/2007/10/9/ACNS) on 9 October, 2007. Then in 2008, the APJN secretariat produced the 64-page report 'Community Transformation: Violence and the Church's Response' (see http://apjn.anglicancommunion.org/reports/index.cfm). Illustrated with nearly 50 photos, the report includes:

- the Burundi/Rwanda meeting summary along with APJN's recommendations and commitments for action
- accounts of Anglican peace conferences and consultations in Korea, South Africa, Melanesia and Sudan
- articles and analyses concerning Pakistan, Palestine, Burundi, Congo, Japan and Brazil
- educational tools and links to various models for conflict transformation.

The report was mailed widely and posted on the Anglican Communion website. Additional copies of the print version may be obtained from the Anglican Communion Office, email networks@anglicancommunion.org, or from the APJN secretary.

At the Lambeth Conference in July 2008, 1,500 copies were distributed to bishops from the APJN exhibit space, along with thousands of bookmarks featuring prayers for justice and peace reprinted from various Anglican and Episcopal prayer books.

APJN members took turns staffing the display and resource table, and networking with passers-by. The Steering Group met to hear reports from regions who could not send representatives to the Great Lakes meeting (eg, Sri Lanka), and to begin planning for APJN's next meeting in 2010 (APJN's 25th anniversary). The convenor, Dr Jenny Te Paa, and secretary, the Revd Dr Brian Grieves, also helped lead or resource special events, bible studies, and workshops.

The invitation to have a presence at the ACC-14 meeting has been eagerly welcomed by the APJN leadership. Mindful of the shocking events in Gaza a few months ago, APJN has invited the Revd Canon Naim Ateek from Palestine to lead APJN's two workshops.

The APJN Steering Group is extremely grateful for the invitations to make a witness at the Lambeth Conference and at Anglican Consultative Council meetings, and believes that such opportunities already have borne fruit and will continue to do so.

Great Lakes meeting

The 2007 meeting began with a welcoming address in Kigali by the Most Revd Emmanuel M Kolini, Primate of Rwanda. The Archbishop told APJN members that their gathering was a 'sacramental moment'. During a four-month period in 1994 more than a million Rwandans were slaughtered. He noted that in a nation such as Rwanda, where 90 per cent of the people are Christian, genocide nevertheless occurred amidst a failure of the church to prevent it. 'It is very easy to be religious, but very difficult to be the people of God. What went wrong is a problem of the soul. The Lord is calling us to be a blessing.'

APJN members were deeply sobered by a visit to the Rwandan genocide museum, and to the Ntarama Church, where 5,000 people were slaughtered after taking refuge. As Bishop Micah Dawidi of Sudan prayed for the victims and their families, members of the Network were enveloped in a spirit of prayer and reverence for the sanctity of life.

Along with a Great Lakes delegation of the International Anglican Women's Network, representatives met with women survivors from Rwanda. One woman told of being systematically hacked by machete and left for dead. When asked if she forgave those who committed these acts, she quietly replied, 'The Bible calls us to forgive'. Another woman spoke of being taken captive to the Congo region where she was brutally gang raped. As a result she became pregnant and infected with HIV at the same time. Her baby subsequently died and she now suffers both the stigma and the pain of AIDS and the grief of losing a child. Both women attributed their ability to give witness about these events to AVEGA, an organisation established with support from the church in Rwanda to assist widows and orphans of the genocide.

APJN members saw many ways in which the church is participating in the hard work of repentance, forgiveness, and reconciliation, and saw encouraging signs of hope in the areas of public health, education, justice, environmental policy, and the official statistic that nearly 50 per cent of the Rwandan parliament is made up of women.

Members of the Network then spent a week in Bujumbura, Burundi, a country wracked by years of civil strife. Bishop Pie Ntukamazina led them to a Roman Catholic seminary in Buta, where 40 seminarians and workers were slaughtered. Rebels had demanded that the seminarians separate themselves along ethnic lines so that one group would be killed and the other spared. In an extraordinarily courageous act of public witness the young men declared they would rather die together than be separated. The memorial serves as a sign of hope and victory over evil.

As in Rwanda, women survivors in Burundi bravely revealed stories of pain and suffering. Though they escaped death, they and thousands of others continue to live in tragically difficult situations of poverty, lack of housing or means to support their children and, for many, HIV and AIDS as a result of infection from sexual abusers.

Other Burundians shared firsthand accounts of the ongoing socio-economic and political impact of violence and conflict giving rise to extreme conditions including poverty, HIV/AIDS and malaria, environmental degradation, and the continued abuse of women and children. Network members also heard poignant accounts of the plight of thousands of internally displaced people traumatised by genocide and conflict in Rwanda, Burundi, and the neighbouring Democratic Republic of Congo.

The Network originally planned to visit Goma in the DRC but had to cancel when travel by road became too dangerous. Instead, Bishop Bahati Bali Busane offered a compelling account of the current situation there, drawing special attention to the ways in which conflict inevitably and often cruelly affects women and children.

Reporting on Sudan, Bishop Micah outlined the background to the long war between north and south, its recent resolution through the signing of a Comprehensive Peace Agreement, and the continuing conflict and humanitarian disaster in Darfur.

APJN members learned that Muslims and Christians of southern Sudan once coexisted in relative harmony. They were encouraged to hear that the Episcopal Church of Sudan now provides training in conflict resolution, and agreed that skills of negotiation, co-operation, mutuality and interdependence should be revived with urgency across the Anglican Communion.

Jessica Nalwoga's report from Uganda indicated there is hope that a 21-year conflict in the north appears to be coming to an end, and that the ongoing peace process hosted by the government of southern Sudan will bear fruit. The report included the story of those bishops from the north who struggled for a long time in isolation until 15 bishops from the south crossed over to the conflict zone and learned how their brother bishops had risked their lives to meet with rebel groups and even slept on the streets with abandoned children to protect them. Seeing the effects of war first hand and praying side by side created the possibility for the whole country and church to take full ownership of their roles in conflict resolution.

From the Central Africa delegate, members heard about further deterioration in Zimbabwe, once the breadbasket of central Africa and now reduced to begging from neighbouring countries for the most basic needs. APJN acknowledged that this tragic situation has a twofold cause: (1) political mismanagement of the country, the blocking of any reform and the suppression of voices of opposition and, (2) the failure of the United States and the United Kingdom to realise the commitments they made in the 1978 Lancaster Agreement, to assist in redistribution of land.

Stirring accounts of situations in Panama, the Democratic Republic of Congo, and the Philippines were reminders of the complicity of the United States and other countries in perpetrating and perpetuating acts of violence and social and economic destruction.

The APJN members also reviewed situations of violence in Myanmar, Israel/Palestine, Iraq, Sri Lanka, and Pakistan, and offered prayers for their people as well as urgent recommendations for reinvigorated peace processes.

In hearing many reports of horrific acts of violence by gunmen and armed militias, APJN members asked themselves who benefits from the sale of small arms, and reflected on the role of makers and sellers of arms in contributing to all conflicts.

The story from Cynthia Patterson and Maylanne Maybee, of the Anglican Church of Canada's effort to seek healing and truth with Aboriginal peoples, pointed to the fact that reconciliation is not only a project in places of visible conflict, but also is called for where historic injustices have not been adequately addressed or resolved.

Dr Jeremiah Yang reported on plans for the upcoming TOPIK conference (Towards Peace in Korea), which was subsequently held in North and South Korea, November 14-21, 2007, under the leadership of the Anglican Church in Korea. The conference focused on reconciliation and reunification of the Korean peninsula, and APJN delegates participated. (In 1999, when APJN met in Seoul, APJN commended the plan for reunification to the Anglican Consultative Council in its 1999 report, see http://apjn.anglicancommunion.org/reports/Coming%20to%20Seoul.pdf.)

Canon Delene Mark made a presentation on the TEAM (Toward Effective Anglican Mission) conference held in March 2007 in Boksburg, South Africa. This conference drew more than 400 participants, representing more than 30 Provinces and extra-provincial churches, to discuss new strategies for eradicating the pervasive scourges of HIV/AIDS and poverty, especially through the Millennium Development Goals. APJN discussed the recommendations of the TEAM conference, specifically Number 9 on strengthening peace and justice initiatives in areas of conflict and human displacement (see http://apjn.anglicancommunion.org/reports/team_oct_2007.pdf).

Recommendations

The Anglican Communion, as a family of churches of more than 77 million members in 165 countries, has the potential for great influence in the world. APJN believes it must increase its voice in advocacy on behalf of the powerless, for those most affected by conditions of suffering.

APJN continues to assert that in all situations of conflict and political violence, the church has the difficult and sometimes dangerous task of speaking out against injustice, especially where political interests are driven primarily by personal greed or ambition; where violence continues due to the unchecked spread of armaments, and where agreements between rebel or minority groups and governments are not being honoured. The Anglican Communion must develop the skills and profile necessary for it to be an effective and boldly prophetic voice for God's justice in all societies.

APJN supports the concept of healing through the processes of truth telling, repentance, and restorative justice. The Anglican Communion has an important role to play in these processes of reconciliation and in the ongoing pursuit of peace.

APJN calls on the Anglican Communion to preach the message of reconciliation by transformative prophetic action, and to continue assisting in the facilitation of peacemaking dialogue in situations of conflict. The Network will continue to identify resources for conflict transformation that can be used in the important work of reconciliation.

APJN celebrates the work of the Peace Centre in Burundi, and encourages the establishment everywhere of programs that support post-conflict reconciliation, rebuilding, and social development.

APJN encourages the Anglican Communion to urge international Anglican development and aid agencies to increase their support where possible to local churches in order to hasten the implementation and flourishing of all social development programs.

On the devastating situation in Darfur, and specifically on the north-south conflict in Sudan, APJN requests that the Communion urge the African Union and United Nations to seek commitment from the Khartoum government to implement the Comprehensive Peace Agreement without further delay.

In all contexts where inter-religious tensions are a factor in ongoing conflict, APJN appeals to those Anglican leaders who are in dialogue with Muslim leaders around the world to share from their experience, insights, and wisdom on how best the inter-religious dimensions of the conflict in Sudan can be reduced. APJN applauds and affirms the efforts of local churches that are endeavouring to bring warring parties together and at the same time to provide training in conflict resolution skills. APJN calls on the Anglican Communion to support these courageous and visionary efforts.

APJN is firmly convinced that the Anglican Communion must increase its presence in regions in conflict, and stand in solidarity with the affected Anglican jurisdictions as they seek to restore peace and achieve reconciliation. We particularly call for increased solidarity with the Anglican Provinces in the Great Lakes region.

APJN challenges all Provinces of the Communion to provide much more generous assistance to those sister and brother members who are being needlessly and undeservedly caught up in seemingly endless cycles of political, economic, and sexual violence. The resultant suffering, displacement, and unbearable poverty leads too often to premature and entirely avoidable death.

APJN sees the critical work for justice and peace in all areas of conflict and violence as being utterly central to the effective and credible mission of the church and therefore to our ability as God's peoples to reconcile all things to Christ.

Anglican Refugee and Migrant Network

Report submitted by the Very Revd Andrew Chan

Introduction

Decades of continuing economic crisis and wars resulted in displacements of peoples creating a huge population of migrant workers, refugees and asylum seekers. Government labour export policies, racial, political and religious repressions and war contingencies further increased the population of this sector practically gravitating towards more affluent and economically advanced countries.

The United Nations estimated the total immigrant population to be 186,579,300 in its World Population Policies 2005 Report. The number has grown to about 205 million in 2008. Tens of millions are undocumented while about 20 million are refugees (International Assembly of Migrants and Refugees (IAMR) - Founding Congress, October 2008).

The UN and its related institutions approved conventions and recommendations setting international standards on handling migration and refugees. These conventions were made possible with the active lobbying of non-governmental and grassroots organizations (e.g. the International Convention on the Protection of the Rights of all Migrant Workers and Members of their Families, the Convention Relating to the Status of Refugees 1951 [revised 1967] and the Geneva Convention).

While there are such international formations that attempt to ensure the protection of rights of migrants, refugees and asylum seekers, there are also similar levels of formations that stand otherwise.

Members of the World Trade Organization (WTO) could not agree on the coverage of its General Agreement on Trades in Services (GATS) Mode 4 – the international movements of persons – regarding a proposal for standard benefits among experts sent by big businesses for the efficient use of their products, vis a vis, labour migrants. Rich countries want their experts to be assured of protection but refuse to provide them to migrant workers.

Realizing the latest economic crisis to be in the offing, a series of high level/inter-governmental meetings resulted in the creation of the Global Forum on Migration and Development (GFMD). The GFMD implies that migration can lead to development because of the enormous remittances being sent by international migrant workers to their families through international banks. It noted some studies made in the past ten years which included a World Bank research showing the huge remittances migrants send back to their homeland amounting to US$2.26 trillion: an amount far more than the combined development assistance given by developed countries to underdeveloped ones. GFMD professes to embrace 'development', but this concept may be remote to the realities of peoples of poor countries who are impoverished.

At present, almost all the global regions have migrant-sending and migrant-receiving countries, war–torn cities and affluent societies that result in migrants and fleeing nationals.

Rationale

The Anglican community in several independent initiatives responded to the local needs of migrants and refugees in their midst.

In 1981, in particular, the Mission for Filipino Migrant Workers (now Mission For Migrant Workers) was adapted by the St. John's Cathedral with the acceptance of the then Anglican Diocese of Hong Kong & Macau (now the Hong Kong Sheng Kung Hui). It was meant to provide pastoral care, paralegal assistance and advocacy for migrants in Hong Kong. This form of direct services eventually expanded to cover several migrant and refugee-receiving countries in Asia and the Pacific through the Asia Pacific Mission for Migrants that was established in 1983.

On a global level, in 1984, following a specific request from the 1983 Primates' Meeting, the Anglican Refugee and Migrant Network (ARMN) was established as an officially-accredited Anglican Communion Network through Resolution 39 of ACC-6.

Essentially, ARMN was set up: 'to encourage coordination, consultation and action in refugee/migration issues with the Anglican Communion, with partner communions with ecumenical agencies and governments within their respective Provinces, to alleviate human suffering, and to determine and eliminate the root causes that lead to forced migration and create refugees.' This development reflected a clear recognition of the growing scale of the global refugee and migrant problem and its challenge to the church.

However, apart from two regional consultations *(Zimbabwe 1985; Jordan 1992);* the publication of two refugee-related Family Network (IAFN) Newsletters; and the development of an informal inter-diocesan network in East Asia, little of substance has happened to establish and activate the envisaged Anglican Network despite the 2007 IAFN Regional Consultation in East Asia and the 2008 Lambeth Conference that provided further evidence of the outstanding need for the Network.

With continuing developments showing an intensified international migration process *(migrant/refugees – receiving countries come up with policies),* concrete plans in the form of responses as part of the Anglican's Christian responsibility should be in place. The creation of the NETWORK will coordinate the different initiatives and further develop possible concrete actions.

Aims and Objectives of the Network

Broadly, the Network shall provide an arena for networking, education and advocacy based on the rich experiences of the network members as a response to the growing number of issues that go with the increase in number of migrants and refugees.

Specifically, the Network will be established to:

1. share information, ideas and experience, and to provide affirmation and mutual support for front-line programme-workers and programme-managers working with refugees and migrants on behalf of the Anglican Church through the creation of an active informal network
2. provide, when appropriate, practice-based information and briefing to the Archbishop of Canterbury, the Primates, other Anglican Church leaders, and the Anglican Observer to the UN, to inform and strengthen their prophetic, advocacy and pastoral work on behalf of refugees and migrants
3. promote awareness, concern and commitment to action within dioceses and parishes, to the benefit of local refugees and migrants
4. encourage and collaborate with the wider ecumenical family and other faiths in promoting active ministry to refugees and migrants
5. help tackle the root causes contributing to the creation of refugees and migrants through advocacy
6. network with other institutions working on behalf of refugees and migrants
7. develop and share theological reflection on the causes, issues and consequences relating to refugees and migrants.

Methodology

The network will set up a DESK that will basically start the communications with the different Primates: introducing the project and explaining the history that will reflect the undiminished enthusiasm of people behind ARMN.

This can be done by first gathering those who are already in the field: those with on-going programmes and activities for migrants and refugees and those that have shown interest in the Network (e.g. the participants in the Asian Migrant Ministry).

A Consultation should be called that will define more clearly and concretely goals and commitment for a strong network.

Activities

- **Newsletter**

    A regular update on the development of efforts in establishing the network will be ensured through the production of a regular newsletter: an announcement of this initiative as a stir-up activity. The same will provide current situations, concrete cases / experiences of migrants and refugees, status of government policies, local norms and national laws, existing international standards/conventions, bilateral and multi-lateral agreements.

- **Consultation**

    A Consultation will be held to define the goals and commitment of the Network. A preparatory working group will be convened to attend to the preparation of documents and materials for the invitation, Consultation Kit and for the discussions in the sessions, and other technical preparations.

    Invitations will be sent to those who showed interest in the several attempts to establish a coordinated migrant ministry; existing service providers for migrants within the Anglican Community; and other interested groups to be identified by a working/preparatory group.

- **Networking**

    Develop a network to gather information on the different initiatives within the Anglican Communion and establish a library of materials that has been developed along the way. Ensure the Network's growth through publications and release of documents, launching of common activities and coordinated actions for advocacy.

Anglican Urban Network

The following is an extract from the Anglican Urban Network's full report which can be found at
www.anglicancommunion.org/communion/acc/meetings/acc14/documents.cf.

The story so far

The international Anglican Urban Network (AUN) was formed as a response to resolutions made by the 1998 Lambeth Conference and the 11th meeting of the Anglican Consultative Council. Both resolutions acknowledge urban areas as critical sites for the engagement of the churches of the Anglican Communion in mission, ministry and social witness in the twenty-first century, as they struggle to prepare and resource ministers and church leaders for unprecedented situations in terms of both human and spiritual need.

At the heart of the Network is a recognition of the need to connect and resource those engaged in urban ministry and mission, and to use the openings available to raise these issues in the Provinces and with the Instruments of Communion. The global profile of the Anglican Communion also offers the opportunity to influence the forces and institutions shaping our cities.

The formation of the Network Reference Group began in June 2001 with a meeting in the wake of the *United Nations Special Assembly on Human Settlements* in New York. The Group began to look at the strategies and ethos of the Network. Subsequent informal meetings have taken place on the fringes of other gatherings. A report and newsletter were published to coincide with the meetings of the Anglican Consultative Council in Hong Kong in September 2002 and Nottingham in June 2005. Reports have been tabled at meetings of the Joint Standing Committee. Bulletins have also been published to coincide with the UN's International Habitat Day.

The Network has published *Impact of the Global: an Urban Theology* by Bishop Laurie Green, a short introduction to some of the issues facing cities and urban churches in an era of globalization. This was distributed widely, particularly with *Anglican World*, and has been translated into Spanish, Tamil and Japanese.

During Lent 2003 the Reference Group met in London within the context of a consultation on *Urban Mission in Globalizing Cities*. The context of London was a vital part of the meeting with members visiting parishes, NGO and academic sites, gaining insights of good practice, struggle and reflection, enabling the group to reflect on their own contexts, activities and resources. The group also met with the members of the steering groups of other Anglican Communion networks and identified possible areas of collaboration. The model of connecting with local higher education and other allies was felt to be one that could be offered for regional consultations and others working in this field.

In July 2004 members of the Reference Group took part in a week of activities organised by the Institute for Urban Ministry and Pretoria Community Ministries on training, networking and developing those involved in urban ministry. Anglicans from South Africa, Kenya, and Mozambique are already involved in programmes run by IUM and UNISA on *Doing Urban Public Theology in Africa: In Conversation with the Global Household of Faith*.

In September 2005 a visit was made to the Methodist University in Sao Paulo for their Congress on the *Public Presence of the Churches in Urban Areas: Discourse and Practice* and to consider partnership opportunities with their *Urbi et Orbi* Network.

The Network played a full part in the 2007 pan-African consultation on *Reimagining the African City*, organised by the Centre for Urban Mission, Carlile College, Nairobi. This was followed by an important consultation on the future of urban mission training in Africa. The work of the college's training centre in the Kibera slum has acquired an international reputation for its engagement within one of the largest slum communities in sub-Saharan Africa.

During 2007 Network members (from Japan, Kenya, UK, India) contributed to the Anglican Family Network *Anglican World* supplement on 'Urban Families'.

A Network consultation on *Faith, Action and Transformation in Indian Cities* was held in Madurai in January 2008. The consultation attracted a broad participation from agencies, NGOs, churches, and colleges.

The Network has provided a framework for consultation and exchange within the Anglican Communion. Resources, models of good practice, areas of concern for prayer and other means of support have been shared informally and formally. The Network has developed good working relations with other Anglican networks, particularly the Peace and Justice, and the Family Networks.

The next decade

The Reference Group has identified a number of key themes for future work, but realise that the sustainability of the Network does depend on establishing a more realistic basis of support and financing. These themes are:

- Training for urban ministry/mission
- Empowerment of the poor
- Interchange and communication
- Theological reflection and social analysis.

We are aware that there is not a consistent understanding of urban mission issues across the Provinces. Initially the Network was conceived through provincial nominations – these have not always been those who are most active or engaged in their urban contexts and it has been difficult to maintain a current database for such nominations. We have found, however, a vigorous constituency of practitioners and institutions wanting to deepen their understanding of people, or institutions, who are not Anglicans but are resourcing a spectrum of churches.

The urban context is an essential arena for collaboration. We are therefore proposing that the Network is known as the Urban Learning Network and that resources are concentrated on developing resources for educators and practitioners, and networking as widely as possible. In the next section we highlight some of the trends and issues which our urban churches are likely to face over the coming decade, and which the Network could address.

Emerging challenges

The Network exists to resourse, to make connections and enable mission in and between some of the most challenging contexts. The life of the Kingdom, which we seek to draw others into, is found in the possibility of being salt and yeast amidst the crowd. It is not rejecting the city but loving it, through refusing to accept that which dehumanises and desecrates creation. We often will have very different stories to tell, to those of government, the private sector or the NGO sector, as we seek the transformation of communities and individuals.

Beyond targets The UN Millennium Development Goals emphasise 'slum reduction' – with targets that many governments will fail to meet. Even if achieved it is a long way from complete slum eradication – people will continue to live, work, seek education, form churches, in such places for many years to come. *How might the Network share the learning and connect Christians in these communities?*

Another city is possible We are aware that significant restructuring is happening in many cities which impacts on the most vulnerable poor communities. Significant eviction and relocation happens around big events such as the Olympic Games, but also in the cause of urban renewal and gentrification. City authorities compete for global positioning, often cutting welfare and education budgets to become 'lean cities'. *Christians are involved in movements for change and solidarity: how might we enable inclusive debates about what makes a good city?*

Resisting harmful urbanisms In some parts of the world new forms of city are emerging, often based on the knowledge economy or financial services. These cities take their toll on the world's poor – many become migrant works in the construction of new cities and face conditions of exploitation, and physical danger. New cities often 'design out' the poor – pushing them to periphery communities, elsewhere their presence is monitored through technologies of surveillance and control in public spaces. *What are our strategies for supporting migrant workers? How do we begin to understand the new urban forms we find in places like Dubai and China?*

Seeking the peace of our cities Urban space is increasingly violent. From the micro violence of the gang, through the intertribal violence of the slum, to the technological warfare and the showcase terrorist atrocities. Domicide (the destruction of homes) and urbicide (the destruction of settlements) have become routine strategies for governments and insurgents. Urban security has become a major business. *How do our strategies for urban engagement contribute to a culture of peace and reconciliation? In what ways do our public interventions resist and condemn domicide and urbicide?*

A new people? Evangelism and church planting can be coupled creatively with community development and popular organising. Peace making, mediation and reconciliation work will become critical as difference becomes exaggerated, particularly in cities coming out of civil conflict. It is in the midst of the urban throng that worship and the sacraments can be offered, as acts of proclamation and solidarity (Ps 109.30), as new communities are nurtured and God's new urban order is glimpsed.

International Anglican Women's Network

Report submitted by Priscilla Julie, IAWN Steering Group Co-ordinator

I would like to thank the IAWN Steering Group (SG) and the Provincial Links (PLs) for their commitment to women across the Communion. Particular thanks are due to the women of Anglican Women's Empowerment (AWE), Ms Kim Robey and the Revd Margaret Rose, without whom the SG and PLs would not have been able to achieve half of what we report below. We pray that this report demonstrates to the ACC the work that God is able to do when Anglicans work together towards a common purpose.

There has been much activity since IAWN was reformed in 2006, as demonstrated by the reports to the ACC Joint Standing Committee in 2006, 2007 and 2008. Most recently, members of the 2009-2012 SG were elected in February 2009, and these are listed at http://iawn.anglicancommunion.org/about/index.cfm. The new SG has already begun its work towards achieving the objectives and vision of IAWN

244

as outlined in the IAWN Mission (see Appendix 1 below). Copies in Spanish or French will be made available on our website www.iawn.org when translated.

The PLs serve as the liaison between the IAWN SG and the Province. They maintain close contact with their respective Primate and build networks with women's groups and individual women. PLs also build awareness and promote implementation of the United Nations Beijing Platform for Action, the UN Millennium Development Goals and Anglican Consultative Council resolution ACC 13.31. Their role of advocacy is expected to complement the Primate's office and strengthen the ministry of the Church as well as bringing the Gospel to the wider society through their work. To date, 34 Provinces have appointed IAWN PLs. We pray that the Primates of the remaining four Provinces and six extra-provincial dioceses will nominate an IAWN PL in 2009.

Activities of IAWN Steering Group 2006-2009

Presentation and/or attendance at meetings, conferences and other Church events:

- 50th - 53rd Sessions of the United Nations Commission on the Status of Women (UNCSW) February/March 2006-2009 (reports available on-line www.iawn.org).
- IAWN Meeting, February 2009, New York (statement on-line, www.iawn.org).
- IAWN Stalls at the Lambeth Conference 2008
- IAWN Steering Group face-to-face meetings during UNCSW February /March 2007 and 2008.
- TEAM Conference in South Africa, March 2007 (IAWN report on-line www.iawn.org), and subsequent follow-up group meetings.
- Joint meeting of Anglican Peace and Justice Network and IAWN in Kigali, Goma and Bujumbura, including a consultation meeting for the Anglican women in the Great Lakes Region to discuss war and conflict and related problems that have degraded the humanity of women and girls, 25 September – 3 October 2007.

ACC Resolution 13.31

- Promoted awareness of ACC 13.31 and collected data from the Provinces on achievements to date (resolution available on-line www.iawn.org).

Electronic communications

- IAWN website updated and now part of the Anglican Communion website.
- UNCSW e-mail distribution list more active and providing information about activities, prayer requests and issues from around the Communion.

Financial

- Established a bank account for IAWN to be operated by the Anglican Communion Office.
- Membership of the Canadian Compass Rose Society (CCRS) and ability to receive donations through CCRS in support of approved IAWN projects. Funds used to develop website and fund IAWN Lambeth attendance, stalls and event.

Publications and media

- IAWN Brochure and Mission reviewed and reproduced by 2006-2009 and 2009-2012 Steering Groups. Available at www.iawn.org. Translations will be made available as soon as practicable.
- IAWN SG and PLs had articles on IAWN, UNCSW and other issues regarding women published in diocesan and national Church newspapers. IAWN also featured in an article in the *Journal of Anglican Studies*, June 2007, 'Anglican Women: Empowering each other to further God's Kingdom', by Mary Sudman Donovan.
- Articles in ACNS 4376, 4387, 4562 and 4581and Mothers' Union *Home and Family.*

Partnerships

- Partnerships were strengthened with the Anglican Peace and Justice Network (APJN), International Anglican Family Network (IAFN), Mothers' Union (MU), and Theological Education in the Anglican Communion (TEAC).

Priorities of 2009-2012 IAWN Steering Group and Provincial Links

At the IAWN meeting in February 2009, the 2009-2012 IAWN SG and PLs committed themselves to work with the ACC to empower women in the Communion by:

- raising awareness of and promoting IAWN and the IAWN Mission
- strengthening relationships and communication with Provinces especially the Primates and Bishops
- continuing IAWN representation as part of the ACC delegation to the United Nation Commission on the Status of Women
- further developing and improving the IAWN website
- partnering with other ACC Networks and other organisations with similar missions
- identifying various sources of funds for the work of IAWN.

In all of the above, the SG and PLs will focus on promoting awareness of activities dealing with the key issues identified at the February 2009 meeting:

- Elimination of all forms of violence against women and children, especially trafficking.
- Elimination of extreme poverty, by ensuring access to health care, safe water and employment opportunities.
- Promotion of gender equality throughout the Anglican Communion.
- Combating HIV/AIDS, malaria and tuberculosis.
- Promotion of gender budgeting, which is a key to all of the above.

IAWN Provincial Link Women Report 2008

The 2008 report (available in full as Annex A in the on-line version of the 2009 IAWN report to the Anglican Consultative Council, www.iawn.org) summarises the progress IAWN PLs and women in their Provinces are making towards empowering Anglican women. They wish to bring your attention to these particular issues that women face in the Communion:

<ul><li>violence against women and girls especially trafficking</li><li>reluctance of women to nominate themselves or be nominated for positions of leadership</li><li>living in a patriarchal society</li><li>rural/urban divide</li><li>illiteracy and lack of education</li><li>HIV/AIDS, malaria, tuberculosis and other health issues including access to safe water</li></ul>	<ul><li>discriminatory laws and policies including unequal distribution of funds to women's programs in budgeting processes</li><li>extreme poverty and financial insecurity</li><li>the digital/electronic divide</li><li>role of women in Church life</li><li>sexuality</li><li>lack of, and under employment environmental issues.</li></ul>

This list is not exhaustive and specific Provinces have their own unique issues.

IAWN Meeting 23-27 February 2009

The IAWN SG and PL women met at the Desmond Tutu Centre, New York City, USA, from 23-27 February 2009. The Statement issued at the end of this meeting is on-line at www.iawn.org. A number of resolutions for ACC's consideration were formed. The 2006-2009 SG met prior to the meeting 18-22 February to finalise plans for the meeting and lay the groundwork for the 2009-2012 SG.

Lambeth Conference 2008

IAWN was represented at Lambeth 2008 by an international group of women who staffed two stalls, held eight fringe events and participated in two Spouses' self select events. A brief report on IAWN's participation at Lambeth 2008 is included as Annex C in the on-line version of the 2009 IAWN report to the Anglican Consultative Council, www.iawn.org.

Progress on ACC resolution 13.31

In 2008 and early 2009, PLs provided initial data on the representation of women on Provincial decision-making bodies. The detailed report (April 2009) is on-line at www.iawn.org. It is important that the ACC notes that many PLs commented on the difficulties women face in participating in these

248

decision-making bodies even once they are elected or appointed. Institutionalised gender bias needs to be addressed at both the highest level and the smallest parish.

Mothers' Union Summary Report 2008

A summary report of Mothers' Union activities in 2008 is included below as Appendix 2. Margaret Jones is the MU World Wide President's representative on the IAWN Steering Group. A new representative will be appointed during 2009.

Appendix 1: IAWN Mission (revised and adopted 23 February 2009)

Our Mandate The mandate of the International Anglican Women's Network (IAWN), as an official network of the Anglican Communion, is to report to the Anglican Consultative Council (ACC) on women's concerns. It serves as the global voice of Anglican women and links Anglican women around the globe.

Our Vision To be a bold and prophetic voice for Anglican women throughout the Anglican Communion and in the wider world.

Our Purpose To enable and empower all women of the Anglican Communion to work cooperatively at national, provincial and Communion-wide levels to strengthen the ministries of women in God's world and to ensure women are influential and equal participants throughout the entire Anglican Communion.

Our Objectives

- To uphold and live out God's mission for the Anglican Communion as expressed by the ACC in the Five Marks of Mission: to proclaim the Good News of the Kingdom; to teach, baptize and nurture new believers; to respond to human need by loving service; to seek to transform unjust structures of society; to strive to safeguard the integrity of creation and sustain and renew the life of the earth. We will do this with respect to the full participation of women, as well as women's rights and needs.
- To bring to the Anglican Consultative Council the perspectives of women and to raise issues that affect women and to communicate to women across the Communion news from their sisters; IAWN reports to the

ACC will include reports from the provincial links and from multi-provincial organizations, including Mothers' Union, Girsl Friendly Society, etc.

- To work with the Anglican Observer at the United Nations and implement initiatives that fulfil the UN Beijing Platform for Action (BPfA), the Millennium Development Goals (MDGs), and other initiatives of the United Nations and its specialized agencies for the benefit of women.
- To partner with the other networks of the Anglican Consultative Council.
- To ensure adequate resources for IAWN.

Organisational Structure

To assist IAWN achieve its purpose, the following structure shall exist:

- **Steering Group with a Coordinator.** The Steering Group shall comprise eight full members. Seven members of the Steering Group will be elected by the Provincial Links and the current Steering Group members of the Network; the eighth member will be the world-wide President of the Mothers' Union or her representative. The members designate a Coordinator from amongst them. The group shall collectively reflect the diversities of age, ethnicity, clerical status, provincial context and professional and life experiences needed to embrace and advance all women's interests. The Focal Point for women designated by the ACC Standing Committee and the Anglican Observer at the United Nations shall have ex-officio status. From time to time additional members with specific and necessary expertise may be co-opted. The Steering Group, in response to issues raised throughout the Anglican Communion, shall identify, prioritise and promote the key issues for the Network. It shall ensure prompt and appropriate follow-up to ACC actions and resolutions and timely reporting to the ACC. The term of office shall be three years, with the possibility of being re-elected for a second term. No member may serve more than six consecutive years. At the end of the first three-year period up to 50% of the initial Steering Group shall be eligible for re-election.
- **Patron and Advisors** The Steering Group may designate a patron. They may invite individuals to serve as advisors for their expertise and capacity to support and assist the work of IAWN.

- **Provincial Links** The Primate of each Province shall appoint an official link person who will be the IAWN Provincial Link. Each Provincial Link shall be the liaison between the Steering Group and the women in her province. The Provincial Link shall ensure that the successes, challenges and concerns of Anglican women within provinces are brought to the attention of the Steering Group and that provincial reports are prepared for the Steering Group. A national and or diocesan network will be organized by each province.
- **All women** All women of the Anglican Communion are invited to voice their concerns and become active in promoting the work of the IAWN.
- **Secretariat** A secretariat, working with the Coordinator of the Steering Group, shall assist with administrative matters, including financial management, fundraising, publicity and communication on behalf of IAWN.

Appendix 2: Mothers' Union Report 2008

Prepared by Margaret Jones, Mothers' Union appointee to IAWN's Steering Group

Mothers' Union is an organisation of 3.6 million Christians in more than 78 countries worldwide, who give money, experience and prayer to support marriage and family life. Our vision is of a world where God's love is shown through loving, respectful and flourishing relationships. In reaching out to communities, we change lives and bring hope to many.

'Time for Relationships' has been the focus this year. A new global branding was launched to reflect the wider support network of MU. The General Meeting was replaced by a series of Roadshows around the United Kingdom and Ireland, in the hope that more members and friends would be able to come and find out more about the work of MU both locally and internationally. A challenging new 'Home' resource pack with DVD, sessions for groups, talk notes, worship and children's resources, is available for use worldwide.

A strategic planning process 'Reaching Out' has been designed to help members meet real needs within their communities. 'Families First', a new magazine was launched, as we aim to encourage strong marriages, good parenting and active faith. In September, 'Families Worldwide' a new members' resource magazine, was also launched. Although society and technology have changed since the organisation was founded by Mary Sumner in 1887, MU's vision and aim remains unchanged.

'Exploring the Spirituality of the MU' is another new resource launched this year. In this paper, spirituality is being considered from a Christian viewpoint and shows how MU's spirituality is a distinctive part of our identity as a charity, where our work is underpinned by prayer.

MU is pushing for change on the global stage as well as at the grassroots level. Delegates attended UN Commission on the Status of Women earlier this year, lobbying the United Nations to ensure the idealism expressed in Millennium Development Goal 3 - the promotion of gender equality and empowering women- is turned into reality. It is essential that members across the world lobby their governments on the commitments made at CSW52.

MU's Adult Literacy Project began in 2000 with pilot studies in Sudan, Burundi and Malawi. So far, 38000 people have been involved worldwide and 26000 are now considered literate. With 1200 trained facilitators, that figure will rise. The scope of the project may be large but the key to its success is that it is plugged in at ground level. The programme aims to empower women and girls because traditionally across the developing world, education has been the preserve of men.

The Family Life Programme in Uganda cares and offers support to those living with HIV/Aids. Alongside millions of volunteering members across the world, MU supports 350 development workers in 33 countries. Since 1999, MU has been training facilitators to run parenting groups and five years ago, this work was extended into the Worldwide Parenting Programme, which operates in Rwanda, Uganda, Kenya, Guyana, Jamaica and Trinidad.

In Tanzania, many children living on the streets are orphans or from families too poor to support them. Local MU women started an outreach programme for those vulnerable children, providing clothing, food, help in accessing schooling and love.

Through the Relief Fund, emergency support has been given to families all over the world, who have been affected by natural or man-made disaster. Supplies of food, medicine, blankets and other essential items are distributed swiftly to those most in need. Relief was sent, eg, to Myanmar as a result of the Nargis Cyclone, to Kenya for the many displaced women and children in the emergency camps set up because of the staggering violence experienced, to Mozambique and Malawi as a response to the severe weather conditions that lead to crop failure.

Poverty, illiteracy, gender inequality, conflict, natural disaster, domestic violence, family breakdown, commercialisation of children, economic injustice, discrimination, HIV/Aids, loneliness, rejection are some of the issues threatening and challenging communities in developed or developing communities across the world and Mothers' Union is committed to healing those fragmented and wounded families.

International Anglican Youth Network

Report submitted by the Ven Michael Lee Tamihere

Introduction

The International Anglican Youth Network (IAYN) is a network of persons involved in ministry among young people at the provincial level uniting young people within the Anglican Communion. The aims of the Network are to:

- raise the profile of youth ministry in the Anglican Communion
- increase resources and support of youth ministry
- create a communion in which young people are strengthened
- develop and support young people in their ministry
- advocate on behalf of young people to ensure participation within the Church, and
- encourage the inclusion of young people at all levels in the decision-making of the Church.

The Network is managed by its Steering Group which aims to meet annually. A full gathering of the Network takes place normally every three years. The Steering Group comprises one representative from each region, two co-ordinators and the two ACC youth representatives. These are listed at http://iayn.anglicancommunion.org/about/index.cfm

Steering Group Meeting, Porto Alegre 2006

The IAYN steering group was appreciative of the hospitality shown by the Iglesia Ecclesia Anglicana do Brasil, in particular by then Primate, the Most Revd Orlando Santos de Oliveira and the Provincial Secretary, Christina Takatsu Winnischofer.

During the meeting the steering group welcomed Sue Parks, Lambeth Conference Manager, and the Revd Canon Kenneth Kearon, Secretary General of the Anglican Communion, who outlined the new shape envisaged for the 2008 Lambeth Conference and the possible role for young adults to act as Stewards. The Network was invited to submit a proposal for a self-select seminar and to join other networks in setting up a display. Following these discussions the Network wrote and reflected its concerns regarding the proposed structure of the Steward Programme, challenging the suggestion that Stewards be drawn only from ordinands, seminarians and other students engaged in theological studies. The Network offered to work with Lambeth Conference staff in delivering the Stewarding Programme, including recruitment and training.

In February 2006, members of the Network took the opportunity to consult with young Anglicans serving in the Stewarding Programme at the World Council of Churches Assembly, meeting simultaneously in Porto Alegre. These young adults expressed their concern regarding the profile of the Network amongst young people and the need for communication to be improved. As a result of this the Steering Group committed themselves to publishing a newsletter; creating a logo; and, establishing a webpage (this was facilitated with the professional support of Michael Ade at the Anglican Communion Office).

A key task of the Steering Group at this time was to plan in detail for the Network meeting to take place in England during September 2007. It was decided that a Youth Officer and a young person from each Province would be invited in order to consider the growth and development of the Network, its contribution to the Lambeth Conference, and to review ministry with young people across the Communion.

The Network was also invited to nominate representatives to attend a Global Young Adult Gathering with the Anglican Observer to the United Nations, to take place in New York from 7-11 June 2006. Mr Wade Aukett, Aotearoa, New Zealand & Polynesia; Ms Sarah Tomlinson, Scotland; Ms Neven Abora, Jerusalem & the Middle East; Mr Richard Whitmill, England; Mr Odwa Gonya, Southern Africa; Tiana Morel, Seychelles; Mr Lucas Andrade, Brazil; Laura Amendola, USA; Ms Mellisa Sim & Ms Rhonda Waters, Canada; and Ms Katrina Stevens, Australia attended.

Summary of Gathering in England, 2007

The most recent gathering of the Network took place from 3 to 7 September, 2007 in England – this was the sixth in a series of gatherings started in the 1980s. Each representative had time to report to the Network on the state of youth ministry in their respective provinces. Time was devoted, both in plenaries and small working groups, to considering specific issues and goals facing the Network including a presence at Lambeth 2008, a response to the formation of an Anglican Covenant, and strengthening the Network in order to fulfil its aims.

Sue Parks, Lambeth Conference Manager, and Deidre Martin from the ACO were welcomed and there was a constructive discussion concerning the Network's proposed presence at the Lambeth Conference and its work supporting the Stewarding Programme. (This is commented on later in the report under 'Reflections on Lambeth 2008'.)

The Network responded to the Anglican Covenant and commended the Covenant Design Group for its efforts and the encouragement provided in the Draft Discussion Document for the Church to remain open and patient in times of challenge. The Network expressed its concern that the spirit of the Covenant does not reveal all intentions of the process, and this may expose it to a number of different interpretations and possible misuse by parties in the future. The Network felt that the document need rewording so that it contained clearer intentions and processes. The Network wondered what the legacy of an Anglican Covenant will be? Will it curtail the mission of the Church in the future, and its membership? Should we not be working towards an inclusive Church which celebrates its diversity, as opposed to creating mechanisms for expelling those we do not agree with? Another key question posed in the Network's discussions was: what will happen to Provinces who choose not to sign up to the Covenant? Young people will inherit this document and the Church it may create.

The Network also affirmed the work of the Steering Committee to strengthen the promotion of the Network and the achievement of its aims through more effective communication. Representatives committed themselves to maintaining an up-to-date database of provincial youth workers – a difficult task as the stability of youth positions across the Communion varies widely while some Provinces have a clear stance of not having youth workers at a provincial level. The IAYN website with comprehensive information about the Network, its history and its work has recently been created. It can be accessed at http://iayn.anglicancommunion.org/index.cfm.

Those who attended the gathering were nurtured in their faith through times of worship, which combined distinctive elements from Anglican traditions across the Provinces represented, a day pilgrimage to the Shrine of our Lady, Walsingham, and through the warmth of fellowship throughout. Strength was also gained through the Network's shared experiences of ministry with youth and young adults in their own areas and participants were renewed for ministry in their own provinces.

A list of participants is available on-line at
http://iayn.anglicancommunion.org/resources/gatherings/england2007.cfm:

Reflections on Lambeth 2008

The Network's presence at Lambeth 2008 was marked by its leadership of a self-select seminar; the provision of a prayer labyrinth and stations in the crypt of Canterbury Cathedral; and a display in a prominent position in the foyer enabled good encounters with conference delegates and raised the profile of the Network. Visual presentations from a number of provinces were on display throughout the Network's time at the Conference.

The Network recieved good feedback from many delegates. There was good attendance at the self-select seminar facilitated by the Network, 'Evangelism and Young People', with a positive exchange of ideas. Members of the Network were disappointed, however, to find that their workshop had not been included in the published programme, nor advertised.

The prayer labyrinth and stations set up in the Cathedral Crypt were well recieved by visitors and greatly appreciated by the Cathedral staff. The focus of the labyrinth was on the place and voice of young people in the church whilst the prayer stations provided an opportunity for individuals to reflect on their own spiritual journey. Unfortunately, the distance from the university campus meant that very few Lambeth Conference delegates were able to benefit from this.

The Network was pleased to contribute to the development of the selection criteria for Lambeth Conference Stewards and supported and encouraged applicants from around the Communion. The feedback the Network has recieved from stewards has been positive. However, there was a concern that the agreed criteria were not universally applied. Our hope and prayer is that the Networks will be more central in the planning and delivery of future conferences. The Network's Lambeth Team included: Mr Jeff Lizardo, Philippines; Ms Maki Nakamura, Japan; Mr Odwa Gonya, Southern Africa; Mr Michael Tamihere, Aotearoa, New Zealand & Polynesia; Ms Sarah Tomlinson and young adult group, Scotland; Revd Peter Ball, England; Revd Douglas Fenton, USA; and, Mrs Pam and Revd Den Richards, Wales.

Details of Steering Group Meeting 2009

The Network was deeply grateful to the Province of Hong Kong Sheng Kung Hui for their generosity and warm welcome, and to the Church of the Holy Carpenter, Kowloon for providing the space for the meeting of the Steering Group. Business included: regional reports; reflections on the Lambeth Conference; the Network's relationship with ACC; discussion of the Anglican Covenant; funding; and, young people and vocations. Time was also devoted to reviewing the work of the Network and identifying future goals.

In addition to the Network's business, the opportunity was taken to visit with the Revd Canon Dr Thomas Pang in the Macau Missionary Area and reflect on the evangelistic outreach and ministry with young people there. The Network also met staff of the Religious Education Centre in Hong Kong. Discussion also took place with Diocesan Youth Ministry Advisors and Workers from across the Province. Members of the Steering Group were particularly delighted to meet formally with the Most Revd Paul Kwong, Archbishop of Hong Kong Sheng Kung Hui, and are grateful to him for his invitation and hospitality.

ACC-13 Resolutions

ACC-13 received the report of the Network and thanked it for its ongoing work in support of the witness of young people across the Communion. It also recommended to dioceses and Provinces that they review their provision for ministry amongst young people and ensure appropriate budgetary provision. The Network has to ask, what progress has been made and what future actions still have to be taken?

The new staffing arrangements that are in place to support Networks are to be welcomed, and the Network looks forward to working more closely with the Anglican Communion staff, in particular Terrie Robinson.

Future Goals

It is increasingly recognised that the Networks make a vital contribution to the work of the Communion; the IAYN in particular has become more effective in supporting and bringing together those who share responsibility for youth ministry. Its work is to continue through:

- **Publication of an IAYN Journal: Buenos Nuevos** This will aim to educate the church about youth ministry and its importance in the formation of Christian leaders and vocational discernment; inspire people who are working in youth ministry and broaden their experience of youth ministry in the Communion; and, resource youth leaders.

- **Increase representation at Network Gatherings** Past gatherings have been well attended but the Network would like to see even wider representation from across the Communion. The Network encourages Provinces to strengthen their commitment to send representatives.

- **Youth Sunday** A number of Provinces already set aside a Sunday dedicated to Young People. The Network would like to see this extended across the Communion. On those Sundays it is suggested that an offering is made to support the work of the Network.

- **Website** The succesful creation and running of the website with the support of ACO, in particular Michael Ade, needs to be built on further. Provinces are invited to submit articles for inclusion on the Network's website.

- **Steering Group Meetings and Network Gatherings** The pattern of Network and Steering Group meetings has proven to be effective in developing its work and plans are in place for a proposed Steering Group Meeting in South Africa in 2010, a full Network meeting in 2011, and a further Steering Group Meeting in 2012 prior to ACC-15.

- **Provincial Contributions** The success of the Network is dependent not only on the commitment of its members but also the financial support it receives from the Provinces. While a number of Provinces respond to the annual Advent request for financial support (US$200), many do not. The good work that has been achieved so far can only be built on and extended further if even more Provinces are willing to contribute. We recognise that not every province would be able to afford this, and that some Provinces might be able to afford more. So we encourage each Province to contribute as much or as little as they can.

Asia Regional Youth Conference

On the suggestion of Archbishop Kwong the Network will explore the possibility of facilitating a regional youth conference in Asia. In addition to strengthening the Asia Region's youth work, it is hoped that this will serve as a model for the other four regions.

Part Five
Appendices

Previous Meetings of the Council
and the title of Reports

ACC-1   Limuru, Kenya, 1971
The Time is Now

ACC-2   Dublin, Ireland, 1973
Partners in Mission

ACC-3   Trinidad, 1976
Report of Third Meeting

ACC-4   London, Ontario, Canada, 1979
Report of the Fourth Meeting 1979

ACC-5   Newcastle, England, 1981
Report of Fifth Meeting

ACC-6   Badagry, Nigeria, 1984
Bonds of Affection

ACC-7   Singapore, 1987
Many Gifts One Spirit

ACC-8   Lampeter, Wales, 1990
Mission in a Broken World

ACC-9   Cape Town, South Africa, 1993
Report of Ninth Meeting

ACC-10 Panama, 1996
Witnessing as Anglicans in the Third Millennium

ACC-11 Dundee, Scotland, 1999
The Communion We Share

ACC-12 Hong Kong, 2002
For the Life of the World

ACC-13 Nottingham, England, 2005
Living Communion

The Provinces of the Anglican Communion

The Anglican Church in Aotearoa, New Zealand and Polynesia
The Anglican Church of Australia
The Church of Bangladesh
The Episcopal Anglican Church of Brazil
The Province of the Anglican Church of Burundi
The Anglican Church of Canada
The Church of the Province of Central Africa
The Anglican Church of the Central America Region
The Anglican Church of Congo
The Church of England
Hong Kong Sheng Kung Hui
The Church of the Province of the Indian Ocean
The Church of Ireland
Nippon Sei Ko Kai - The Anglican Communion in Japan
The Anglican/Episcopal Church in Jerusalem and the Middle East
The Anglican Church of Kenya
The Anglican Church of Korea
The Church of the Province of Melanesia
The Anglican Church of Mexico
The Church of the Province of Myanmar (Burma)
The Church of Nigeria (Anglican Communion)
The Church of North India
The Church of Pakistan
The Anglican Church of Papua New Guinea
The Episcopal Church in the Philippines
The Episcopal Church of Rwanda
The Scottish Episcopal Church
The Church of the Province of South East Asia

The Anglican Church of Southern Africa
The Anglican Church of the Southern Cone of America
The Church of South India
The Episcopal Church of Sudan
The Anglican Church of Tanzania
The Church of the Province of Uganda
The Episcopal Church
The Church in Wales
The Church of the Province of West Africa
The Church in the Province of the West Indies

Extra-Provincial Dioceses and Other Churches
The Anglican Church of Bermuda
The Anglican Church in Ceylon (Sri Lanka)
The Episcopal Church of Cuba
The Lusitanian Church (Portugal)
The Spanish Reformed Episcopal Church
Falkland Islands

Index of the Resolutions of ACC-14

Abbreviations

ACC	Anglican Consultative Council
ACEN	Anglican Communion Environmental Network
ACLAN	Anglican Communion Legal Advisers' Network
ACO	Anglican Communion Office
AIN	Anglican Indigenous Network
ALIC	Anglican-Lutheran International Commission
AMICUM	Anglican-Methodist International Commission for Unity in Mission
AOCICC	Anglican-Old Catholic International Co-ordinating Council
AOUN	Anglican Observer at the United Nations
APJN	Anglican Peace and Justice Network

ARCIC	Anglican-Roman Catholic International Commission
AUN	Anglican Urban Network
BCP	Book of Common Prayer
CMS	Church Mission Society
CUAC	Colleges and Universities of the Anglican Communion
IAFAC	Inter-Anglican Finance & Administration Committee
IAFN	International Anglican Family Network
IALC	International Anglican Liturgical Consultation
IARCCUM	International Anglican-Roman Catholic Commission for Unity and Mission
IASCUFO	Inter-Anglican Standing Commission for Unity, Faith and Order
IATDC	Inter-Anglican Theological and Doctrinal Commission
IAWN	International Anglican Women's Network
IAYN	International Anglican Youth Network
ICAOTD	International Commission for Anglican-Orthodox Theological Dialogue
NIFCON	Network for Inter Faith Concerns of the Anglican Communion
NGO	Non-governmental Organisation (United Nations)
NRSV	New Revised Standard Version of the Bible
SCAC	Standing Committee of the Anglican Communion
SOCMS	Selly Oak Centre for Mission Studies
TEAC	Theological Education for the Anglican Communion
TEC	The Episcopal Church
UMCA	Universities' Mission to Central Africa
UN	United Nations
USPG	United Society for the Propagation of the Gospel
WCC	World Council of Churches

Provincial Secretaries and Offices
of the Anglican Communion

The Anglican Church in Aotearoa, New Zealand & Polynesia
The Revd Michael Hughes
General Secretary
PO BOX 87188, Meadowbank, Auckland, 1742, New Zealand

Office	+64 (0)9 521 4439
Fax	+64 (0)9 521 4490
Email 1	gensecm@ang.org.nz
Email 2	gensec@ang.org.nz

The Anglican Church of Australia
Mr Martin Drevikovsky
General Secretary,
General Synod Office, Level 9, 51 Druitt Street, Sydney, New South Wales, 2000, Australia

Office	+61 2 8267 2700
Fax	+61 2 8267 2727
Email	gsoffice@anglican.org.au

The Church of Bangladesh
Mr Augustine Dipak Karmakar
Provincial Secretary, Church of Bangladesh
St Thomas' Church, 54 Johnson Road, Dhaka-1100, Bangladesh

Office	+880 (0)2 711 6546
Fax	+880 (0)2 711 8218
Email	cbdacdio@bangla.net

Igreja Episcopal Anglicana do Brasil
The Revd Canon Francisco de Assis Da Silva
Provincial Secretary, Centro de Estudos Anglicanos
Av Eng Ludolfo Boehl 256, Teresopolis 91720-150, Porto Alegre RS, Brazil

Office	+55 51 3318 6200

Fax   +55 51 3318 6200
Email   fassis@ieab.org.br

The Anglican Church of Burundi
The Revd Pédaçuli Birakengana
Provincial Secretary, The Episcopal Church of Burundi
BP 2098, Bujumbura, Burundi

Office   +257 22 22 4389
Fax   +257 22 22 9129
Email   peab@cbinf.com

The Anglican Church of Canada
The Ven Michael Pollesel
General Secretary of the General Synod,
Anglican Church of Canada, 80 Hayden Street, Toronto, ON, M4Y 3G2,
Canada

Office   +1 416 924 9199
Fax   +1 416 924 0211
Email1   mpollesel@national.anglican.ca
Email 2   general.secretary@national.anglican.ca

The Church of the Province of Central Africa
The Rt Revd William Mchombo
Bishop of Eastern Zambia & Acting Provincial Secretary,
PO Box 510154, Chipata, Zambia

Office   +260 216 221 294
Email 1   dioeastzm@zamnet.zm
Email 2   m_william1962@yahoo.com

Iglesia Anglicana de la Region Central de America
The Rt Revd Hector Monterroso Gonzalez
Bishop of Costa Rica,
De Plaza Cemaco, 75 Metros Notre Sobre, Calle Paralela, San José, Costa
Rica

Office	+506 253 0790/
Fax	+506 253 8331
Email 1	iarca@amnet.co.cr
Email 2	iarcahfm@hotmail.com

Province de L'Eglise Anglicane Du Congo
The Rt Revd Molanga Jean Botola
Suffragan Bishop of Kinshasa & Provincial Secretary, Province de L'Eglise
Anglicane Du Congo
PO Box 16482, Kinshasa, D R Congo

Office	+243 99 862 3508
Email	moranga2k@yahoo.co.uk

The Church of England
Mr William Robert Fittall
Provincial Secretary,
Church House, Great Smith Street, London, SW1P 3AZ, England

Office	+44 (0)20 7898 1360
Fax	+44 (0)20 7898 1369
Email	william.fittall@c-of-e.org.uk

Hong Kong Sheng Kung Hui
The Revd Peter Douglas Koon
Provincial Secretary,
1 Lower Albert Road, Central, Hong Kong, People's Republic of China

Office	+852 25 265 355
Fax	+852 25 212 199
Email 1	peter.koon@hkskh.org
Email 2	peterkoon@email.com

The Church of the Province of the Indian Ocean
The Revd Canon Samitiana Jhonson Razafindralambo
Provincial Secretary, Anglican Diocese of Mauritius
Diocesan Church House, 37th St Paul Road, Vacoas, Mauritius

Office	+230 686 5158

| Email 1 | gen.sec.cpio@gmail.com |
| Email 2 | eemtma@hotmail.com |

The Church of Ireland
Mr Denis Reardon
Chief Officer and Secretary,
Church of Ireland House, Church Avenue, Rathmines, Dublin, 6, Republic of Ireland

Office	+353 (0)1 497 8422
Fax	+353 (0)1 497 8792
Email 1	denis.reardon@rcbdub.org
Email 2	chief@rcbdub.org

Ms Janet Maxwell
General Secretary,
Church of Ireland House, 61-67 Donegall Street, Belfast, BT1 2QH, Northern Ireland

| Email 1 | communications@ireland.anglican.org |
| Email 2 | janet.maxwell@rcbdub.org |

Nippon Sei Ko Kai (The Anglican Communion in Japan)
The Revd John Makito Aizawa
General Secretary,
65-3 Yarai Cho, Shinjuku-Ku, Tokyo, 162-0805, Japan

Office	+81 (0)3 5228 3171
Fax	+81 (0)3 5228 3175
Email	general-sec.po@nskk.org

The Episcopal Church in Jerusalem & The Middle East
The Revd Hanna Mansour
Provincial Secretary,
Diocesan Office, PO Box 87, Zamalek Distribution 11211, Cairo, Egypt
Office +20 (0)2 738 0821/3/9

| Email | fr_hannamansour@hotmail.com |

The Anglican Church of Kenya
The Revd Canon Rosemary Mbogo
Provincial Secretary,
Ag. Provincial Secretary, P. O. Box 40502 - 00100, Nairobi, Kenya

Office	+254 (0)20 271 4752/3
Email 1	ackpsoffice@swiftkenya.com
Email 2	mission@ackenya.org

The Anglican Church of Korea
The Revd Abraham Gwang Joon Kim
Provincial Secretary, Anglican Church of Korea
3 Chong-dong, Chung-ku, Seoul, 100-120, Republic of Korea

Office	+82 2 738 8952
Fax	+82 2 737 4210
Email	abgwk@hanmail.net

The Church of the Province of Melanesia
Mr George S Kiriau
Provincial Secretary,
PO Box 19, Honiara, Solomon Islands

Office	+677 241 34
Email 1	kiriau_g@comphq.org.sb
Email 2	gkiriau@comphq.org.sb

La Iglesia Anglicana de Mexico
The Ven Habacuc Ramos-Huerta
General Secretary, La Iglesia Anglicana de Mexico
Calle La Otra Banda #40, San Angel, 01090 Mexico, DF, Mexico

Office 1	+52 (0)5 550 4073
Office 2	+52 (0)5 616 2490
Fax	+52 (0)5 616 4063
Email 1	habacuc_mx@yahoo.es
Email 2	ofipam@adetel.net.mx

The Church of the Province of Myanmar (Burma)
Mr Kenneth Saw
Provincial Secretary,
140 Pyidaungsu Yeiktha Road, Dagon PO 11191, Yangon, Myanmar

Office 1	+95 1 395 279
Office 2	+95 1 395 350
Email	kennethkyawaye@gmail.com

The Church of Nigeria (Anglican Communion)
The Ven Emmaunel Adekunle
General Secretary,
24, Douala Street, Wuse Zone 5, P. O. Box 212, ADCP, Abuja, Nigeria

Office	+234 09 523 6950
Fax	+234 09 523 0987
Email 1	general_secretary@anglican-nig.org
Email 2	emmanuel_adekunle@yahoo.com

The Church of North India (United)
The Revd Enos Das Pradhan
Provincial Secretary,
General Secretarys Office, CNI Bhawan 311, 16 Pandit Pant Marg, New
Delhi, 110001, India

Office	+91 (0)11 2373 1079
Fax	+91 (0)11 2371 3710
Email 1	enos@cnisynod.org
Email 2	cnisynod@nda.vsnl.net.in

The Anglican Church of Papua New Guinea
Mr Richard Rabiafi
General Secretary & Provincial Secretary, Papua New Guinea Church
Anglican National Office, PO Box 673, Lae, Morobe Province, 411, Papua
New Guinea

Office	+675 472 4111
Fax	+675 472 1852
Email 1	acpng@acpng.org.pg

Email 2   richard@acpng.org.pg

The Church of Pakistan (United)
The Revd Nasim Fayyaz
Acting General Secretary, 17 Waris Road, Lahore, Pakistan
Office   +92 (0)42 758 8950
Fax   +92 (0)42 757 7255
Email: info@dioceseofraiwand.org

The Episcopal Church in the Philippines
The Rt Revd Miguel Paredes Yamoyam
Suffragan Bishop of the Northern Philippines and Provincial Secretary,
PO Box 10321, Broadway Centrum, Quezon City, 1112, Philippines

Office   +63 (0)2 722
Fax   +63 (0)2 721 1923
Email   ecpnational@yahoo.co.ph

L'Eglise Episcopal au Rwanda
The Revd Emmanuel Gatera
Provincial Secretary, L'Eglise Episcopal au Rwanda
PO BOX 2487, Kigali, Rwanda

Office   +250 514 160
Fax 1   +250 514 160
Email 1   egapeer@yahoo.com
Email 2   peer1925@yahoo.fr

The Scottish Episcopal Church
Mr John Stuart
Secretary General, Scottish Episcopal Church
21 Grosvenor Crescent, Edinburgh, EH12 5EE, Scotland
Office   +44 (0)131 225 6357
Fax   +44 (0)131 346 7247
Email   secgen@scotland.anglican.org

Church of the Province of South East Asia
Mr Caldwell David Joseph
Provincial Secretary,
16 Jalan Pudu, 50200 Kuala Lumpur, Malaysia

Office	+60 03 2031 2728
Fax	+60 03 2031 3225
Email	anglican@streamyx.com

The Church of South India (United)
The Revd Moses Jayakumar
General Secretary,
CSI Centre, No. 5 Whites Road, Royapettah, Chennai, 600 014, India

Office 1	+44 2 852 4166
Office 2	+44 2 852 3763
Email 1	jayakumaran17@rediff.com
Email 2	csi@vsnl.com

The Anglican Church of Southern Africa
The Revd Rob A Butterworth
Acting Provincial Executive Officer,
Provincial Executive Office, 20 Bishopcourt Drive, Bishopcourt, Western
Cape, 7708, South Africa

Office	+27 (0)21 763 1300
Fax	+27 (0)21 797 1329
Email	peo@anglicanchurchsa.org.za

Iglesia Anglicana del Cono Sur de America
The Revd Nelson Ojeda
Provincial Secretary,
Casilla 50675, Correo Central, Santiago, Chile

Email	ojedanel@gmail.com

The Episcopal Church of Sudan
The Revd Canon Enock Tombe
Provincial Secretary, Provincial Liaison Office
PO Box 604, Amarat, Street 1, Khartoum, Sudan

Office	+249 811 820 065
Fax	+249 183 564 724
Email	ecsprovince@hotmail.com

The Anglican Church of Tanzania
The Revd Canon Dr Dickson Chilongani
General Secretary, Church of the Province of Tanzania
PO Box 899, Dodoma, Tanzania

Office	+255 262 324 574
Fax	+255 262 324 565
Email	chilonganid@hotmail.com

The Church of the Province of Uganda
The Revd Aaron Mwesigye
Provincial Secretary, Church of the Province of Uganda
P.O. Box 14123, Kampala, Uganda

Office 1	+256 772 455 129
Email	ankundarev@yahoo.com

The Episcopal Church
The Revd Dr Gregory Stephen Straub
Executive Officer & Secretary of the General Convention,
815 Second Avenue, New York City, NY, 10017, USA

Office	+1 212 922 5184
Email	gstraub@episcopalchurch.org

The Rt Revd Herbert Alcorn Donovan Jr.
Deputy to the Presiding Bishop for Anglican Communion Relations,
815 Second Avenue, New York City, NY, 10017, USA

Office	+1 212 922 5282
Email	hdonovan@episcopalchurch.org

The Church in Wales
Mr John M Shirley
Provincial Secretary, The Church In Wales
39 Cathedral Road, Cardiff, CF11 9XF, Wales

Office	+44 (0)2920 348 200
Fax	+44 (0)2920 387 835
Email	johnshirley@churchinwales.org.uk

The Church of the Province of West Africa
The Revd Canon Fr Anthony M Eiwuley
Provincial Secretary, The Church of the Province of West Africa
PO Box KN 2023, Kaneshie, Accra, Ghana

Office	+233 (0)21 662 292
Email 1	cpwa@4u.com.gh
Email 2	morkeiwuley@gmail.com

The Church in the Province of the West Indies
Mrs Elenor Lawrence
Provincial Secretary, Provincial Secretariat
Bamford House, Society Hill, St John, Barbados, 2008, West Indies

Office	+1 246 423 0842
Fax	+1 246 423 0855
Email	bamford@sunbeach.net

The Church of Ceylon
Mrs Mary Thanja Peiris
Provincial Secretary,
368/3A Bauddhaloka, Mawathe, Colombo 7, Sri Lanka

Office 1	+94 1 684 810
Office 2	+94 1 696 208
Fax	+94 1 684 811
Email	sec_diocese_tr@yahoo.com

Iglesia Episcopal de Cuba
Mr Francisco De Arazoza
Provincial Secretary,
Calle 6 No 273 Vedado, Plaza de la revolucion, Ciudad de la Habana, Cuba

Office	+53 7 832 1120
Fax	+53 7 834 3293
Email 1	episcopal@enet.cu
Email 2	episcopal@ip.etecsa.cu

Bermuda (Extra-Provincial to the Archbishop of Canterbury)
Mrs Ruth Allen
Provincial Treasurer,
PO BOX 769, Hamilton, Bermuda

Office	+1 441 292 6987
Fax	+1 441 292 5421

The Lusitanian Church (Extra-Provincial to the Archbishop of Canterbury)
The Rt Revd Fernando Soares
Bishop of the Lusitanian Church,
Secretaria Diocesana, Apartado 392, P - 4430 Vila Nova de Gaia, Portugal

Office	+351 (0)22 375 4018
Fax	+351 (0)22 375 2016
Email 1	bisposoares@igreja-lusitana.org
Email 2	ilcae@mail.telepac.pt

The Reformed Episcopal Church of Spain
(Extra-Privincial to the Archbishop of Canterbury)
The Rt Revd Carlos López-Lozano
Bishop of Spanish Reformed Episcopal Church,
Calle Beneficencia 18, 28004 Madrid, Spain

Office	+34 (0)91 445 2560
Fax	+34 (0)91 594 4572
Email	eclesiae@arrakis.es